DERRICK NAPIER

READ ROMAN MOSAICS

BIGNOR, LULLINGSTONE, CHEDWORTH, BRADING & NEWPORT ROMAN VILLAS

First published in Great Britain as a softback original in 2015

Typeset in Century Schoolbook

Editing, design and publishing by UK Book Publishing

UK Book Publishing is a trading name of Consilience Media

www.ukbookpublishing.com

ISBN: 978-1-910223-46-8

Contents

Introduction

Mosaics and mythology

Today Greek myths are known primarily from Greek literature, with the oldest known works credited to the Greek poet Homer (birth and death dates unknown). His poems in the Iliad tell the story of the siege of Troy, the Trojan war and Paris' kidnapping of Helen, said to be the world's most beautiful woman. Homer's poems, found in the Odyssey, pick up after the fall of Troy. But we should seek out Hesiod, another Greek poet, who offers us in his 'Theogony' (origin of the gods) a full account of the earliest Greek myths.

For Roman mythology we look to the Roman poet Virgil (70-19 BC) and his work 'The Aeneid', which follows the Trojan refugee Aeneas as he begins to fulfil his destiny to arrive on the shores of Italy, which in Roman mythology was the founding act of Rome. Another Roman poet, Ovid (43 BC-AD 14), tells us engaging stories of the transformation of humans and nymphs into animals and plants.

Many of the Greek and Roman gods of mythology are similar, which is possibly explained by the adoption of the Greek gods by the Romans as they conquered the Hellenistic world. The Celts, unlike the Greeks and the Romans, did not record their myths in the written word. The bards were the Celtic historians, passing down orally, from generation to generation, the history, fables and tales of their people. It was only in the 5th Century AD that their myths were written down and recorded by the monks of Christianity.

The art of mosaic construction seems to have spread through the Hellenistic world and was brought to Italy by Greek craftsmen. Consequently the Romans carried the art further afield as their empire expanded and eventually to England. In England the first mosaic floors were laid in the 1st Century AD and it was only in the later mosaic floors, laid between 150-360 AD, that Greek/Roman mythology was noticed in the Romano-British villas. Because of this timeline there is an absence of any Celtic myths, although I feel that within these mosaic floors there are decorative motifs that appear to derive from pre-Roman tradition and could be credited to the Celts. The Celts had been around for many hundreds of years and they inhabited the spirit of the landscape, which include fertility, the seasons of the year, flowers, healing and life-giving water. We see nothing until we understand it. So join me in this journey of discovery – I therefore invite you to read on.

Chapter I

Bignor Roman Villa

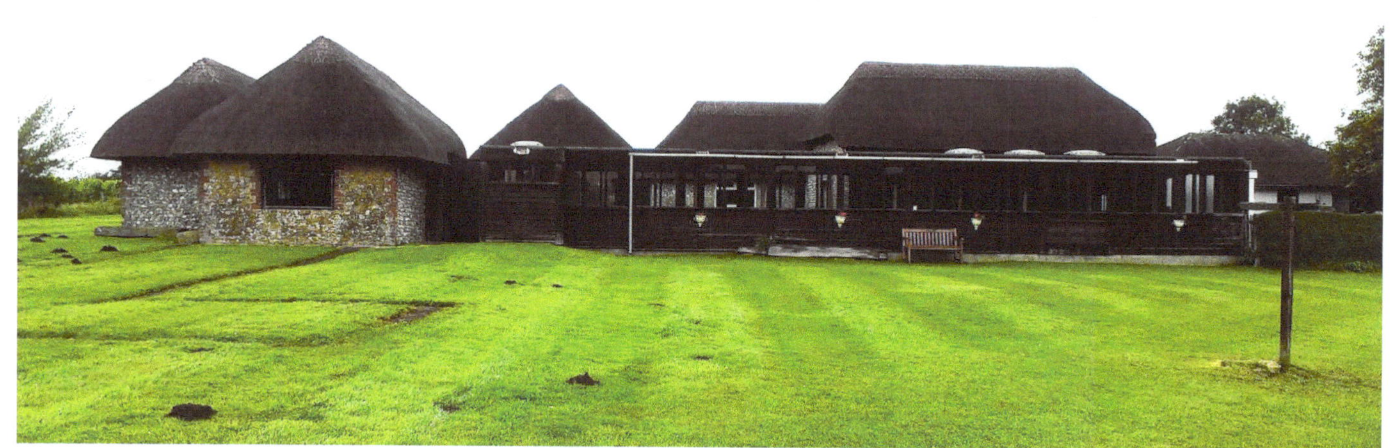

Villa cover-building

The Bignor Villa lies a little east of the village of Bignor, on a slope of a ridge of upper greensand and sits in a downland setting in the centre of the South Downs National Park. It has stunning views to the south, east and west. The place name 'Bignor' could be derived from the old English 'Bican Yfer', perhaps meaning 'Bica's slope' – signifying that a Saxon named Bica owned the land on this crest. The site chosen for the villa gave close access to Stane Street, which gave direct communication with the Roman market town of Chichester and of London. The villa's owners would, therefore, have had the opportunity to sell their agricultural produce in both of these developing towns. As both these settlements became more populated the villa's owners had expanding markets and, no doubt, they would have become more and more wealthy. There was also the possibility that they could have exported grain to the Roman military on the Continent. With more prosperity, the villa would have expanded in size and grandeur and by the 4th century AD had become extensively integrated in Roman culture, as borne out by the mosaics now on view.

It seems that the villa was resurrected on 18 July 1811, when a farmer, by the name of George Tupper, was ploughing and his plough struck a large stone. In all probability, this was part of the external rim of the six-sided ornamental fountain constructed of white limestone. The fountain can be viewed in the Ganymede Room. The site was open to public viewing on 13 October 1814 and the records show that nearly a thousand entries were made in the visitors' book between March and November 1815. After the villa's discovery, a Mr John Hawkins took responsibility for its excavation. He invited a Mr Samuel Lysons to supervise the excavations which he did until his death in 1819. The site then remained sleeping until 1925, when a Mr S E Winbolt re-excavated and repaired the cold bath and then in 1929 part of the Venus mosaic was relaid. Between 1956 and 1962, Professor S S Frere was engaged in re-excavating part of the north, south and west wings of the courtyard villa. At present the Villa is a Scheduled Historic Monument (73) and is privately owned by Mr Jack R Tupper.

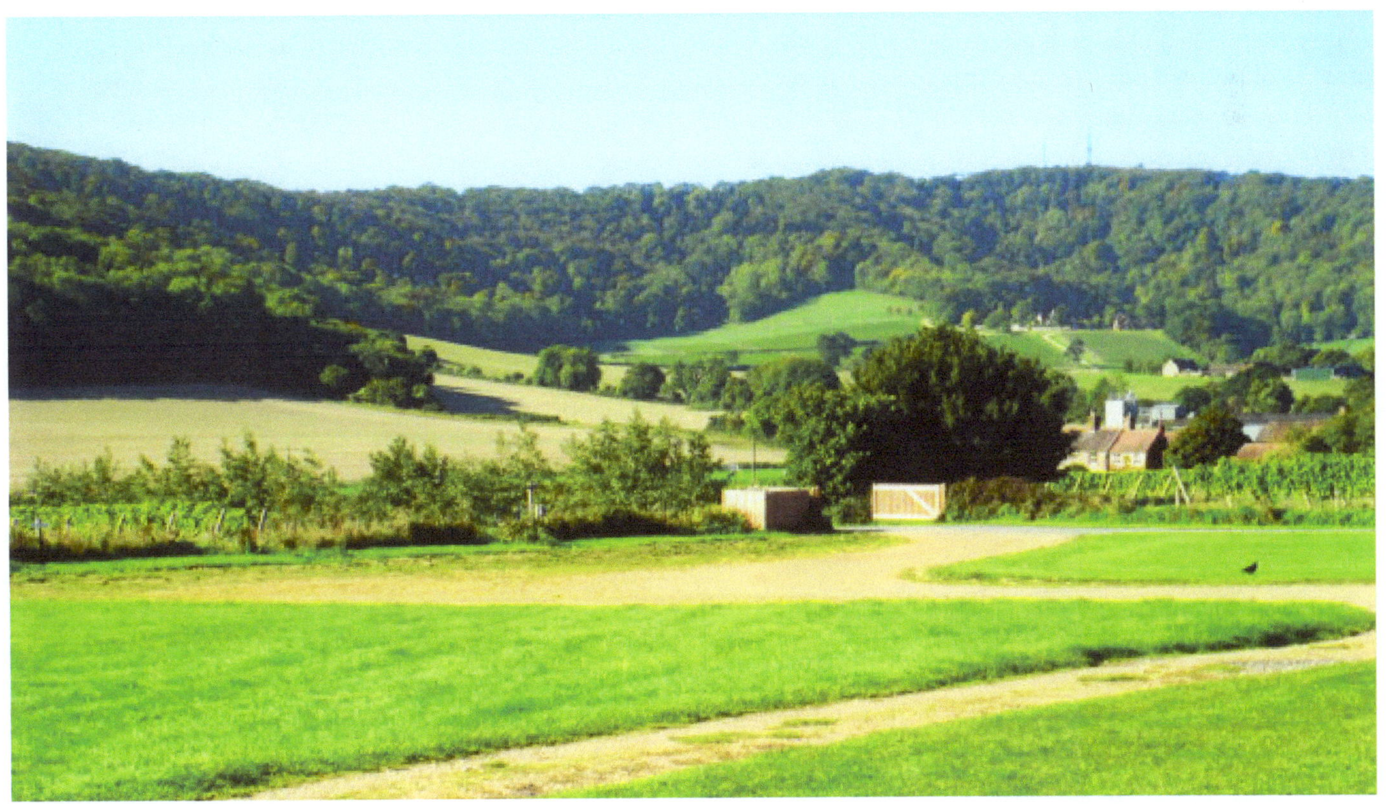

View of surrounding countryside

OVERVIEW

I think it is appropriate, because of the vast rainbow of colours of the tesserae that can be seen in the mosaics at Bignor, I should make reference to them now rather than when I am discussing the individual room mosaics. The cretaceous and Jurassic rock formations of south east England, in all probability, would have provided most of the subtle shades of colours used in the mosaics at Bignor. Liassic rocks of the lower Jurassic provide the sandstones. These can be yellow, blue, black/grey and a brownish red. The white tesserae could have been chalk from the cretaceous deposits of southern England. Jurassic shale, from Kimmeridge in Dorset, would have been the grey/black tesserae. Also, Jurassic limestone from the Purbeck beds in Dorset can be seen in the varying shades of grey and blue. Some tile and brick account for most of the orange/red tesserae. The mineral content of all these rocks are responsible for the nearly new, fresh and bright viewing when they are gently wiped with a damp mop. Blue and green glass is also present as tesserae but, unlike Fishbourne, no samian tesserae are seen here. The tesserae vary in size from one inch square on the red/orange borders, but within the mosaic floors they can be one fifth of an inch square, a quarter of an inch square, or a third of an inch square, although the standard size is a half an inch square. All the mosaics at Bignor, in all probability, were constructed in the late third century AD, or early fourth century AD.

THE TOUR

The first room to view is the museum, just to the right after entering the villa complex. This room houses the model of the villa which depicts how the villa would have been laid out in about 350 AD. It is wonderfully crafted and was constructed in 1972 and is the work of Mr J Morgan, the then curator of the site. The model stands on a geometrical mosaic eight and a half feet square, sitting in a tessellated pavement constructed from red brick/tiles.

Four rows of white tesserae lead the eye into a surrounding two rows of black tesserae. Beyond that we see a white background containing two black diminishing boxes. The smaller box in its centre contains a solid black box. Another design is a black triangle containing three smaller white and one black triangle. Next to that can be noticed a black bow contained in a box. The bow touches the surrounding black tesserae on the north, south, east and west of the box. The design teases and tantalizes the eye as it all seems to interlock. Underneath one of the white legs which help to support the model a circular setting of black tesserae can be noticed. Within that – do I detect some coloured tesserae…? The centre of this mosaic has collapsed onto the under floor heating system, hypocaust, which is a huge disappointment, for it would have been interesting to see how the missing inner design would have related to the outer design, described above. This mosaic is of quality workmanship, not just for the design, but also the black and white tesserae are very neatly laid and pleasing to the eye.

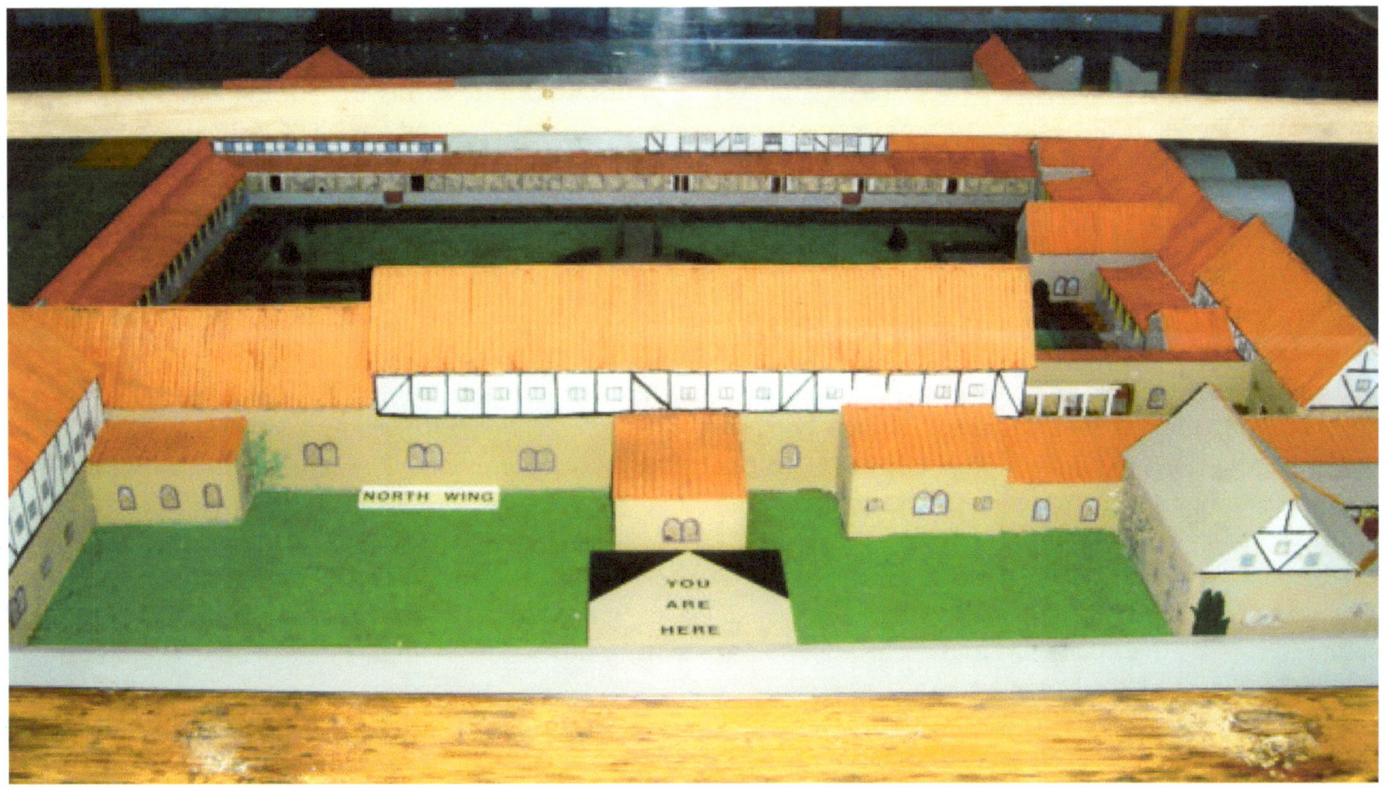

Model of the Villa

If we now exit this room, opposite we can view the Ganymede and Dancers Mosaic. A large room of two compartments, this is a triclinium/dining-room and at the southern and larger end we view a six sided piscine/water basin constructed from white limestone. The external rim of each side measures two feet eleven inches. It is four feet in diameter, and one foot eight inches deep and has a step about half way down. Within the six hexagonal panels would have been dancing girls (maenads) erotically dressed with veils. Green glass can be observed in their veils. This colourful room had no under floor heating and in all probability was a summer room of entertainment, where the wine flowed and was followed by erotic activity. Then perhaps during the winter months the proprietor of the villa could flaunt his knowledge of Greek/ Roman mythology. I view this room with excited eyes and with stimulated thoughts and imagination, for in Greek mythology maenads were the immortal female followers of Dionysus which translates as the raving ones. They could be immortal goddesses of natural manifestations being the extremes of pleasurable emotions and actions fuelled by drunken intoxication.

In the northern part of the room Ganymede is abducted by Zeus in the form of an eagle to serve as a cup-bearer in Olympus. There Zeus granted him eternal youth and immortality and Ganymede became the symbol for the beautiful young male who attracted homosexual desire and love. The red cap worn by Ganymede is associated in antiquity with the inhabitants of Phrygia, now modern day Turkey, centred around the Sakarya river. Sadly, all that is left for us to view of the dancing girls is the following – in the north panel there is a girl with a veil who is looking backwards, in the south a similar figure looking left, and in the south east there is another.

The next room to view contains an almost complete geometrical mosaic pavement which measures 13 feet 4 inches by 5 feet 7 inches and within it sits two squares separated by a rectangle. As this room had under floor heating, I feel that this area could have been a cosy bedroom. The multi coloured tesserae are eye catching and they invite one's eyes to begin to engage with the complete floor. The contents of the rectangle are protected by a continuing interlocking guilloche.

Within it a cup/vase can be noticed, out of which grow acorns/lotus flowers (?) and heart-shaped leaves. The western square has a quatrefoil of heart-shaped leaves, with a circle in the centre, surrounded by four squares set diamond-wise and enclosing two intercepting links. Also seen in the cubes are swastikas, adjoining hearts and solomon knots.

All of these three motifs, I think, have a symbolic meaning. The Solomon knot has no visible beginning or ending and therefore it may represent immortality and eternity. The swastika is an equilateral cross with four arms bent at 90 degrees and would have been well recognised by both Greek/Roman and Celtic cultures. It could be read as life, power, strength and good luck radiating in all four directions – north, south, east and west as depicted on this mosaic. Perhaps the heart-shaped motifs symbolise the spirit, emotion and morals, therefore the heart becomes the seat of one's soul. The eastern square contains a smaller centre square and a smaller circle set diamond-wise with a protective guilloche border and a four-pointed flower pattern. The winged flower motif, in all probability, is another symbol of good fortune.

Moving on from this room we can now view the 'Venus and Gladiators' mosaic. As I enter this room, the mosaic begins to suck me in and the eyes of the female bust follow me wherever I roam within this room. The feeling of ambiguity shimmers into my mind … is this the head of the Goddess Venus or the Goddess

Juno? Juno was worshipped by the ancient Romans who, with her consort, the God Jupiter, rules over all aspects of Roman life, including the military. This could explain the gladiators being depicted beneath her in this mosaic. Beneath her we view a panel 14 feet long and two feet three inches wide filled with winged cupids playing the parts of gladiators at a training school. It seems that it was a Roman custom to represent phases of life playfully – here depicting the actors as cupids. It seems that the most popular duel was between the retiarius and the secutor. The retiarius is armed with a net, trident and a short sword.

He is lightly clad in a tunic and a girdle. The secutor wears a helmet with a visor, a breast plate, a leather leg guard on his left leg and holds a curved shield and a short sword. A retired gladiator performs the role of instructor/umpire and can be seen holding a rudus. From left to right we view the following scenes:

1. A secutor and a retiarius are fighting, with the instructor acting as umpire (magister).
2. A secutor has disarmed the retiarius but the magister seems to intervene.
3. A secutor being armed and a retiarius being led to fight.
4. A secutor is about to kill the wounded retiarius.

   The two stones with an iron ring attached would have probably both held a watching apprentice gladiator. The Goddess Juno also looked after the women of Rome and this deity was an embodiment of the traditional female roles of wife and mother. Her main festival, the Matronalia, was held on the first of March and each Roman woman was said to have her own image of Juno which represented her female spirit. Perhaps this heated room was, at certain times, strictly for the use of women only.

The head of the Goddess is one foot 11 inches high and sits in the middle of a circle. It shows a blue nimbus surrounding her head indicating her deity and she wears a headdress with a wreath of flowers. Most scholars are adamant that this is the head depicting the Goddess Venus. However, the accompanying symbols of birds are ambiguous as they are not distinctive enough to be confirmed as being peacocks, the bird which usually accompanies Juno, or pheasants which accompany Venus. The Goddess Venus is one of the most widely referenced deities in Greek/Roman mythology and embodies all the female attributes of enticement, seduction, sex and beauty. Surrounding the head of the Goddess, and sealed between two separate rows of continuing guilloche, a number of small motifs can be noticed. Above her head is a Solomon knot; this and all the small motifs originate from the cup/vase on a continuing and never ending trailing vine with leaves. What can we notice in these never ending circles? Hearts? Lotus flower? Seeds? Acorns? Ivy leaves? They all seem to be sealed together by the numerous hearts positioned outside but touching the circles. This 32 feet by 19 feet 10 inches mosaic is a wonderful piece of craftsmanship in both its design, neatness and impacting way the tesserae are laid. The passing of time has taken its toll and part of this mosaic was lifted and restored by the Art, Pavements and Decoration Company in the summer of 1929. All this was paid for by Mr Maurice Tupper. The Society of Antiquities also did some restoration work in the area around the head of the Goddess. A keen eye should be able to distinguish between the original mosaic and the restored part. Less can be seen of the southern part of this mosaic because the pilae of the hypocaust, which support the floor, have collapsed, thus destroying that part of the mosaic – although parts of dancing cupids in panels are still visible around the cavity. Nevertheless, this mosaic still holds on to its intrigue and mystery, for there is so much to be viewed and discussed.

If we wander on we can now visit a large room 40 feet long and 19 feet wide (known as Winter). This room had contained a hypocaust. To the north we can view a small geometric mosaic which leads us towards the only remaining figure of a four seasons mosaic. This figure, on a white background, sits in an octagon of intersecting squares of guilloche and the bust stands one foot 10 inches high.

It depicts winter and shows a sad face. The cold effect has been highlighted by the use of brown, blue-grey and black tesserae. The figure wears an expensive, British, hooded cloak well recognised in the third century AD. The cloak is mentioned in Diocletian's Edit of Prices in 301 AD. My mind wanders to how the mosaisist would have laid out the three missing figures representing Spring, Summer and Autumn. With the wide range of coloured tesserae available and matched with the sensitivity of how the winter figure is depicted, I feel they would have been a joy to view. Let's dwell for a moment or two on the concept of this popular mosaic design of the four seasons. There is a close correspondence between the seasons and the stages of life – from birth to death, with spring being the birth, summer being one's youth and autumn one's adulthood and finally, winter being old age and eventually death. One of the motifs laid close to the winter figure is the Solomon knot, the symbol of eternal motion and the intertwining of space and time. Is this just a coincidence? Or is it to reinforce what the mosaisist is being instructed to show by the proprietor of this villa? This is, in all probability, a 4th century AD mosaic. In the southern part of this room only a fragment of mosaic remains. It depicts a dolphin enclosed in a white rectangular box contained in a surround of black tesserae. Surrounding the box is a continuing interlocking guilloche. Above the guilloche is a white triangle and contained within it is a smaller black triangle which houses the letters T R. The villa guide book (2012) offers up the possibility that this may be the signature of Terentius, who could be responsible for the design of this mosaic and the other 4th century AD mosaic seen in this villa. It is an intriguing suggestion – but if this person did exist he seems to have been lost in the fog of the past. To keep this chapter within certain boundaries, I suggest that for more information on the inscription, the reader seeks out an article written by Dr Stephen R Cosh called the Bignor Inscription Reconsidered.

We can now enter a room, 10 feet by 12 feet, containing an earlier mosaic known as the Four Seasons. This mosaic was probably constructed in the 3rd century AD and is mainly constructed with black and white tesserae. Of the four heads depicted here only the head of winter is recognisable as it wears a black hood. Within the centre of the mosaic the black head of Medusa can be viewed, with spikes protruding from the head, representing snakes. One of the many stories from mythology regarding Medusa was that she was the only mortal of three sisters, known as the Gorgons. Medusa accused the Goddess Athena of being jealous of her beauty. Athena/Minerva, angered, responded by turning Medusa's fair hair into snakes and cursed her by making Medusa so ugly that whoever looked into her eyes would be turned into stone. In classical antiquity the image of the Medusa head would, therefore, become a powerful protective amulet against all forms of evil spirits. The symbolism of this could be read as to protect the four seasons of the year and the occupants of this room from evil influences. Interestingly, when this room was first excavated, the walls remained up to two feet 10 inches in height. They were plastered with colour in five panels, the centre panel being white with two red panels on either side of the white. The panels were divided by blue bands and a wide band of black was noticed around the bottom of the panels. I am very fond of this mosaic as it still has lots to view and much to ponder over. Part of the mat survives and this leads the eye into the main layout of the floor. Within the first two black circles a black box and black diamond designs can be noticed. Also a dolphin and a fish can be seen near the head of winter. The two black circles are joined intermittently by interlocking thin bands of black tesserae. Beyond this a continuing, interlocking circle of guilloche constructed using red/orange, white and black tesserae surround the third black circle. Within the third black circle leaves/flower designs are viewed and the head of Medusa sits alone surrounded by the fourth black circle. Note that the two inner black circles are wider than the first two black circles.

We now find our way to the north corridor to view a geometric mosaic, 78 feet 9 inches long by nine feet six inches wide. This is one of the mosaics at the villa that has been lifted and relaid on a bed of concrete to help ensure its long-term preservation. The lead pipe draining the piscina (in the Ganymede room) can be seen in the channel below the floor. Looking at the mosaic we view an outer border of red/orange cubes which leads the eye to three rows of white tesserae. Beyond that a continuing guilloche rests in a blue/grey background. Further in is a pattern of blue/grey labyrinth and red/orange squares with internal red dots on a white background. To the east, but now sadly lost, the design was similar but blues took the place of the red/orange and it was edged with a blue and white triangular pattern.

We now venture outside and proceed in a south easterly direction to view the Medusa mosaic in the bath suite. This room is 25 feet square and was probably an apodyterium (dressing room); in its centre rests a head of Medusa. Protruding in a lively fashion from the head are 14 snakes. Surrounding the mosaic is a chequerboard pattern of six inch squares consisting of red tiles and black kimmeridge shale. This room contained a hypercaust, no doubt to keep the bathers warm as they changed their clothes in readiness for a body-cleansing experience. The room next to this was the frigidarium (cold bath). The Medusa mosaic is a colourful piece of craftsmanship with a number of interesting, interlocking patterns to view. The Medusa head is in a central circle set in an octagon and is protected by a never ending and continuing red/orange, brown and white guilloche. The outer square of this mosaic consisted of a key and guilloche pattern, parts of which can still be viewed today. This encloses an inner square within which were five octagons formed by interlaced squares, four half octagons and four quarter octagons; the smaller spaces between these contained lozenges of black and white, some of which are still visible today.

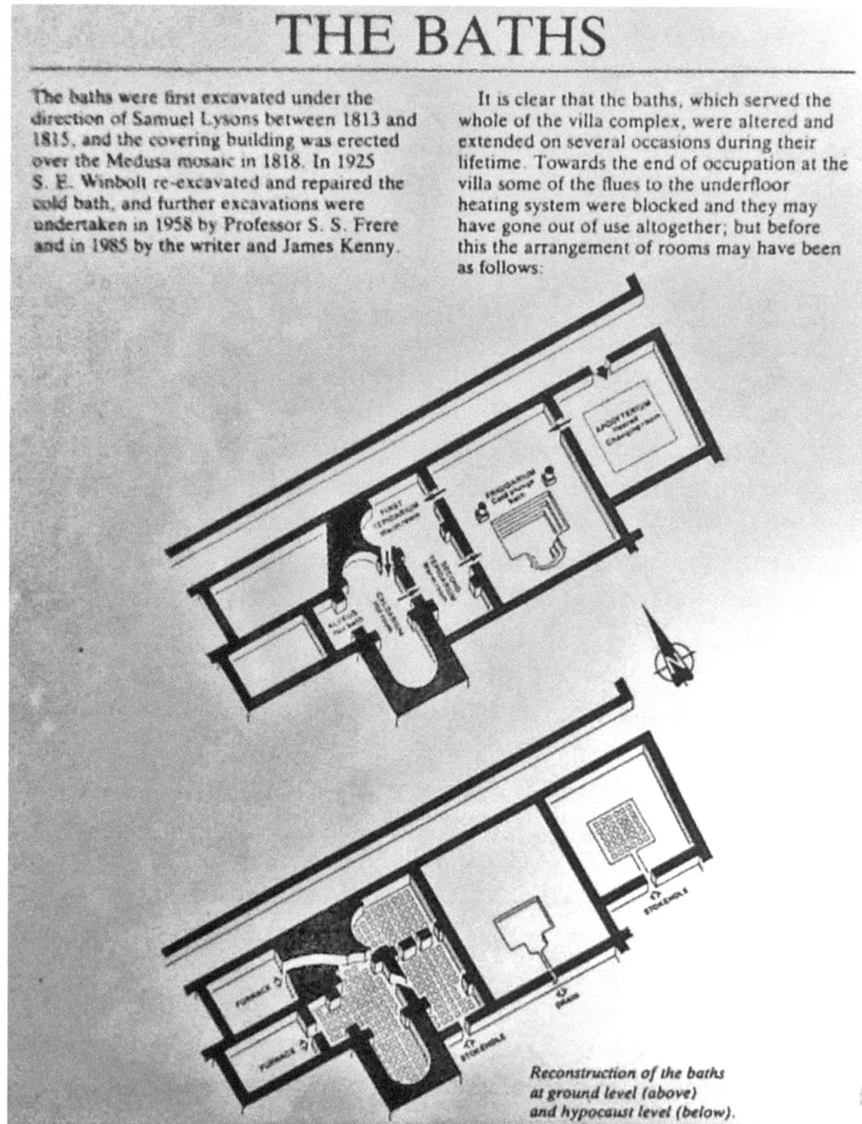

THE BATHS

The baths were first excavated under the direction of Samuel Lysons between 1813 and 1815, and the covering building was erected over the Medusa mosaic in 1818. In 1925 S. E. Winbolt re-excavated and repaired the cold bath, and further excavations were undertaken in 1958 by Professor S. S. Frere and in 1985 by the writer and James Kenny.

It is clear that the baths, which served the whole of the villa complex, were altered and extended on several occasions during their lifetime. Towards the end of occupation at the villa some of the flues to the underfloor heating system were blocked and they may have gone out of use altogether; but before this the arrangement of rooms may have been as follows:

Reconstruction of the baths at ground level (above) and hypocaust level (below).

Plan of the Bath House

Each octagon contained a circle, some containing a central motif. These motifs were surrounded by circles of triangles, coloured guilloche, and finished with wave patterns of black and white. The full design of this mosaic is superbly drawn in Samuel Lysons' Volume Three of his Reliquiae Britannico – Romane. The Bignor Villa in its final form covered four and a half acres, making it one of the largest in Britain. The owners were wealthy and were perhaps men of prominence who played their part in the administration of the Civitas of the Regnenses, centred at Chichester.

I highly recommend a visit to the remains of this Roman villa, whether you are a resident or a visitor to this island. If you are blessed with a sunny day, just dwell for a few minutes and view the beautiful countryside that surrounds you. Then enter, arm yourself with a guide book, and let your eyes and mind be seduced by what awaits to be viewed. Afterwards, in the Bignor café, enjoy a pot of fresh coffee and a homemade cake. What then may enter into your mind is the thought of how many generations of the Tupper family have nourished, maintained and financially supported, from their own resources, the well-being of this establishment. Without them, perhaps all we would have left to view today are the wonderfully crafted drawings of Samuel Lysons, completed nearly 200 years ago for his third volume of Reliquiae Britannico – Romane.

CONCLUSION

I wonder if there is a family connection between the Bignor villa and the huge villa/ Roman palace at Fishbourne. The distance between the two villas, by modern roads, is only 18 miles. Archaeological evidence seems to suggest that a Romanised farm at Bignor existed there by the early 2nd century AD. Samian pottery, of the late 1st century AD and two coins of Trajan (98-117 AD) were excavated there. The first stone building is believed to have been erected sometime after 250 AD. The Fishbourne Villa experienced a destructive fire between 270-290 AD. The archaeological excavations at Fishbourne, during the 1960s, uncovered a stack of glass window panes, tesserae and mortar in preparation for use in the near future. Around the time of the fire at Fishbourne the Franks and the Saxons were harassing sea traffic in the English Channel, impeding trade with the Continent. Importing and exporting was becoming less financially productive, therefore more intensive farming could have been a more worthwhile and financially rewarding option. By the late 3rd century AD the Romans were beginning to build, what is now known as, the Saxon shore forts all along the south coast of England to offer protection from the potential threat of invading Germanic tribes. The villa at Bignor would therefore have offered more security as it is further away from the coast and in return there would have been readymade building material to be taken from the remains at Fishbourne. I feel there is an opportunity here for a graduate of archaeology to do a research paper to compare the sourcing of the building material at Fishbourne with that at Bignor.

Mosaic beneath the Villa Model

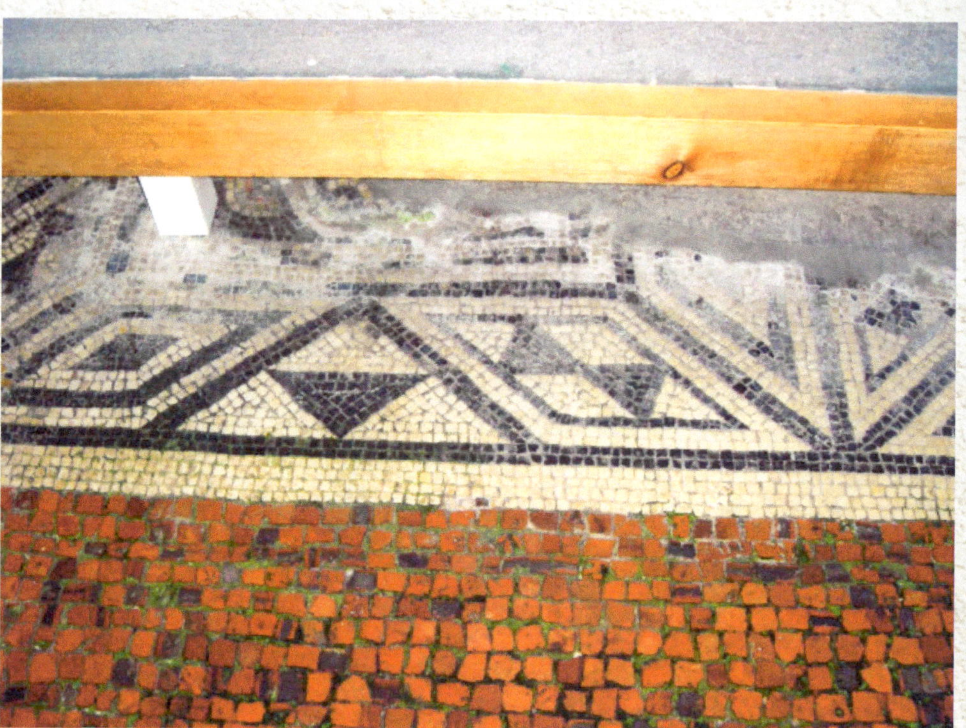

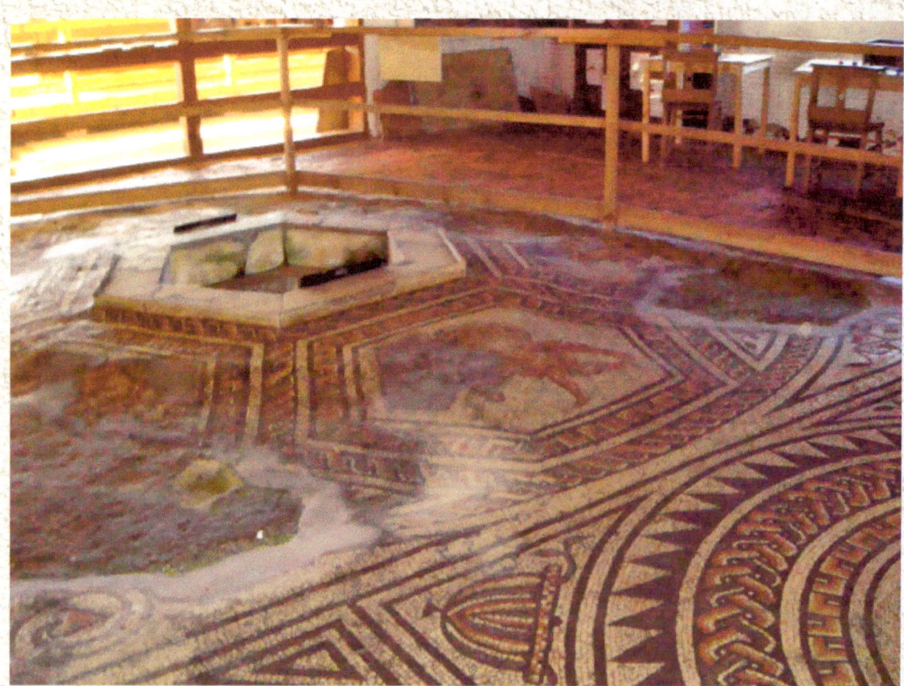

Ganymede and Dancers Mosaic

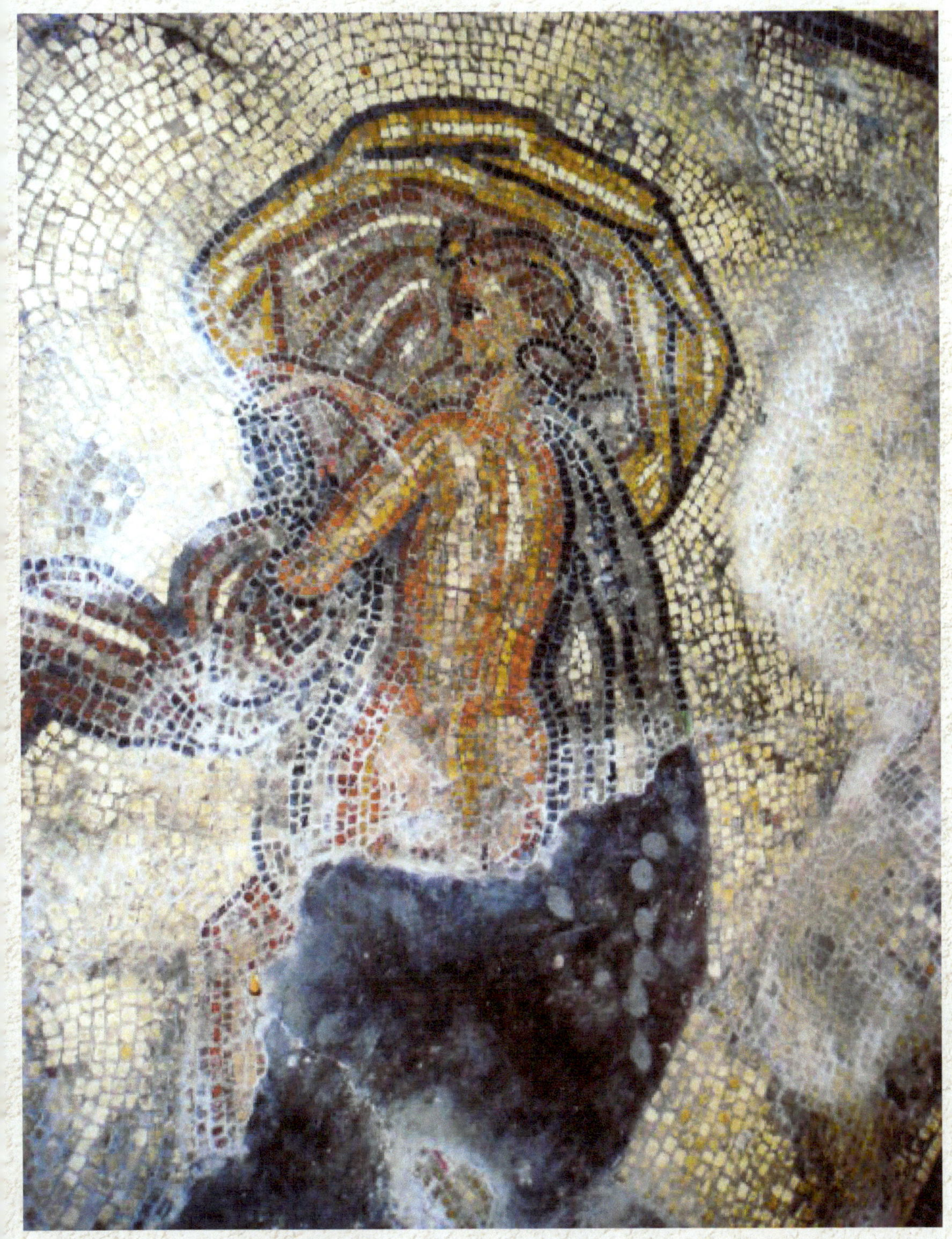

Ganymede and Dancers Mosaic

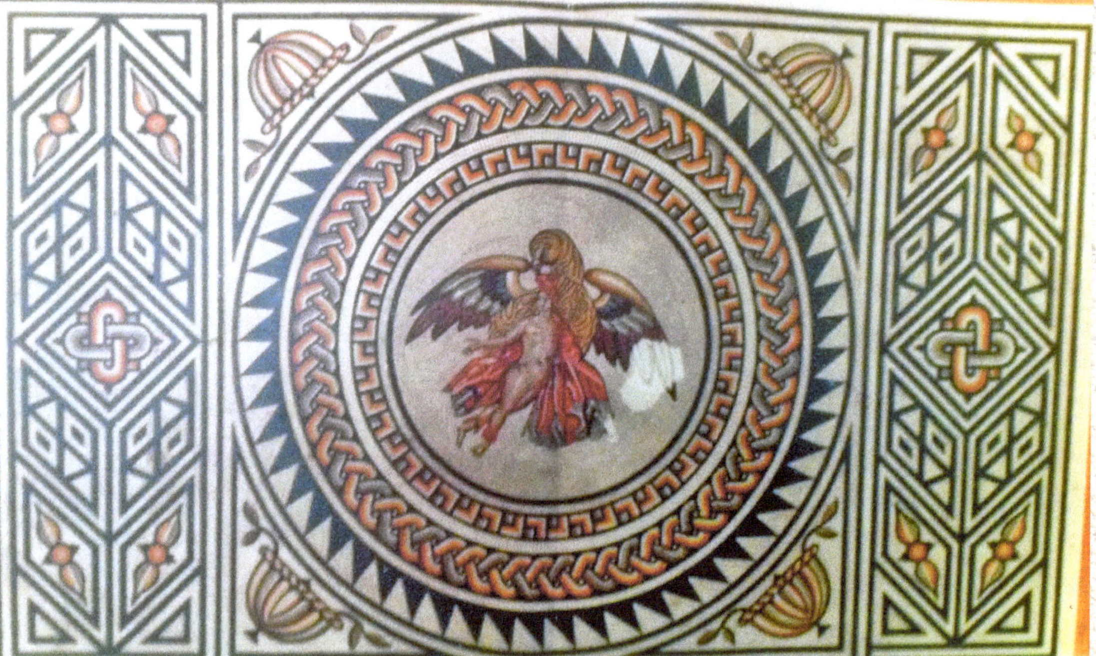

Ganymede being abducted by Zeus
Drawing by Samuel Lysons

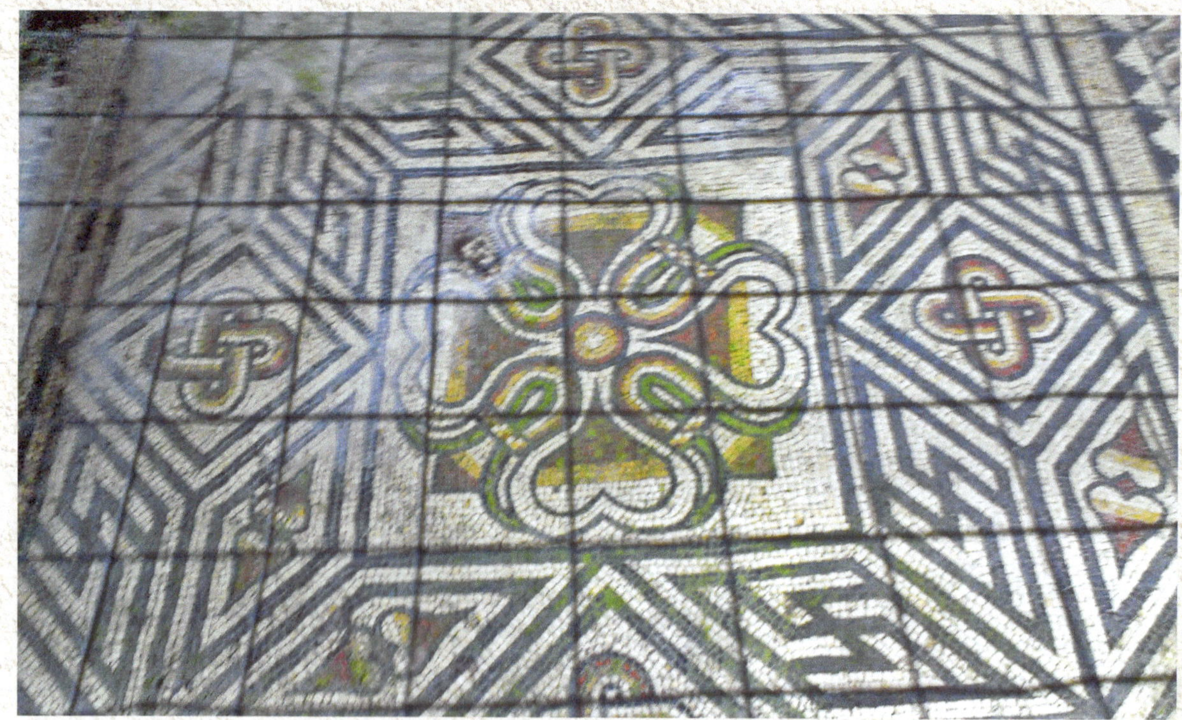

Geometric Mosaic. Room 6

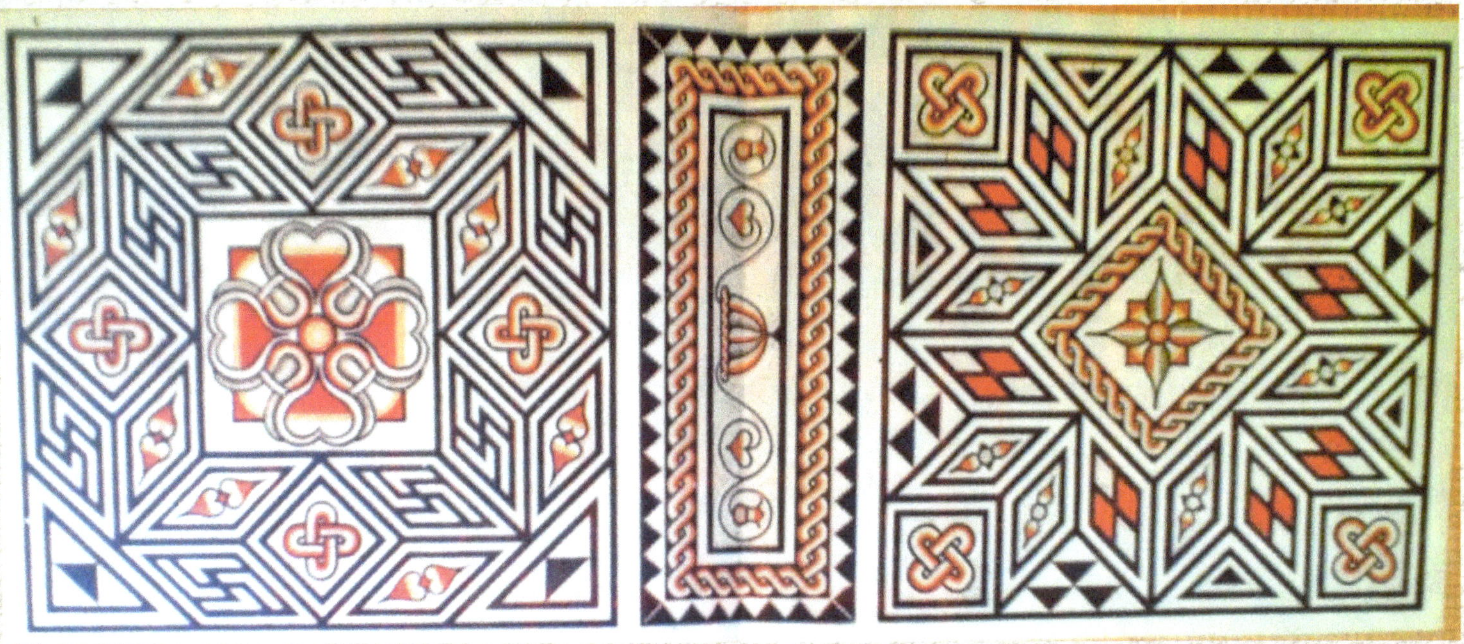

Geometric Mosaic Room 6
Drawing by Samuel Lysons

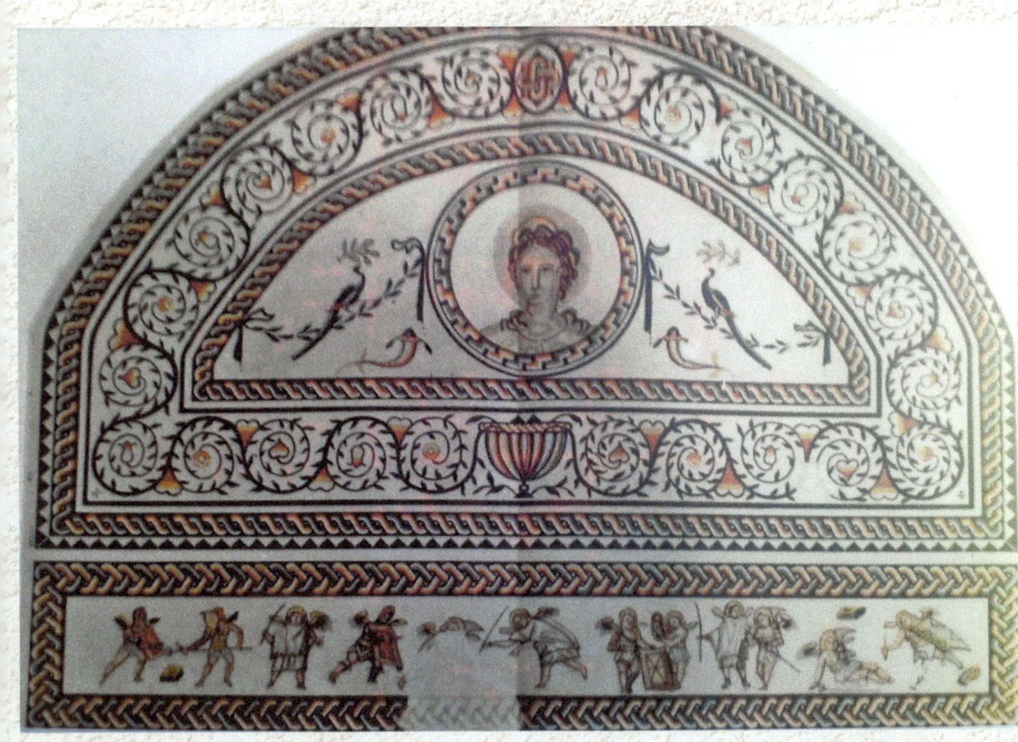

Part of Room 7
Drawing by Samuel Lysons

Venus and Gladiators Mosaic. Room 7

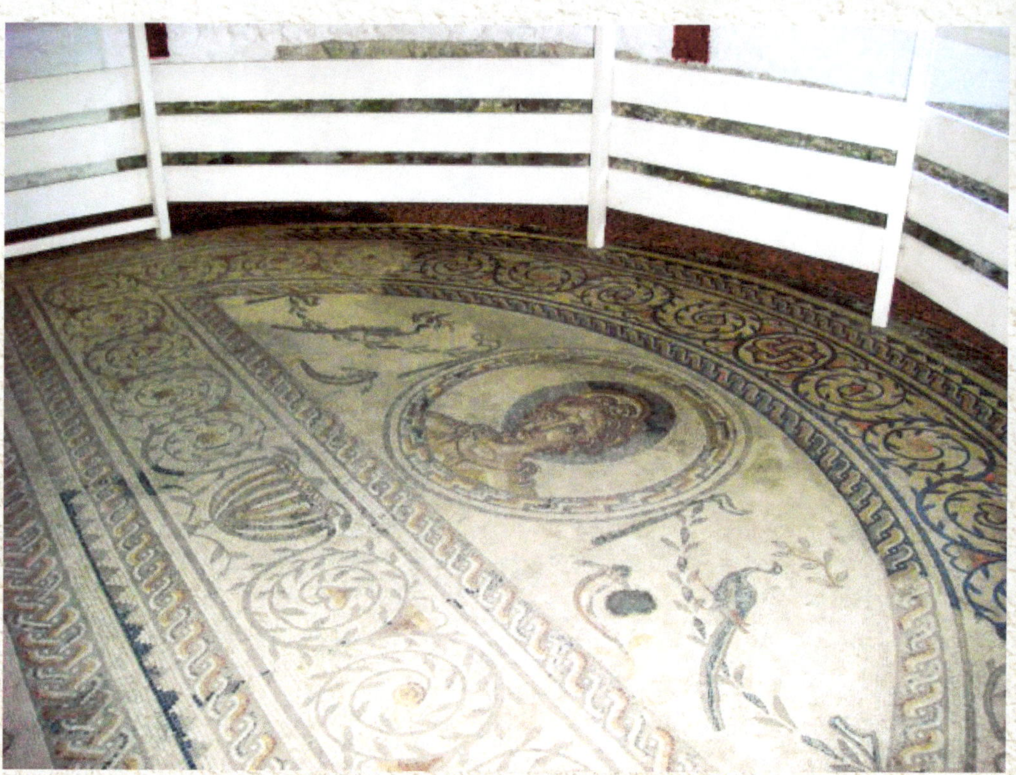

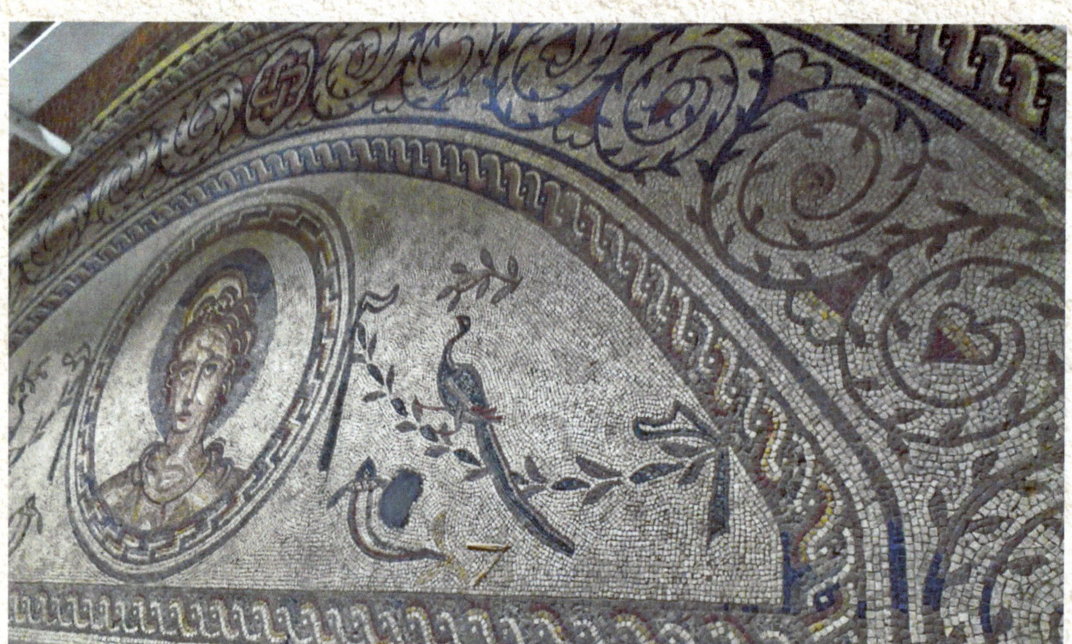

Venus and Gladiators Mosaic. Room 7

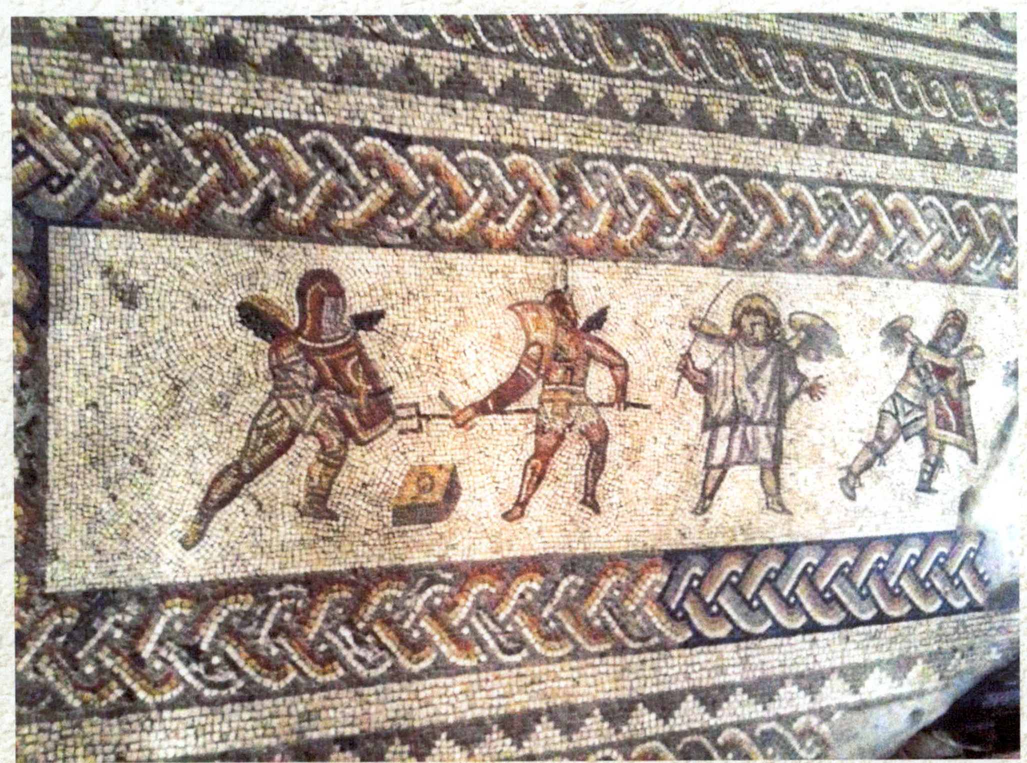

Venus and Gladiators Mosaic Room 7

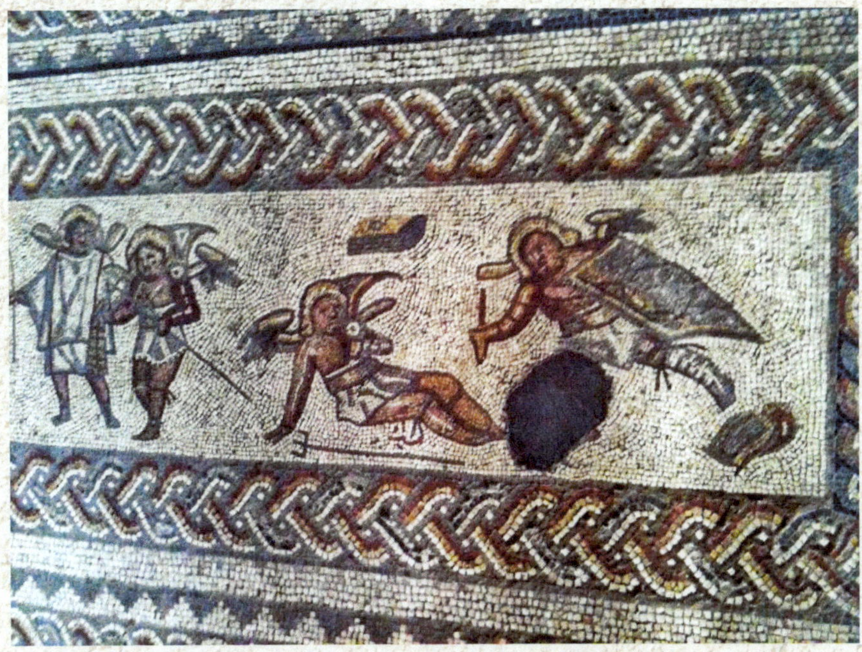

Venus and Gladiators Mosaic Room 7

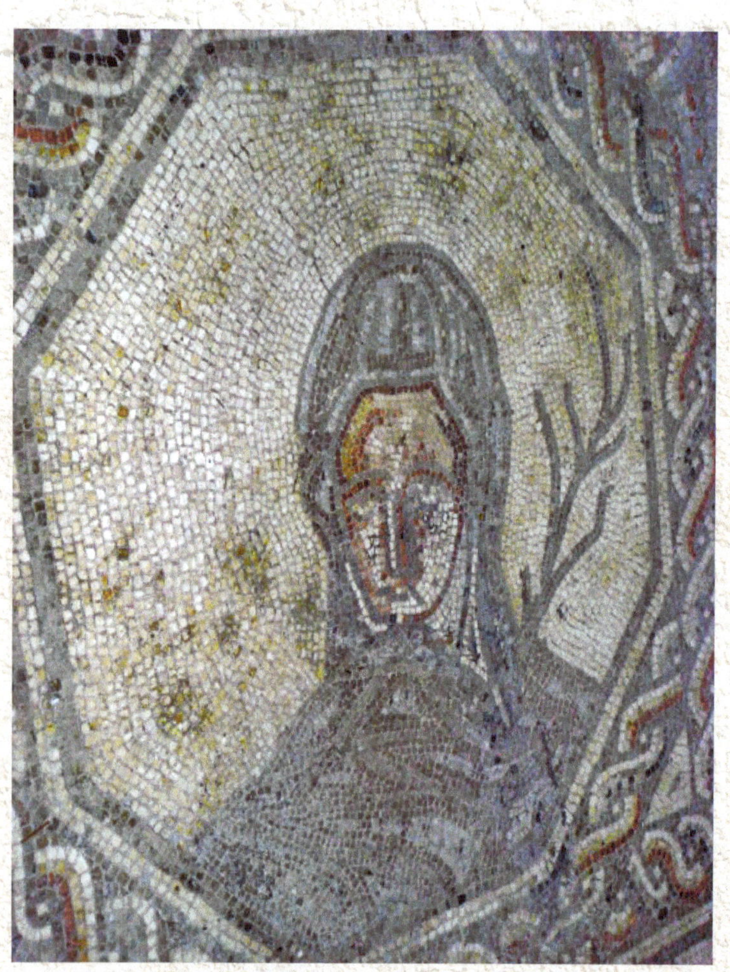

Head of Winter. Room 8

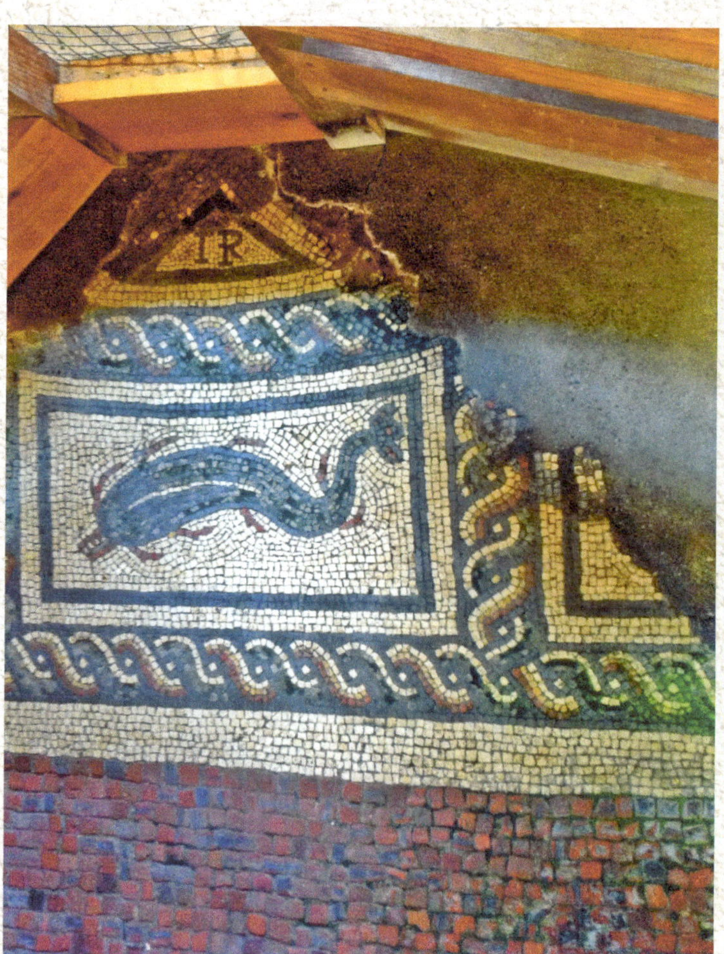

Dolphin and signature mosaic room 9

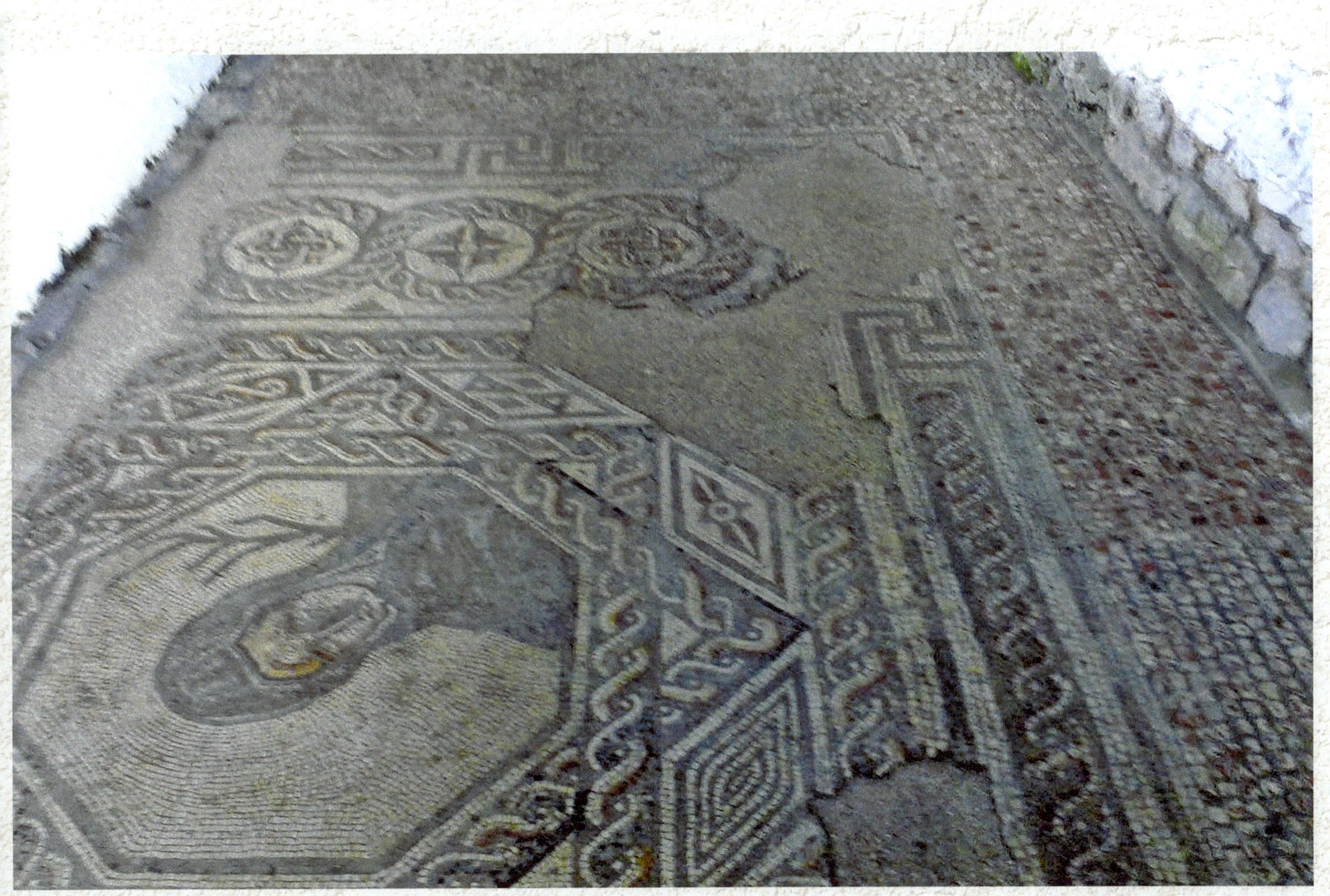

Winter-Room 8

Four Seasons Mosaic Room 33
Drawing by Samuel Lysons and Richard Smirke

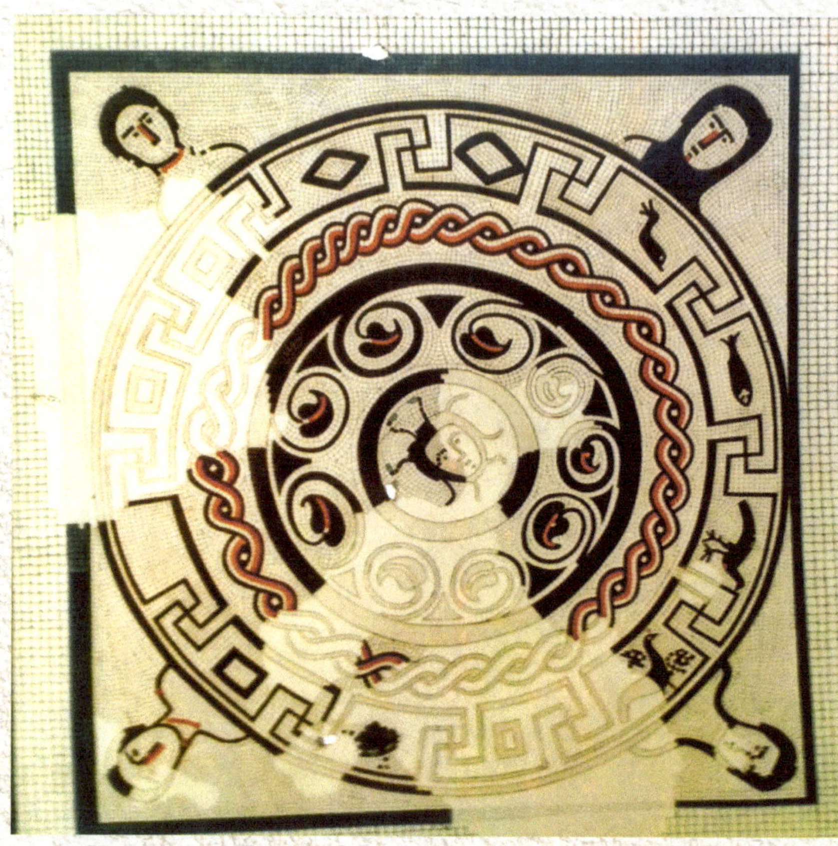

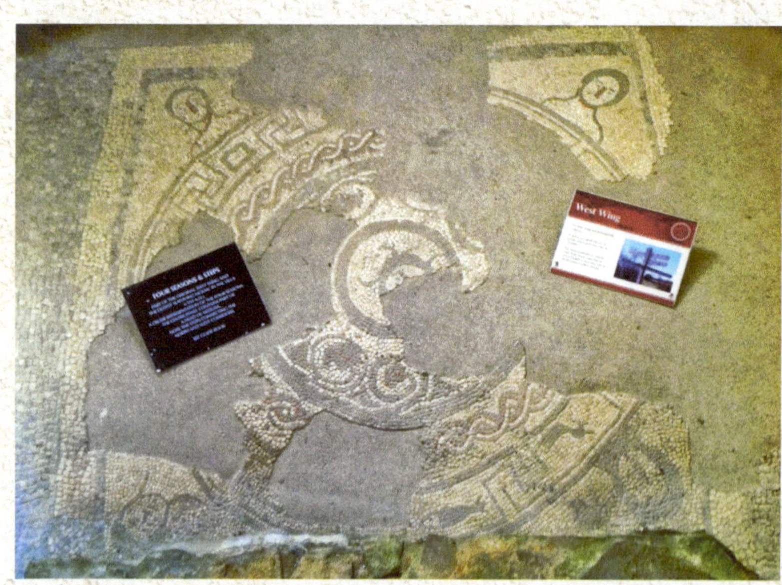

Four Seasons Mosaic Room 33

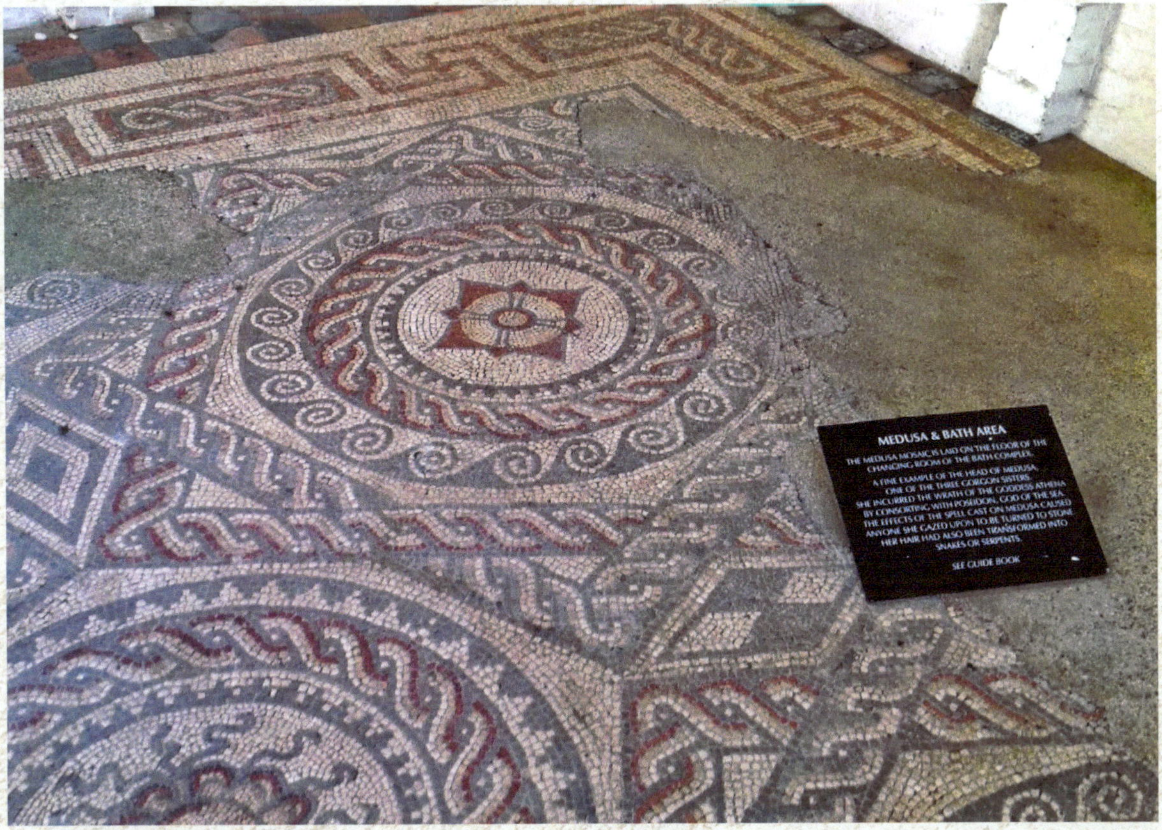

Mosaic from the Bath-House

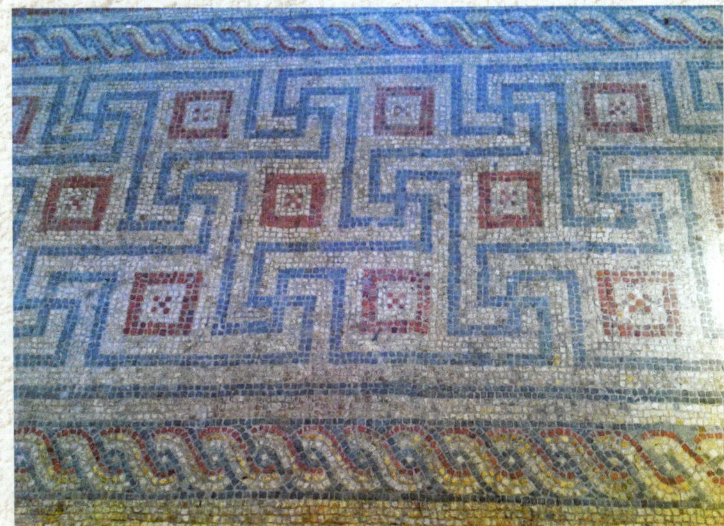

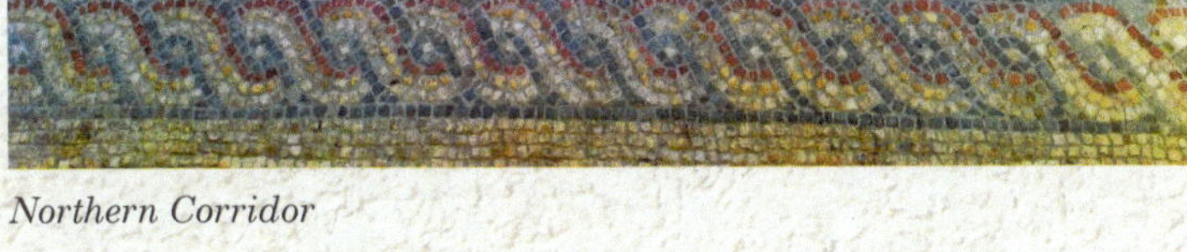

Northern Corridor

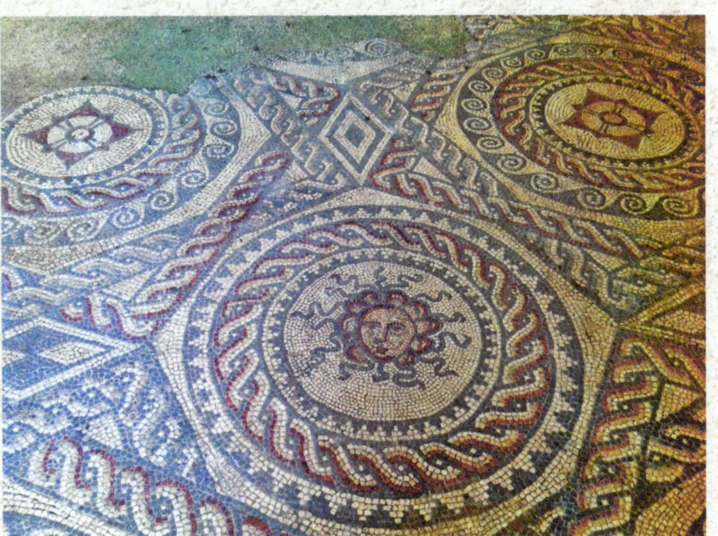

Mosaic Floor in the Bath-House

Chapter II
Lullingstone Roman Villa

This chapter discusses the discovery and interpretation of Lullingstone Roman Villa. The villa is located within the delightful countryside of South Eastern England, in the county of Kent. The Lullingstone villa nestles contentedly in the valley of Darent and, if we take a straight line from the villa to London, we would have travelled only 18 miles. The villa is situated near the village of Eynsford. Lullingstone, in the Textus Roffensis (the book of the church of Rochester, a mediaeval manuscript), was known as Lullineston, and in the Doomsday, Lolingestone. The Parish was small; it had no village, consisting only of three houses, one being known as Lullingstone House.

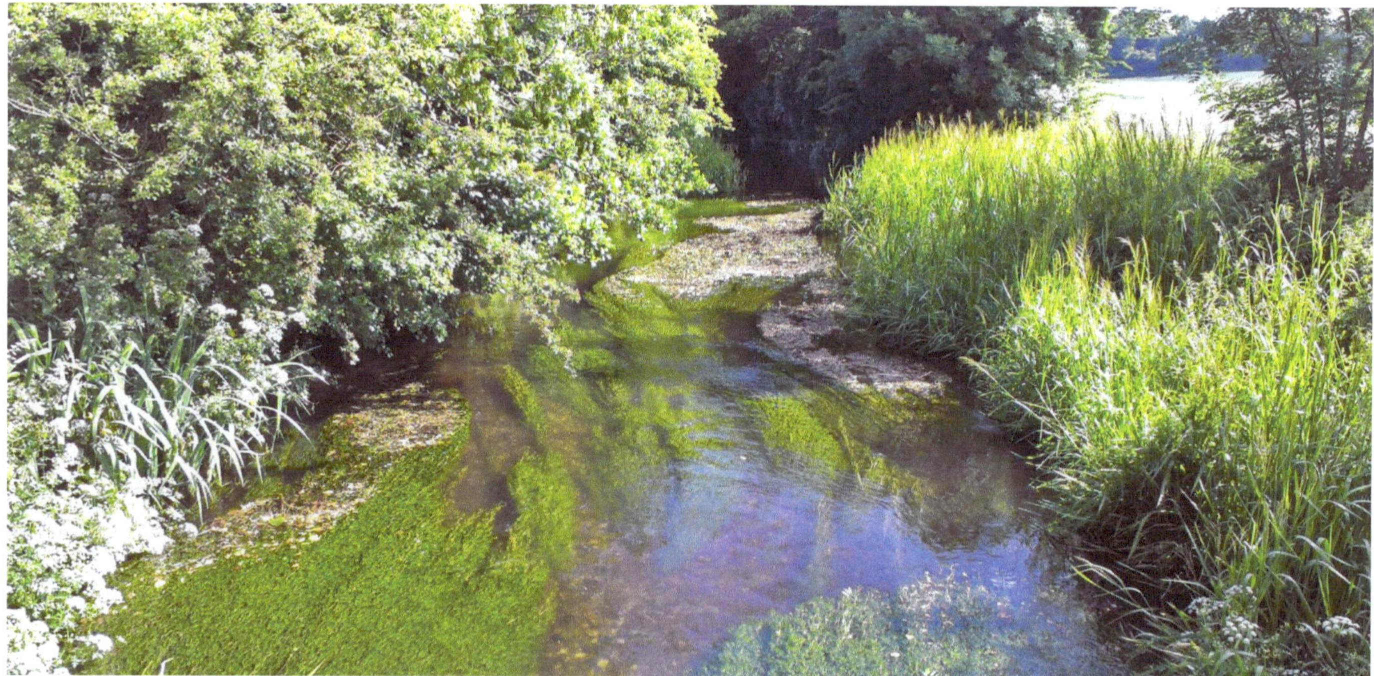

Country view of River Darant

The Lullingstone villa lies close to the west bank of the River Darent and is terraced into the east facing slope, its boundary extending down to the river bank.The villa was situated above it, upon a low terrace, cut back into the hillside.

To the north and south deeper compartments were built. Behind it to the west and 20 feet higher, a second terrace was constructed, this also being cut into the hillside. Upon this second terrace two religious buildings, a small circular temple and a temple-mausoleum were built. After the villa went out of habitation, hundreds of years of clay and flint hill-wash cascaded down to form a steep slope and consequently buried the ancient building, thus preserving some of the constructed walls up to eight feet in height.

This welcoming valley, secluded within the North Downs, offers up many inviting temptations to encourage homo sapiens to begin to lay down some permanent life roots and construct a positive and rewarding future. To the east of the River Darent is the River Medway and to the Darent's west is the River Cray.

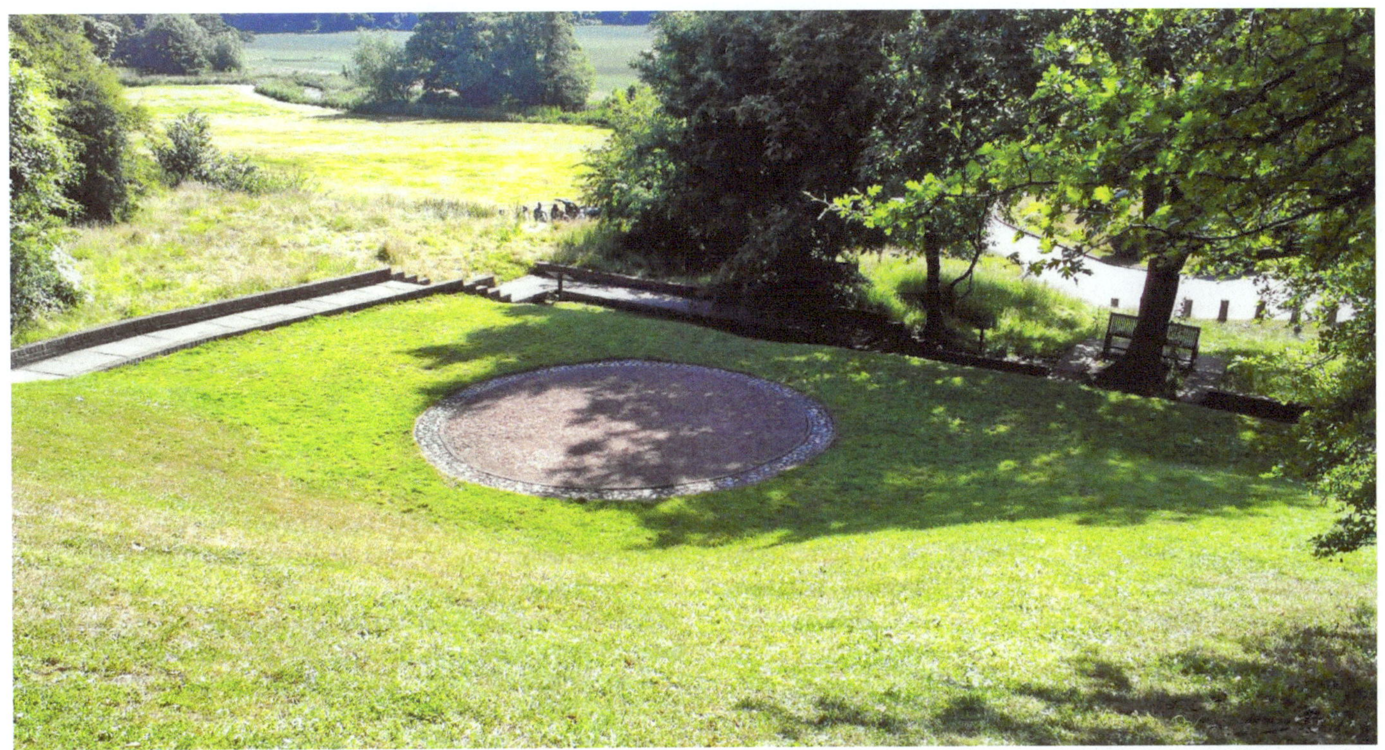

Position of the circular shrine

These three rivers meander through copses and a number of water meadows and eventually flow into the larger River Thames east of London. Within this abundance of clear running water, trout and other edible fish would have been found. This, with other natural attributes, including hundreds of acres of land for extensive farming, the flat valley bottom offering a lush pasture for cattle and finally, to the east of the valley, the wooded heights would have supplied fuel and oak for the construction of buildings – all of these would have provided an ideal environment for a rewarding, sustainable future. In such an environment the native/indigenous peoples would have flourished. In all probability the valley would have sustained a number of family units for many generations of the past, well before the main arrival of Vespasian and his conquering Legions in AD 43. But with their homes being constructed of wood, thatch and clay, all of which is degradable, their presence would have faded with the passing of time. Only the agricultural terrace, to the high ground to the west, is where their past is betrayed, caused by their ploughing activities. Over many generations of tilling, these great plough banks and lynchets were formed. Then, on closer inspection, Belgic pottery is to be found dated to before 80 AD.

Prior to Lullingstone Roman Villa being discovered and excavated, a small group of local archaeologists, inspired by the knowledge of other known Roman buildings in the valley, began a field survey of the upper part of the valley from Farningham working south to Otford. Evidence of any Roman building materials, including brick, tile and pottery fragments, were inserted on a map. When the whole of the valley map was scrutinised it became evident that every 2-3 miles, from Otford to Dartford, Roman buildings of some size existed. It seemed possible that land had been parcelled out for individual farming units, but a gap seemed to occur at Lullingstone. Two members of the field survey team continued their survey around that area of Lullingstone. Driven on by their passion, fuelled by a lusting curiosity for the past, they began to search dense undergrowth and came upon trees that had bowed to the storms of the past and noticed that the roots of one of the trees had levered up red brick, tile, tesserae and shards of Roman pottery. This was noted and filed. Then with the threat of instability to the people of the nation, caused by Hitler's military massing upon the horizon, the files were laid to rest and for the next ten years gathered dust.

When the universal interruption of the war receded from the shores of Britain, the search for the Romano-British villa resumed with renewed vigour. Many new faces emerged from the mists of memory to form the Darent Valley Archaeological Research Group. With the completion of the field survey, a watershed of detective work descended upon the literary works of the past. These were scrutinized and hiding away in the Archaeologia Cantiana Volume XXXIX, page 158, was a reference to a Roman Villa 'at Lullingstone at the north eastern boundary of the park (Gentleman's Magazine, 1823, Pt 1, pages 577-580)'. This article talks about the discovery of a tessellated pavement, coins and other relics of Roman occupation all brought back to the eye by the plough. This illuminating piece of literary source drove on towards the work of John

Thorpe, the antiquary, and his monumental work Custumale Roffense published in 1788. Through viewing this work, it eventually became apparent that the two members of the field survey before the war, who had mapped out the remains of the Roman material from the roots of the felled tree, that what they had found related to the Lullingstone Villa itself. Permission to excavate was sought and consequently granted by the landowners and in the spring of 1949 archaeological excavations began.

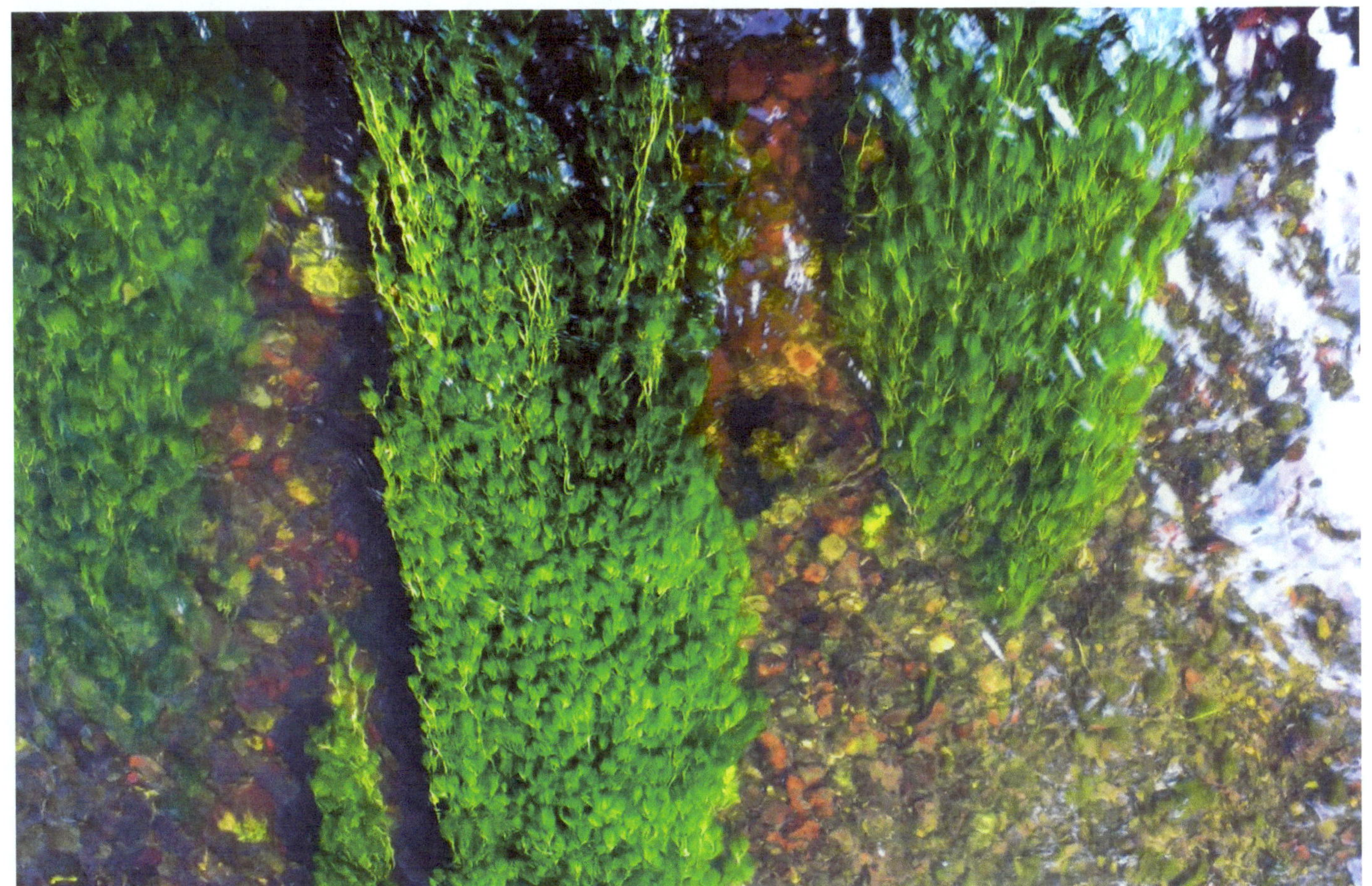

Roman building material on the river bed

I can only imagine the weeks prior to the first day of the excavation, for many of the excavators would have been filled with the emotions of impatience and excitement. Perhaps some of the more romantic excavators offered up silent prayers to Apollo – the Roman sun God, so the fire of their enthusiasm, fuelled by expectancy, would not be dampened with grey skies and rain. It was within this atmosphere of expectancy, in the spring of 1949, that the first spade penetrated the ground. Little did these early excavators realise that eventually their efforts would expose to the nation one of the earliest chapels of Christian worship as yet known in England. The excavations at Lullingstone continued up until 1961.

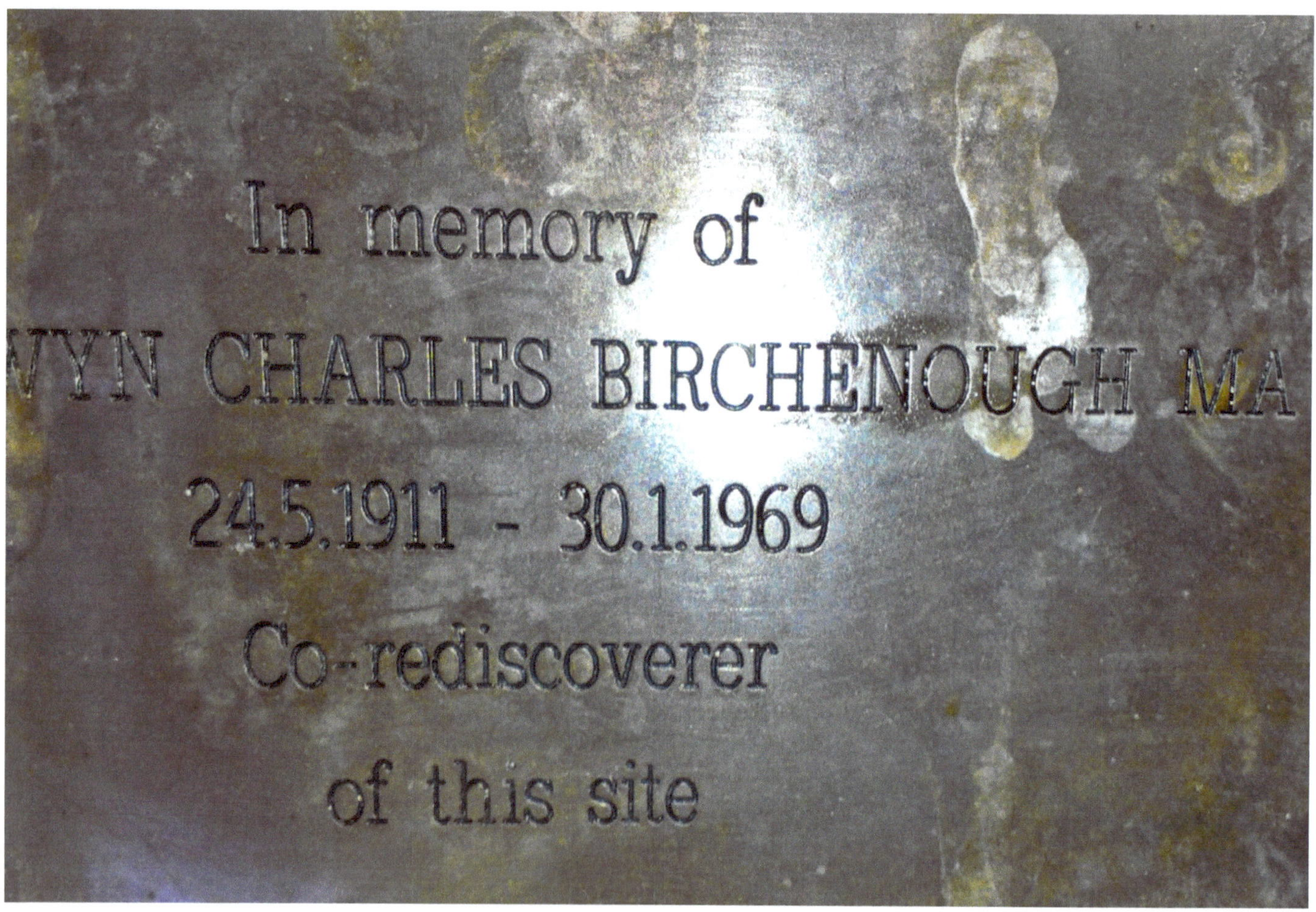

Memorial Plaque

The site was excavated by the Darent Valley Archaeological group, directed by Earnest Greenfield and Edwyn Birchenough and subsequently, solely, by Lt Col GW Meates – until 1961. Greenfield and Birchenough were the two archaeologists who had recognised the Roman deposits within the roots of the fallen tree, on the bank of the River Darent. In 1958, it became apparent that this villa was of national importance and, consequently, the then Ministry of Works erected a specially designed cover building over the remains and opened the villa to public viewing in 1963. Sadly, by the late 20th century, the original cover building was beginning to show its age and a number of leaks appeared. Under the guidance of English Heritage a £1.8 million renovation took place to safeguard all that the visitor can see today.

EVOLUTION AND HISTORY OF THE VILLA

The first substantial building on this site was possibly constructed in the early 70s AD. The villa underwent a great deal of expansion and remodelling and, without doubt, the occasional change of ownership. The political and the archaeological evidence seem to tell a story of prosperity and recession. Changes were made by architectural fashions, fuelled by prosperity. Perhaps the first inhabitants were of tribal aristocracy, but later in the villa's life the owners were more affiliated to the Roman/Greek legacy in literature, as borne out by the mosaic floors and busts of marble, sourced from the Mediterranean.

To fully comprehend the evolution of this villa we have to take a long look back over our shoulder and understand why the Romans, under Claudius, breached the shores of Britain in AD 43. They were driven by Britain's rich resources in copper, silver, gold, tin, lead and salt. Lead

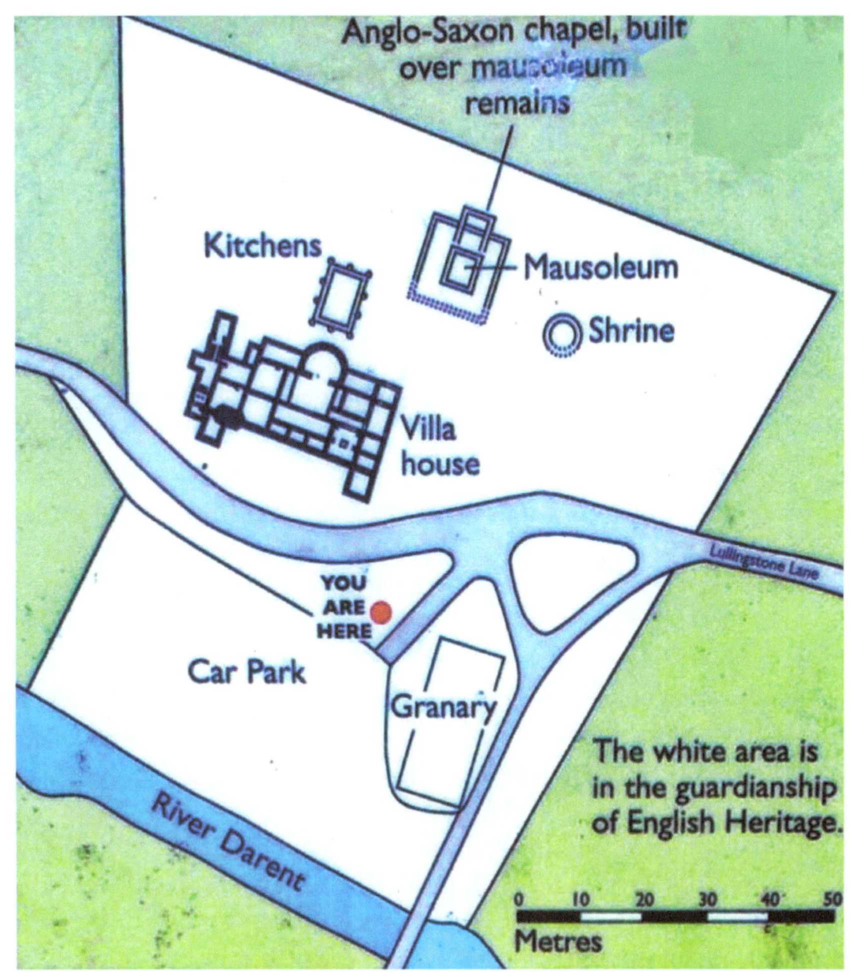

The villa in its grounds

mining in Somerset, North West England and Wales was highly productive by AD 49. By AD 70 Britain was the leading lead producing province within the Empire. Silver and lead were found together, the silver being encased in lead ore. The silver was especially important to the Roman economy as it was used for the production of coins. Gold was mined in Wales at Dolaucothi, and iron was mined from the Weald and the Forest of Dean. With the economy prospering, a workable administration system would have needed to be in place. It seems that Colchester (Camulodunum) and St Albans (Verulamium) were on course to succeed in this endeavour. Then, suddenly, the volcano of Boudicca erupted! With hindsight the following destruction and loss of life could have been avoided but, unfortunately, Roman greed prevailed. Boudicca, the queen of the Iceni tribe, in East Anglia, and her two daughters – Camorra and Tasca – suffered a political and humiliating rape. These combined events resulted in the future holocaust. Prasutagus, the king of the Iceni tribe, died in AD 61 and his will left half of his estate to the Roman Emperor and the other half to his wife and daughters. This was legal by British law, but the Roman administrator, Catus Decianus, chose to apply Roman law, as Britain was a province of the Roman Empire, which only allowed inheritance to male descendants. Underlying this event, the Romans had seized the lead mines within Iceni territory which cut off the financial benefit to the Iceni royal family. Consequently Prasutagus was forced to borrow money from Seneca, a wealthy Roman philosopher. Under Roman law, Seneca would not have been allowed to lend money to a fellow Roman, but the Iceni tribe were classed as foreigners, therefore this loan would have been legal. At the death of Prasutagus, Seneca informed the Roman administrator Catus Decianus that he wished to call in his loan. This, therefore, would have put pressure on the administrator to apply Roman law to Prasutagus' will.

The public flogging of Boudica and the loss of her daughters' virginity, taken by the Roman soldiers, was the final humiliation that forced the bubbling magma of discontent to the surface. In consequence to this, other tribes, also disillusioned with the heavy hand of Rome, joined together with Boudica's Iceni tribe and the destruction of anything, or anybody, allied to Romanisation was imminent. Colchester (Camulodunum), London (Londinium) and St Albans (Verulamium) were ransacked, burnt to the ground and inhabitants were destroyed by the violence of the sword. Roman control of Britain became fragile and the political stability of the Island was in the balance. News of the rebellion rippled through to the then Governor of Britain, Gaius Suetonius Paulinus, who was engaged with his army on the Island of Anglesey (Mona), off the north west coast of Wales, where the vicious veins of his Legions, with their heavy-soled, hobnailed caligae, were stamping the life out of the Druids. The Druids, the priestly class in Britain, welded more power over the Celtic tribes than the Celtic kings themselves. This religious order was responsible for organising worship, judicial procedures and the practice of divination. They preached that the human soul was indestructible and this teaching developed a high level of human courage when the tribes were engaged in combat. Without the influence of the Druids, the tribes would be under the control of their various kings whom the Romans could manipulate.

Paulinus' intrusion on the Isle of Anglesey was interrupted by the uprising of the native tribes and after a short period of assessment of the situation, Paulinus marched his Legions north east and, at a battlefield not as yet identified by archaeologists, extinguished the Boudicca-led revolt. The waves of the after-shock of this revolt eventually reached Rome and the Emperor Nero. His response was to recall Paulinus back to Rome and replace him with the more conciliatory Publius Petronius Turpilianus, whose policy was one of appeasement. This policy of appeasement began to be more consolidated in the late summer of AD 77 when Gnaeus Julius Agricola became the Roman Governor of Britain. He was a reputable administrator as well as a commander, and his reforms encouraged the expansion of Roman ways, including education for the native nobility. He reformed the corn levy which then became financially of more benefit to the community rather than to specific individuals. These measures encouraged the growth of towns to be established on the Roman model, culminating with the opening of St Albans (Verulamium) civic centre. It comprised a forum with colonnaded shops, basilica and official cult temples.

With the growth of the population in the towns, more food would have been required. This accelerated the evolution of the farmsteads in the Darent valley. Some farmsteads grasped the opportunity to expand and gain more wealth. This, combined with Romanisation, was reflected in the living quarters of the families which became more substantial, sophisticated and elegant. They became known as villas.

TOUR OF THE VILLA

The gurgling of the flowing water from the River Darent pleasantly welcomes me to the villa, as I alight from my car in the villa's car park. On viewing this part of the river, now relatively narrow, some of the bits and pieces of the villa's past stare back at me through the rippling water. As I approach the entrance to the villa and glance to the right, the steep wooded west bank of the river valley becomes clearly visible. The entrance doors of the modern building which houses the villa open before me and I am greeted by a welcoming and pleasant atmosphere. Before reaching the pay desk I view to the left and the right an abundance of neatly presented possible purchases. I do recommend the purchase of a guide book as this explains in some detail the alterations made to the villa during its lifetime. I make my way to the far left of the lobby and, as a second set of doors close behind me, the atmosphere changes to one of serenity, which is subtly supported by thoughtfully placed artificial lighting. As I view to my right, I gaze down upon the skeletal remains of the home of a once wealthy and prosperous family. Upon the right end-wall, above the remains, a ground plan can be seen which depicts in colour the changing design of the villa over its lifetime. Information boards placed on the right-hand side of the walkway assist the visitor to understand the layout of the rooms. On the left wall are reconstructed wall-paintings and two marble busts from the deep room which add to the increasing intrigue that has begun to bubble up in my mind.

There is a balcony walkway from which the visitor has a deeper view into the rooms below. The walkway floor space is adorned with cabinets housing interesting artefacts. Also on view is a lead sarcophagus containing the remains of a young man. This coffin was excavated from the mausoleum within the villa grounds. The mausoleum's Roman ruins were incorporated into the late Anglo Saxon chapel of Lullingstane.

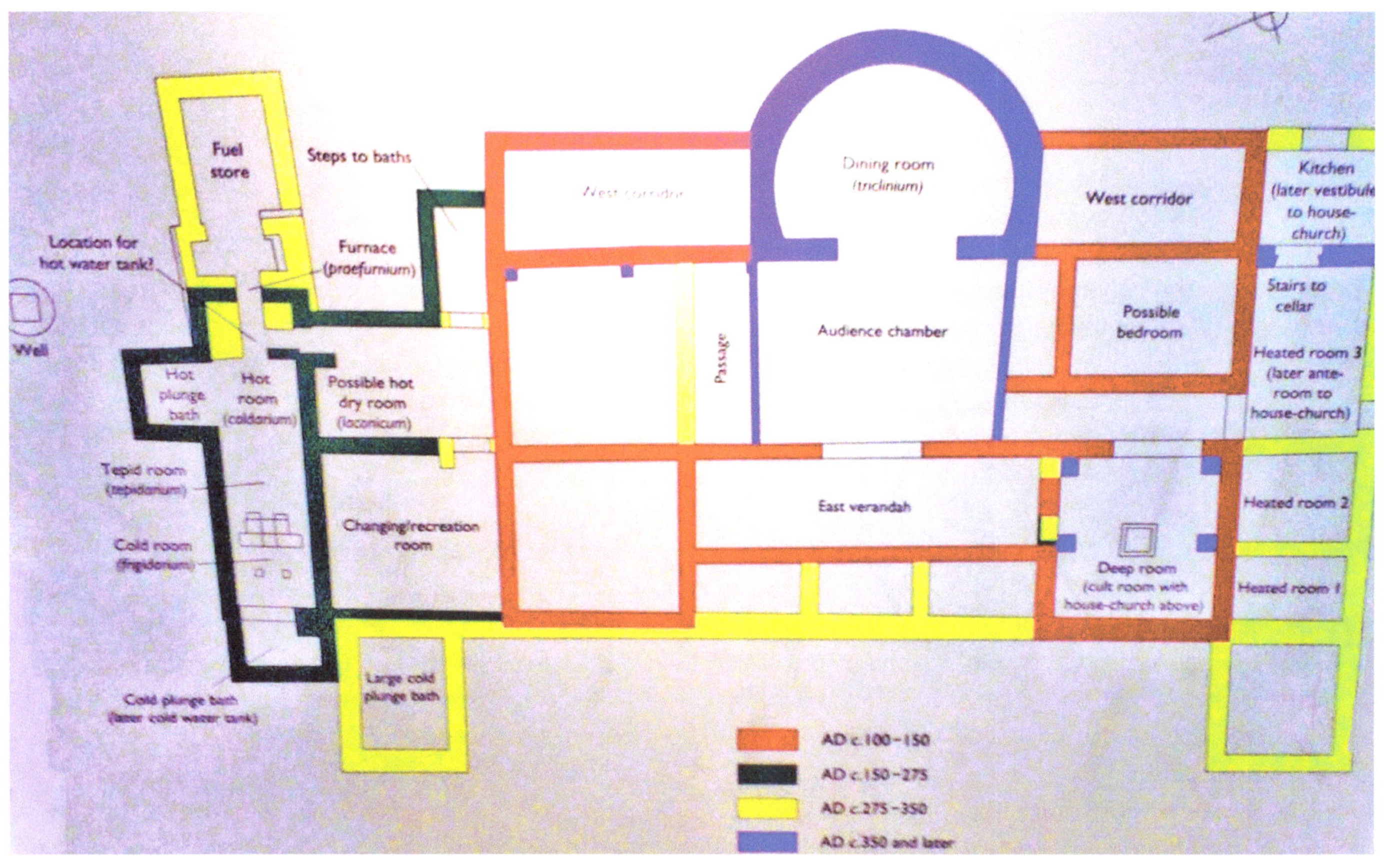

Time-line of the villa

Interestingly, upon the young man's coffin a bone inlay head of Medusa was found. This was, possibly, the lid of the now degraded wooden box which contained a gaming set of dice and glass counters. This Medusa's head could have been an amulet to protect the coffin and ward off evil spirits. All this adds a welcoming human presence to the site. Further on, and decorating the wall on the left, are colourful depictions of figures and medallions from the mosaic floors.

THE MOSAICS

Archaeology has revealed that there was a succession of mosaic floors constructed in Room 19 (frigidarium). Although no design of the later mosaic was revealed a large number of tesserae were excavated. Some were fragments of samian ware which was dated to the mid 2nd century AD. Perhaps then this mosaic was constructed in the later years of the second century AD. The white tesserae within the Lullingstone mosaics are of chalk. Some red clay tile has been recognised and the dark blue/grey tesserae were created from the oxidised core of the tile. Yellow ochre is present, as is tesserae of dark grey, brown, yellow, pink and buff. The various deposits of sandstone from the Weald of south east England could have provided the variety of

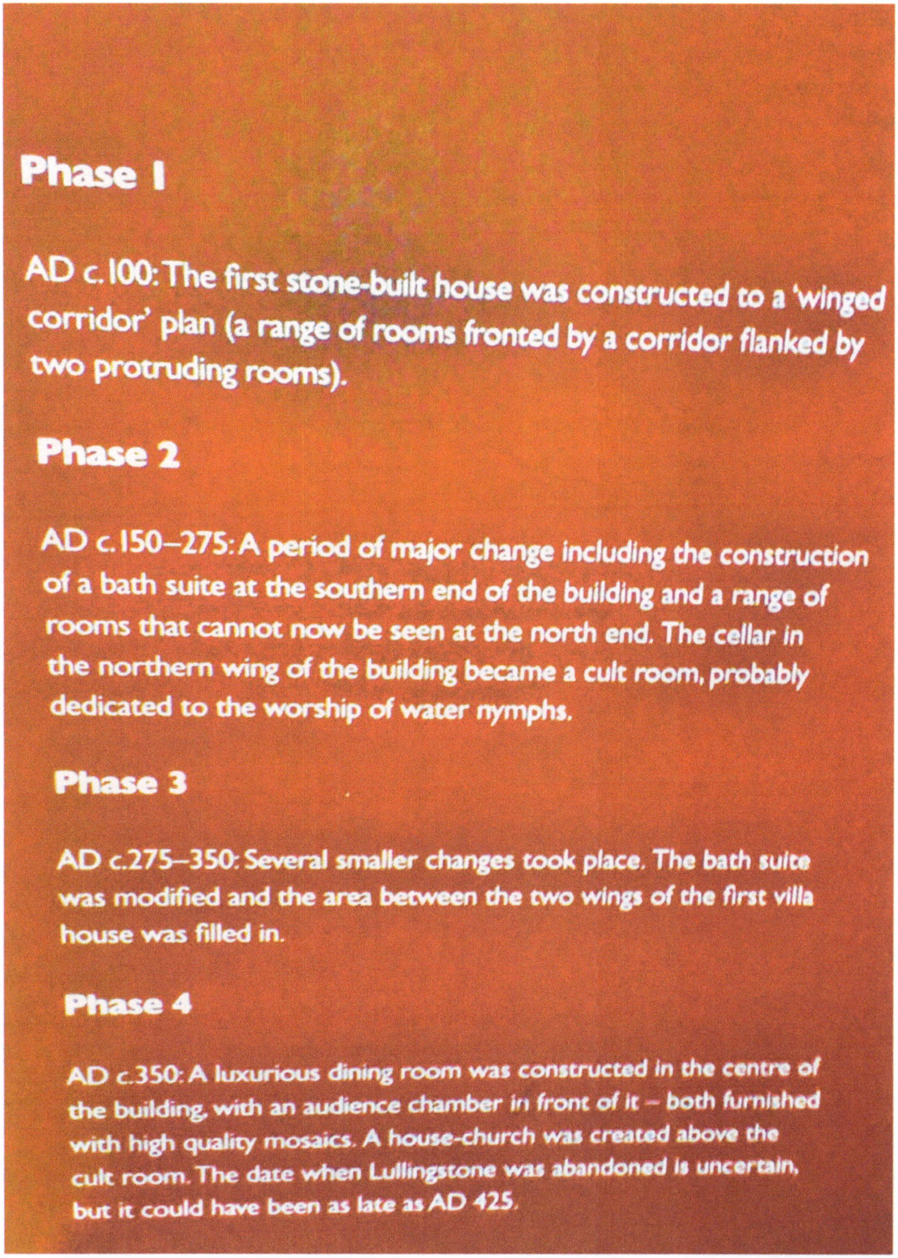

Phase 1

AD c.100: The first stone-built house was constructed to a 'winged corridor' plan (a range of rooms fronted by a corridor flanked by two protruding rooms).

Phase 2

AD c.150–275: A period of major change including the construction of a bath suite at the southern end of the building and a range of rooms that cannot now be seen at the north end. The cellar in the northern wing of the building became a cult room, probably dedicated to the worship of water nymphs.

Phase 3

AD c.275–350: Several smaller changes took place. The bath suite was modified and the area between the two wings of the first villa house was filled in.

Phase 4

AD c.350: A luxurious dining room was constructed in the centre of the building, with an audience chamber in front of it – both furnished with high quality mosaics. A house-church was created above the cult room. The date when Lullingstone was abandoned is uncertain, but it could have been as late as AD 425.

Phases of the villa

colours. These deposits could also have been responsible for some of the red and purple tesserae. I seek out these coloured stones and there before me and laid down by ancient hands, they appear, all grouped together to tell two engaging stores from classical Greek mythology. I glide my eyes over the whole mosaic and my mind is eventually impacted by irregularities contained in the Greek key border. The outer border of the Greek key design is roughly executed and in the south east corner there is no link to the southern side. On the opposite side, a dog-leg is noticed. The infill of the design on the northern side is of white tesserae, as is the east side, but on the south side some of the background tesserae are of yellow. On the outer boundary of the east side, a single line of white tesserae suddenly ceases at a point a little over halfway towards the south. This can possibly be explained away by the presence of a doorway, ten feet wide, which stood centrally in the east wall when this mosaic was first constructed.

The two remaining mosaics on view today are to be found in the apsed dining/reception room. Both mosaics, as I have previously said, depict scenes from mythological stories. In the semi-circular apse we view the 'abduction of Europa'. In the mosaic seen above this we view 'Bellerophon riding Pegasus and killing the Chimera'. In three of the four corners of this mosaic are roundels depicting the seasons. The missing roundel and part of the border were disfigured and destroyed by two post holes erected in the 18th century. These two mosaics are separated by an intriguing rectangular panel containing 40 squares and octagons laid out in four rows of ten. The boxes contain a medley of crosses, swastikas, one of which is reversed, and heart-shaped leaves. Intriguingly, towards the southern end, a cantharus/cup, composed of brown tesserae with a red background, can be seen.

I feel that the viewing of these mosaics is enhanced if the story of the myth is known and one can therefore appreciate the skill of the mosaicist in his interpretation of it. Bellerophon is depicted wearing red, over-the-ankle boots and sporting an elegant red tunic (chlamys) as worn by the Greeks when hunting. It was worn across the chest and was thrown backwards over the left shoulder. The right arm was therefore free to carry a weapon of destruction. Small red tesserae make up the garment which also contains lines of dark blue tesserae, used to highlight the folds within it. Pegasus, the winged horse, gallops in haste across the white background, elegantly controlled and ridden by the composed looking Bellerophon., who drives a long thin lance into the Chimera.

The Chimera is depicted here as an insignificant small yellow lion and seems to be trying to outrun the magnificent and proud Pegasus. In the myth, this beast was a combination of the frightful and the grotesque. It vomited fire from its lion's mouth, the tail was fanged and poisonous, while a goat's head protruded from the middle of its back. The myth unwinds as follows: Bellerophon was born in Korinthos/Corinth and was sired by the God Poseidon. Bellerophon's mother was Eurynome but he was raised by

Eurynome's husband, the King Glaucus. Under King Glaucus' guidance Bellerophon matured into a talented horseman. He was handsome, athletic, had an enquiring mind and longed for adventure. Bellerophon seems to have been exiled for an unintentional killing, possibly one of his brothers named Deliades. By means of atonement for this crime he is sent as a suppliant to Proetus, a king in Tiryns. Proetus, by virtue of his kingship, cleanses Bellerophon of his crime. The king's wife Anteia/Stheneboca falls in love with Bellerophon who, being a man of honour, declines her advances. In revenge for this rejection, Anteia confides to her husband that Bellerophon had tried to seduce her. Proetus, enraged and possibly envious and jealous of Bellerophon's charisma, composes a letter to his father-in-law, Iobates, king of Lycia, requesting that Bellerophon be put to death. Bellerophon is instructed by Proetus to carry and deliver the sealed letter to Iobates. When the king reads the letter he is faced with a dilemma. Although he wants to please his son-in-law, he also did not wish to enrage the wrath of Erinyes, three avenger goddesses of crime. So, slyly, he instructs Bellerophon to slay the Chimera, a monster who terrified and preyed upon the local community – the bones of his victims were left strewn along the mountainside where the Chimera lived. Bellerophon sought out and engaged the wisdom of Polyidus, the wisest man in Lycia. Bellerophon felt he needed a horse to be able to fulfil the task and therefore Polyidus informed him about Pegasus, the immortal winged horse. To obtain the horse Polyidus advised him to spend the night in Athena's temple and to pay her much homage. In a dream Athena came to him and left him a golden bridle and instructed him about the location of the well where Pegasus drank. In the morning, as Pegasus knelt to drink from the well, Bellerophon slipped the bridle onto the horse's head. Consequently, Bellerophon and Pegasus were united for the quest and in due course the people of the village were delivered salvation.

If we dwell on this story, we can recognise that unconditional love is offered to a child by a man who was not a blood relative. Also, we see righteousness, evil and the rejection of temptation. Wisdom is there as is salvation and even a miracle or two. Perhaps then, when the proprietor of this villa and his family, and possibly some friends, enjoyed some food in this dining room, a fleeting glance at this mosaic would serve to remind them of their Christian values.

If we feed our eyes once more upon the scene within the cushion-shaped part of the mosaic, we are viewing a construction of quality and of forceful and rhythmic action. Bellerophon and the soaring Pegasus are accompanied by dolphins and marine molluscs. Perhaps this scene symbolises the part of the myth where Bellerophon has to travel across the Aegean to Lycia to deliver the letter requesting his death. The four, long-whiskered, bulbous dolphins face each other in two pairs, one of dark blue/grey, one of yellow and two of yellow ochre. The open marine molluscs are depicted in red. On the outside of this depiction of Bellerophon and Pegasus, but still contained within the dark blue/grey square panel, three medallions outlined in red rest intriguingly in the corners. Each medallion contains a human head and perhaps, by the style of their hair, they depict women. The portraits on the medallions represent the seasons of the year, although the head depicting summer is lost. Winter, clad in a warming cloak, constructed of dark blue tesserae and with a cold, stern, white face seems to stare with envy and disapproval in the direction of Spring. Spring is skilfully constructed showing clearly a face of innocence, kindliness and of contentment as she gazes at the swallow perching on her shoulder. She wears a tunic of orange/yellow, tight fitting to her throat and over her left shoulder is flung a red cloak. Some lines of small, dark blue tesserae represent the folds within the garment. The face of Autumn is beautifully portrayed, perhaps reddened by the sun and shows a reserved and pensive expression. She has more hair than Spring and it seems to be braided. Interwoven into her hair and drooping in a downward curve are strands of corn and straw. Autumn wears the same attire as Spring although her tunic seems to be in a shade of pink. How to interpret these medallions within the context of the whole mosaic floor is open to interesting debate. Bellerophon and Pegasus have been associated in conjunction with the four seasons of the year in mosaics in France and Italy. There is also a correspondence between the seasons and the stages of human life, from birth to death. Spring is the birth, Summer is youth, Autumn is adulthood and Winter brings old age and death.

A second mosaic scene which occupies the apse, is a representation of the abduction of Europa by Jupiter, in the form of a white bull. It is a story of lustful, wayward love and the jealous emotions of the betrayed wife, Juno. The mosaicist's hand shows his talent in the execution of this scene. All is delicately outlined in red (possibly tile) on a white ground. The depiction of the bull's face shows eagerness in his role of abduction, while Europa, adorned with armlets, bracelet and a necklace, seems serene in her innocence. Her transparent gown, folded and anchored around her leg, billows out behind her in the breeze from her outstretched hands. The hind hooves of the bull penetrate the sea as he starts his journey to the island of Crete. The cupids indicate emotions; the one holding the bull's tail represents caution. The leading cupid, bearing in his left hand a flaming torch, urges abandonment to her forthcoming fate. The mosaic is a wonderful medley of the subtle use of colours and is of high technical ability. Within the cupids' wings dark blue and red stripes can be seen. The robe billowing out behind Europa's head contains tesserae of pink, blue and yellow. The hair of the three figures is delicately constructed with blue, orange, yellow and pink.

If we return to the myth, it gives an intriguing insight to the loves and lives of the Gods and Goddesses of mythology. Jupiter, the husband of the Goddess Juno, has his passions stirred by Europa, the beautiful daughter of Agenor, king of Phoenicia. Jupiter, in the guise of a placid white bull, places himself within the herds of the cattle of Europa's father. When Europa comes across the bull, when attending her father's herd, she is seduced by his beauty of the purest white and starts to caress him. When she decides to place herself upon the bull's back he arises and with all haste carries her off across the sea to the island of Crete. On arrival at Crete, Jupiter changes himself to his human and godlike form. He declares his love for her, and

Europa, in due course, bears him three sons. Juno, Jupiter's wife, seems to be having a less successful time of seduction than her husband. Rejected by the Trojan, Paris, in favour of the fascinating charms of Venus, Juno, in an act of jealousy, calls upon Aeolus, king of the winds, to destroy the fleet of galleys of the Trojan Aeneas, which was carrying the national Gods and the sacred fire of Troy. With all this in mind we should now view the Latin inscription which refers to a passage in the Aeneid of Virgil and its translation.

INVIDA SI TA(VRI) VIDISSET INVO NATATVS IVSTIVS AEOLIAS ISSET ADVSQVE DOMOS
("If jealous Juno had seen the swimming of the bull, she might more justly have gone to the halls of Aeolus")

All is then revealed symbolising, perhaps with irony and some humour, the perils awaiting the emotions of deceit and revenge …and love? This mosaic perhaps portrays the very opposite of the Christian message within the mosaic of Bellerophon and Pegasus.

The mosaic of the 'abduction of Europa' is enclosed in a semi-circular border which frames the scene like a necklace. The border is based on the form of twisted guilloche, with each of the enclosed circles filled with alternate red and white discs. This rests on a dark blue background. In all probability, this border would have contained the seating arrangements, so the mosaic and its inscription could be viewed with interest and discussed by visiting guests.

I feel that the most intriguing part of this mosaic floor is the extraordinary panel of 40 spaced squares, which sits in between the two figured mosaic scenes like a Persian rug. It seems perhaps too easy to dismiss this creation as a random piece of work. The panel is best viewed from the south side. It contains a number of motifs used within mosaics over many hundreds of years. If we dwell for a moment or two we perhaps realise that the inhabitants of this establishment are all-embracing of the past and of the modern. Greek and Roman influences are abundant as is the worship of pagan gods and the modern religion of Christianity. But what of the native Celts, the indigenous people of this Island? Have they really been forgotten and consequently faded into obscurity? By now, after many generations of Roman rule, the local men would have mastered the skills of the mosaicists. Perhaps then, one was commissioned to lay a mosaic panel to their memory. With no written history of Celtic traditions, myths or stories they can only be recognised by the decorative motifs which adorned their metalwork. A display of Celtic metalwork can be seen at the museum in Cirencester, Gloucestershire. Some of their metalwork within this museum contain patterns which are replicated within the panel of 40 squares at this villa. Coin evidence suggests that these mosaics were constructed in the middle part of the 4^{th}Century AD.

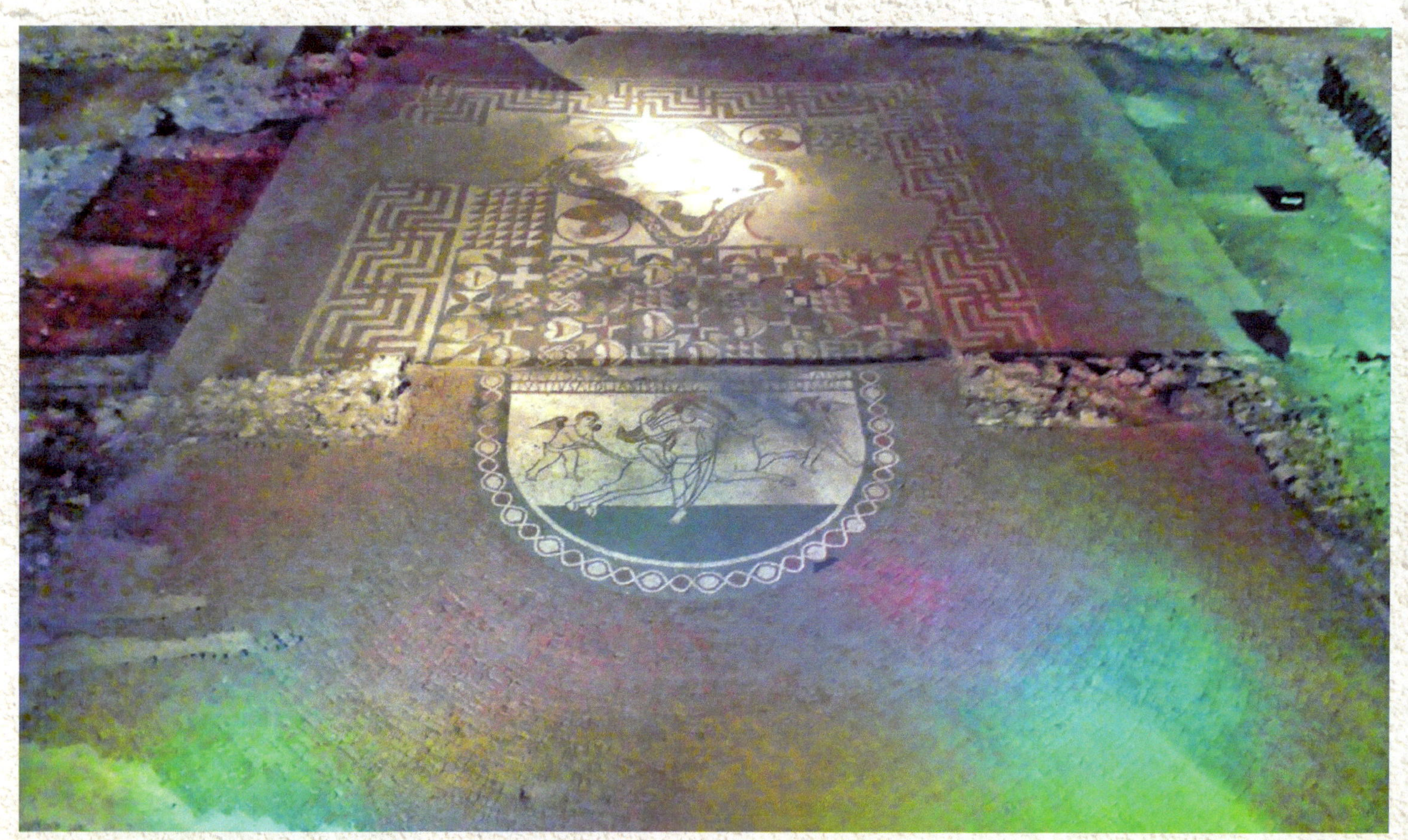

The mosaic floor of the reception room

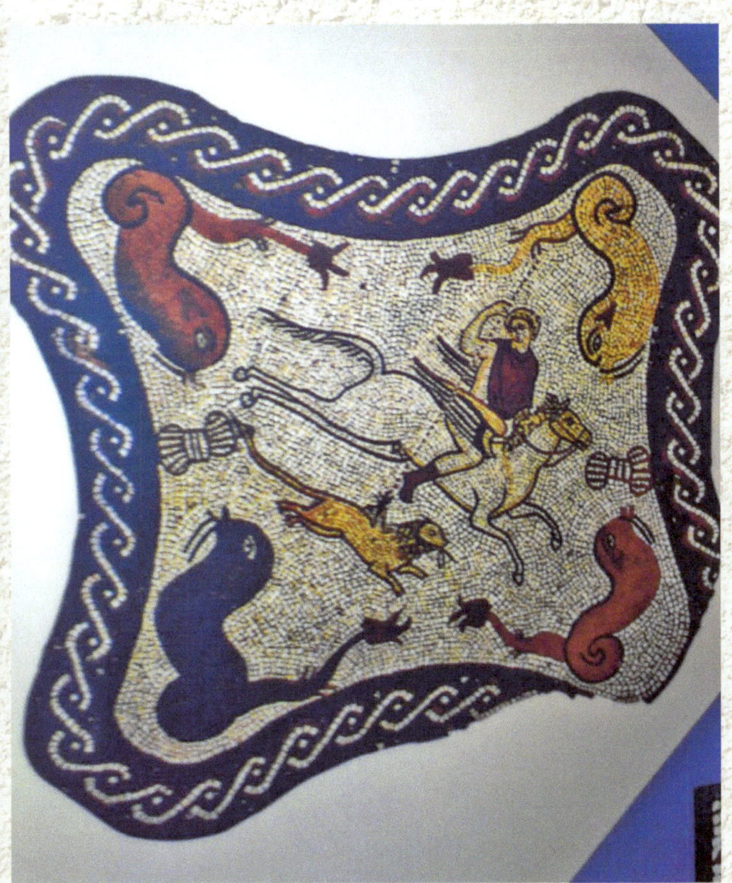

Bellerophon killing the Chimera

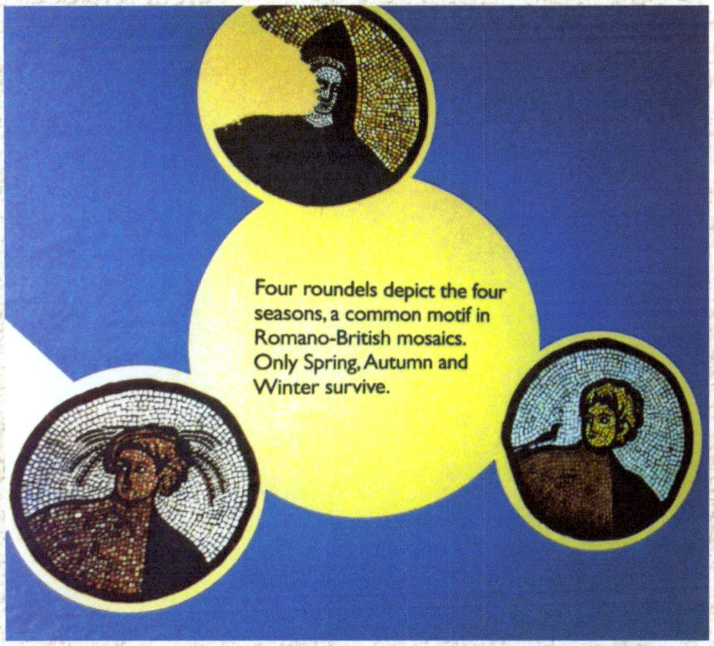

Spring-Autumn-Winter

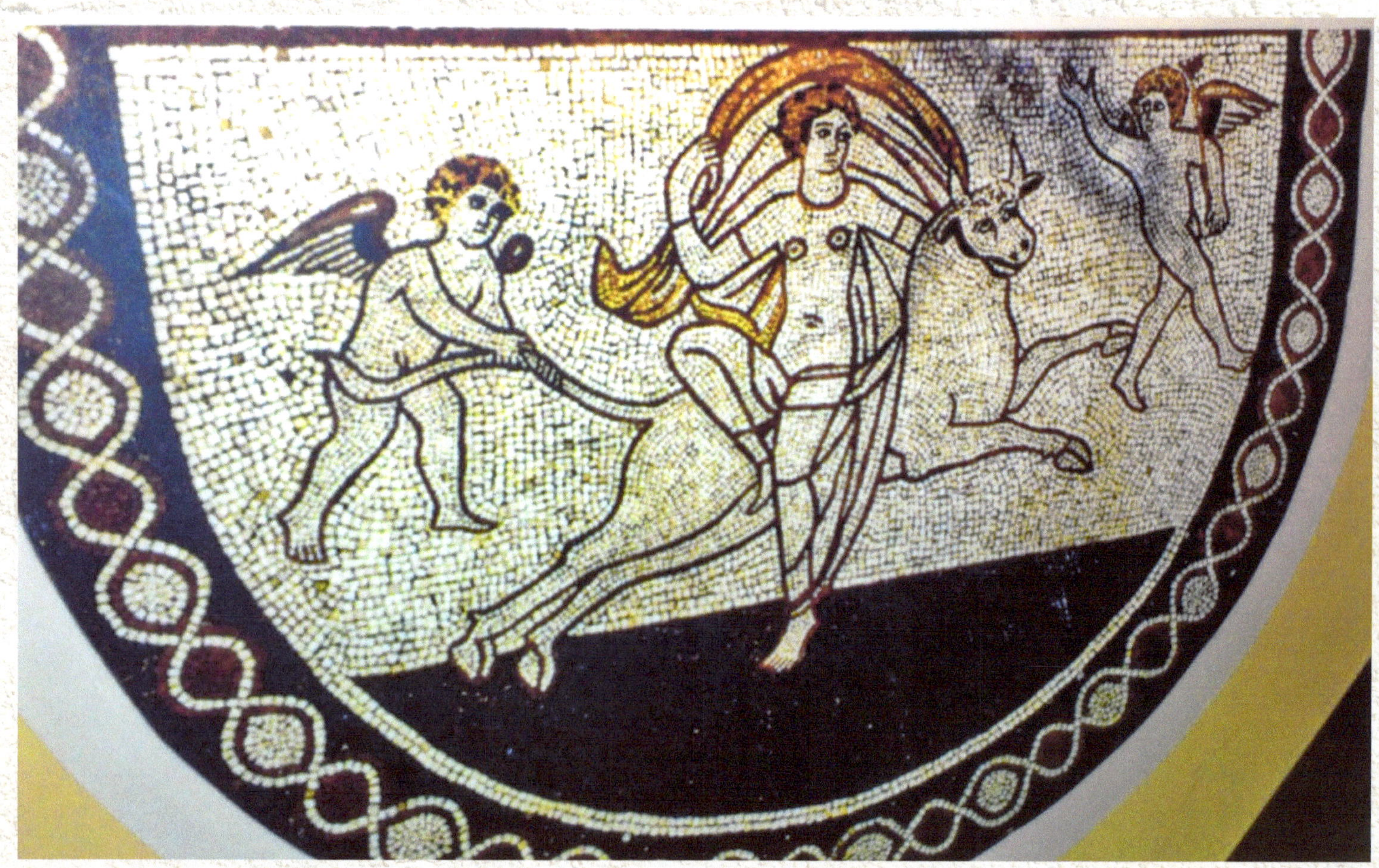

The abduction of Europa by Jupiter

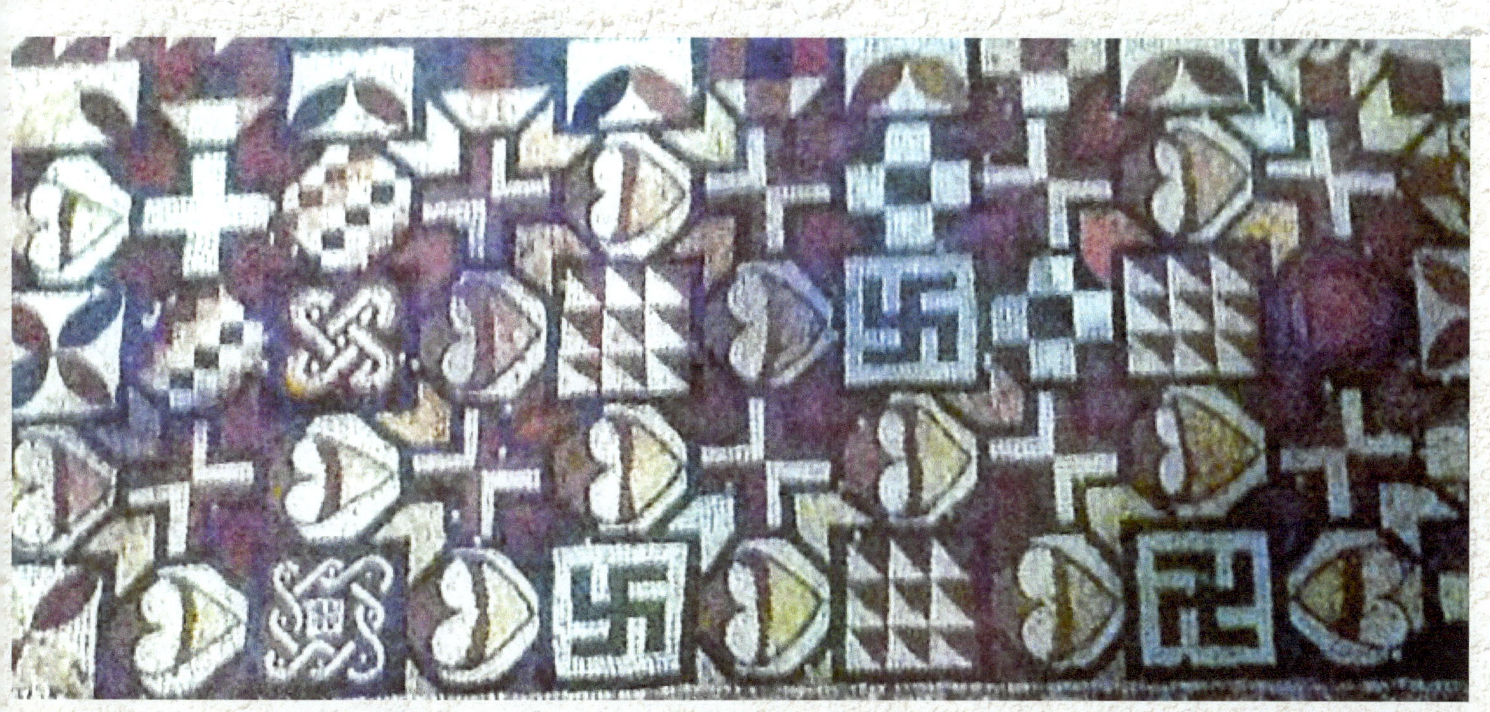

The panel of forty squares from the reception room

THE DEEP ROOM

Eventually, during and after the excavation of what was known as the 'deep room', a huge window of the past was slowly opened for us. Built as part of the original villa, the deep/cult room remained a prominent feature of this villa in all its phases. The archaeology also revealed that above this room an upper chamber, dedicated to Christian worship, had been constructed. Adjoining this upper chamber from the north was an ante-room. Fortunately, as the final destructive fire of the villa took hold, billowing out smoke and showers of sparks towards the stars, some of the blistering and peeling wall-plaster from these upper rooms fell conveniently into the sanctuary of the deep room. Thus, in the aftermath of the excavations, the chronological order of the human use of the rooms was eventually resurrected into the present. It seems that the deep room was a place of pagan worship, the focus being on a water deity/cult. In the niche on the southern wall the remains of a fresco of three water nymphs came to light. Also, a well had been dug in the middle of the floor in this room. An exquisite water-colour reproduction painting of two of the nymphs revealed that water was flowing from the breasts of one of the nymphs. Her sad gaze seems to be focused to her right upon an over-turned vessel, spilling out its contents. This room was redecorated and the niche containing the nymphs disappeared underneath mortared flints which consequently severely damaged the fresco. The deep room, at the time of its excavation, revealed to the world the decorative fashion of the period. Panels were noted of red, orange and green. Rising within them were yellow vines and deep red drooping grapes.

Amongst all the collapsed building material of roof tiles, carbonised wooden beams and many thousands of pieces of wall plaster, two bearded busts revealed themselves. These busts were fashioned from fine white Greek marble and possibly sourced from the ancient quarries on Mount Pentelicus, near Athens. It is highly probable that these busts were carved in the area of the eastern Mediterranean. These busts could well have been images for veneration within this pagan/cult room. One seems to be wearing a tunic and cloak/sagum, a semi-military garment, pinned on the right by a circular brooch, as worn by Romans of distinction. It has been suggested that this bust is of P Helvius Successus. Interestingly, Richard de Kind, on examination of the other bust, has identified it (bust with head only) as that of Publius Helvius Pertinax, Governor of Britain in 185-186 AD, and briefly Emperor in 193 AD, and son of P Helvius Successus. Also within this room four pottery vessels were revealed. Two were in holes in the underlying concrete floor and sealed down by the later clay floor. The other two were within the clay floor, but with their rims protruding several inches above it. Perhaps then these pots were votive in nature. The busts of these two prominent Romans, from the distant past, were, after cleaning, deposited for safekeeping and public viewing at Lullingstone Castle. Today they reside in the sanctuary of the Roman Room within the British Museum, in London.

Six to seven thousand pieces of painted wall-plaster from six different walls, relating to the two rooms above the deep room, were now required to be sorted out to see if there was any information to be gathered from their reconstruction. The heat of the fire was responsible for the change in the colours of reds and blues to dark olive or green, which greatly increased the difficulty of reconstructing the original designs. The responsibility for this challenge was taken on by Mr C D P Nicholson, Professor of classical archaeology at Cambridge University.

After two and a half years of dedication, patience and a sensitive mind and an eagle eye to the cause, it became possible to reconstruct the main outlines of the design painted on the west wall of the upper room. Six robed human figures set within a portico, with their arms extended in a gracious and submissive manner and vividly portrayed in varying colours, were resurrected. Their robes, perhaps ceremonial, have long sleeves, fitted tightly at the wrists and have curving necklines. Although all the robes conform in type, they are all of different colours… they include blue, purple and brown, bright blue and ochre, deep lilac and pale brown, pale blue and scarlet. The six figures are set between ornamental pillars and the pillars are themselves colourful in their decoration. The portico is, like the pillars, bordered in red. The dado upon which the portico rests was roughly painted with flowers of purple, red and pink. The whole length of the west wall of this room was filled with this scene, a length of 14 feet and the dado itself stood three feet high.

If we take a closer look at the human figures, the figure depicted within the pillars on the far left seems to have the countenance of a woman. Perhaps, she is the wife of the proprietor who, diminutive with age and a receding hairline, sits within the pillars on the far right. Between them, perhaps, are their four children. If we focus on the background of the figure next to the woman, a pulled curtain can be noticed; this is the only figure with this feature. This curtain/veil could symbolise the passing of this young man from his life on Earth to his continued life in Heaven. He, in all probability, had died before this columned portico was painted.

His body, after his death, was laid to rest in the in the villa's mausoleum. Now, after nearly 2,000 years, his skeletal remains can be seen within the villa's museum.

The painstaking reconstruction of the fragments of wall-plaster continued and eventually the breakthrough was made which confirmed that these upper rooms were places of Christian worship. Two large-scale representations of the Chi-Rho monogram were reconstructed. This sacred monogram, the earliest sign of Christianity, was found to be on the south wall of the chapel. Another was found in the ante- chamber/ narthex. Mr E Greenfield was responsible for the reconstruction of the monogram within the ante-chamber. Yes, the same gentleman whose eyes had penetrated the roots of the fallen tree many years before and that had led to the excavation of this villa. Sadly, Mr Greenfield died at the age of 58 and a plaque in his memory can be viewed in the villa's grounds. The reconstruction of the richly coloured portico, containing the Romano-British worshipers and one of the Chi-Rho monograms, can now be viewed in the Roman room (49) within the British Museum in London.

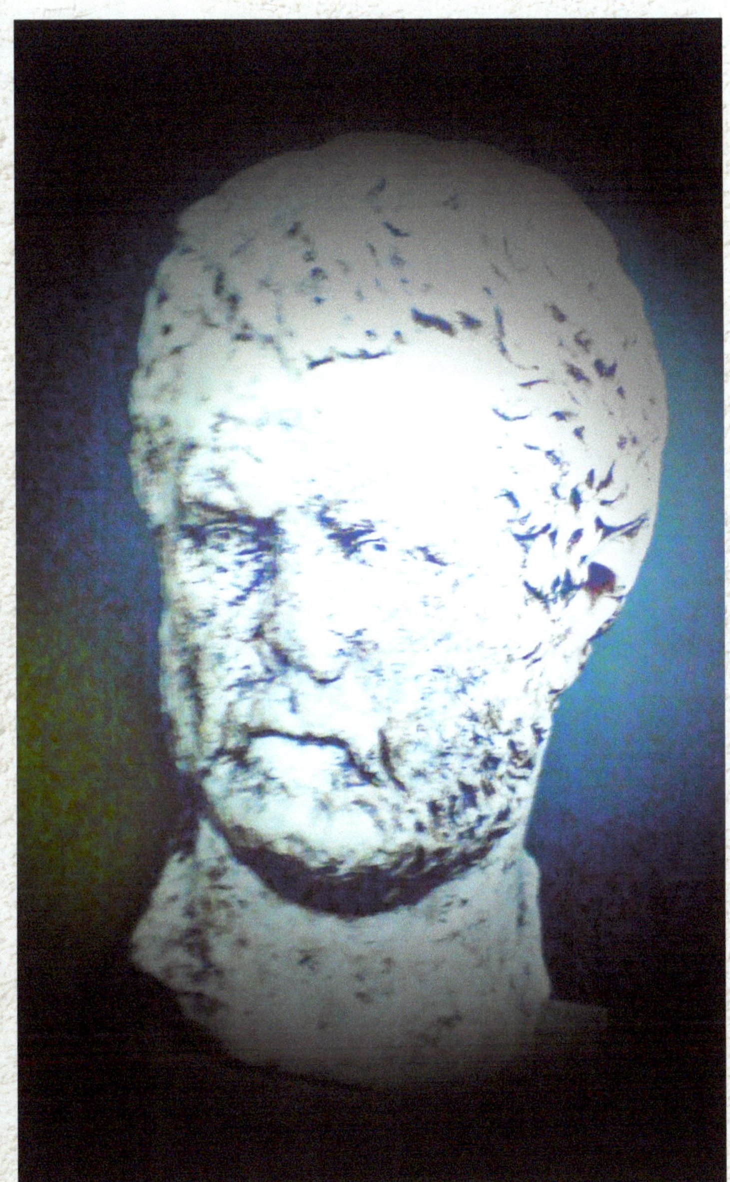

Marble Bust

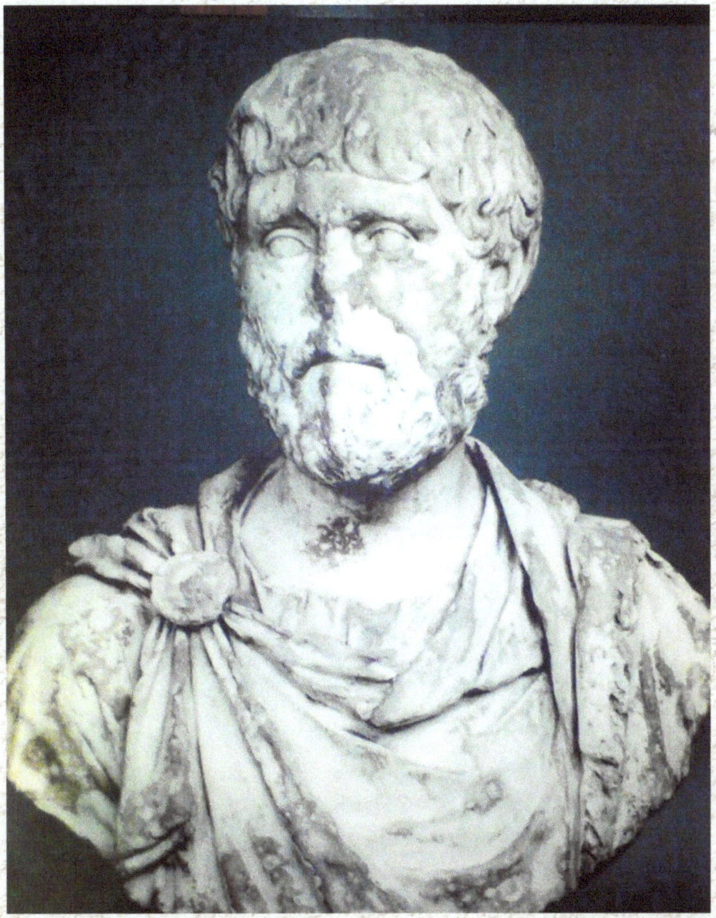

Marble Bust

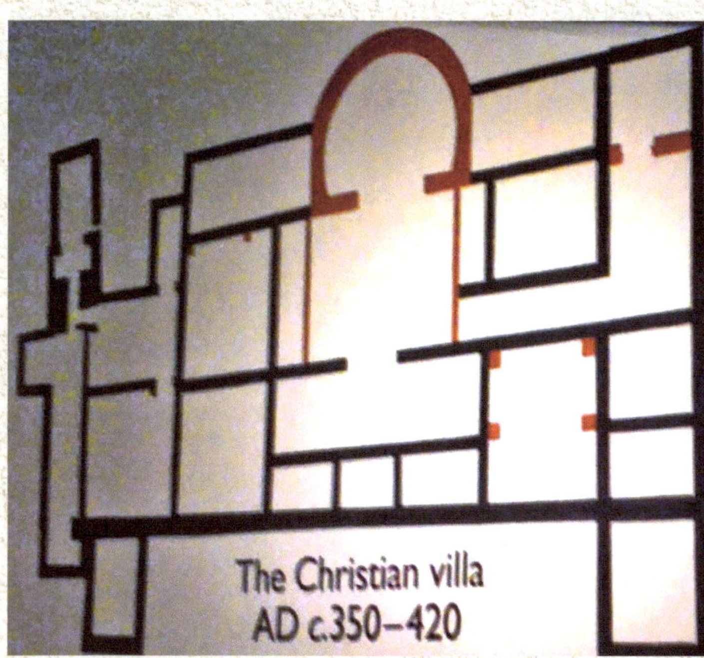

The Christian villa

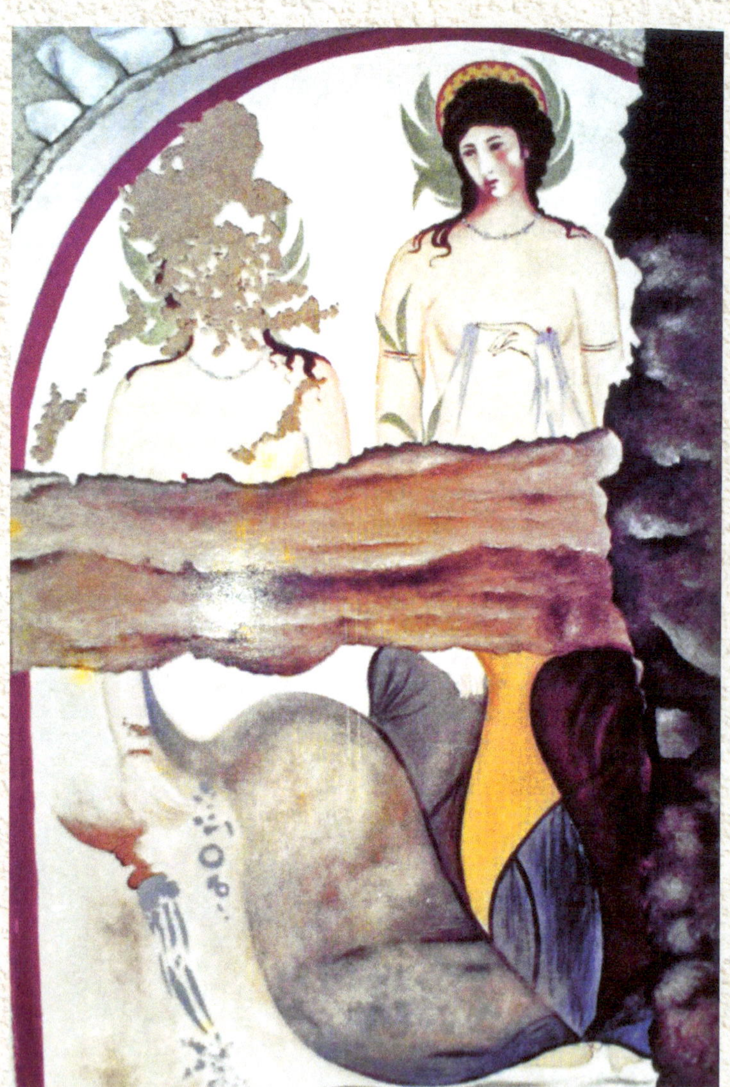

The Water Nymphs.Oil painting by A.J.Rook

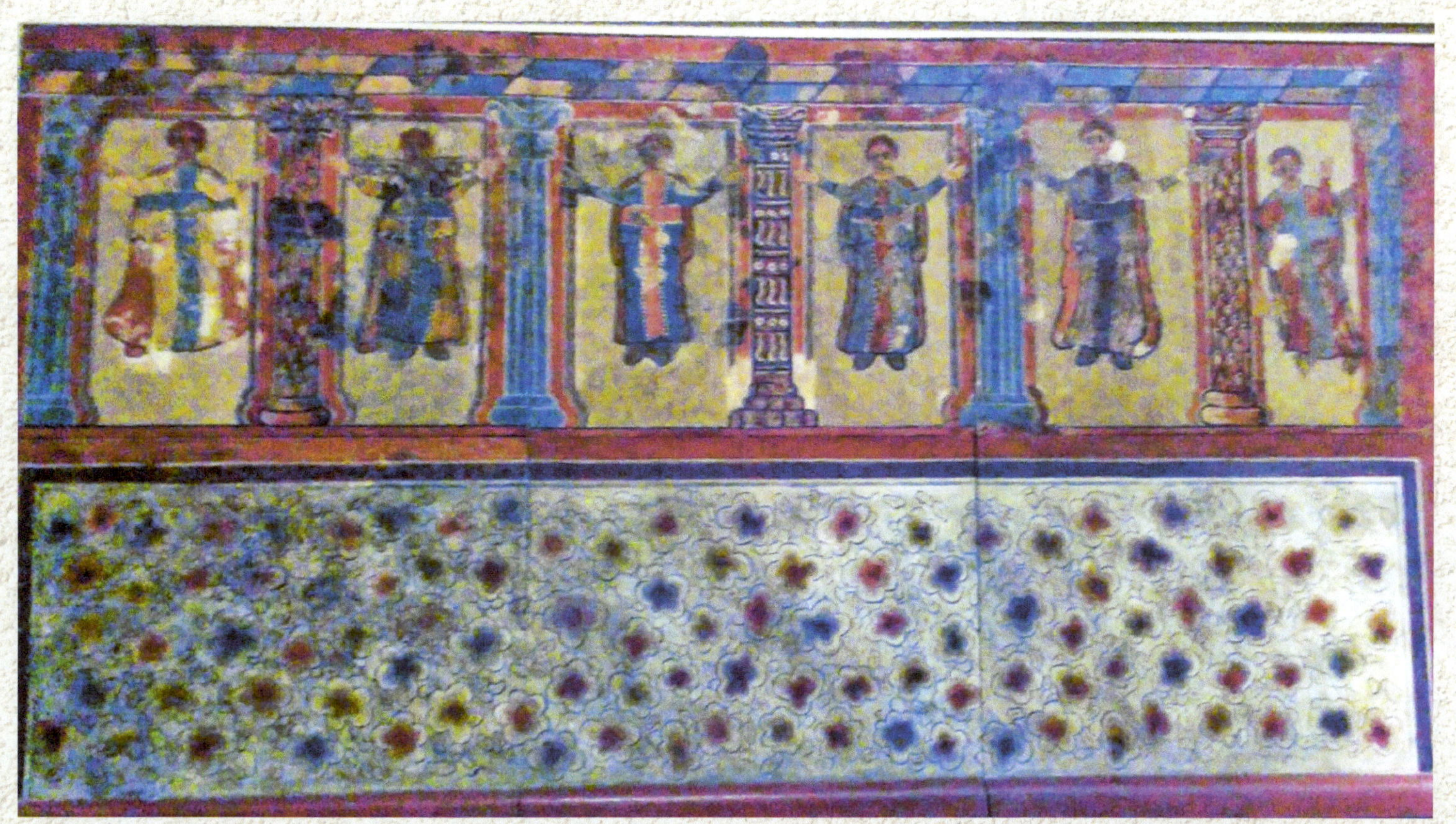

Reconstruction of wall painting from the Chapel

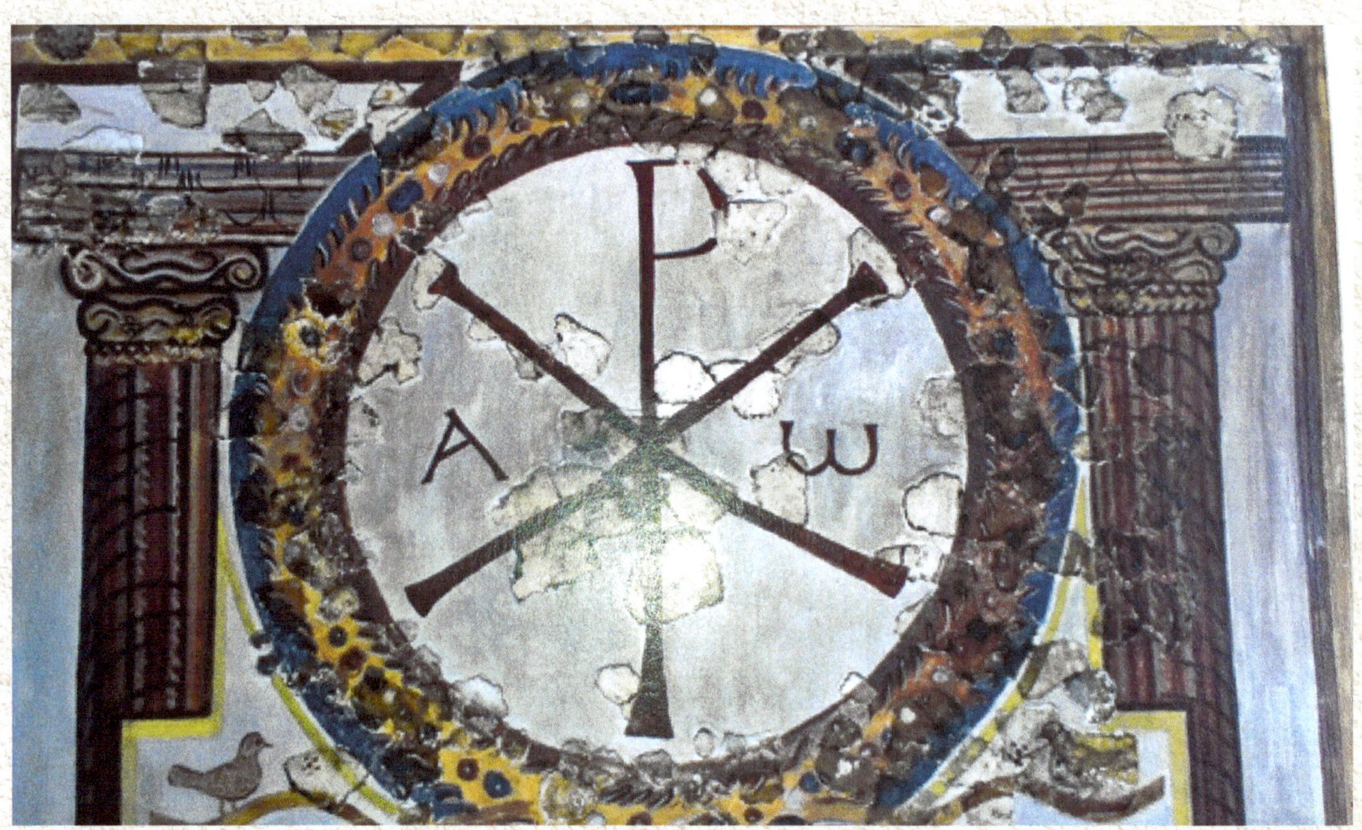

Chi-Rho/Christian monogram

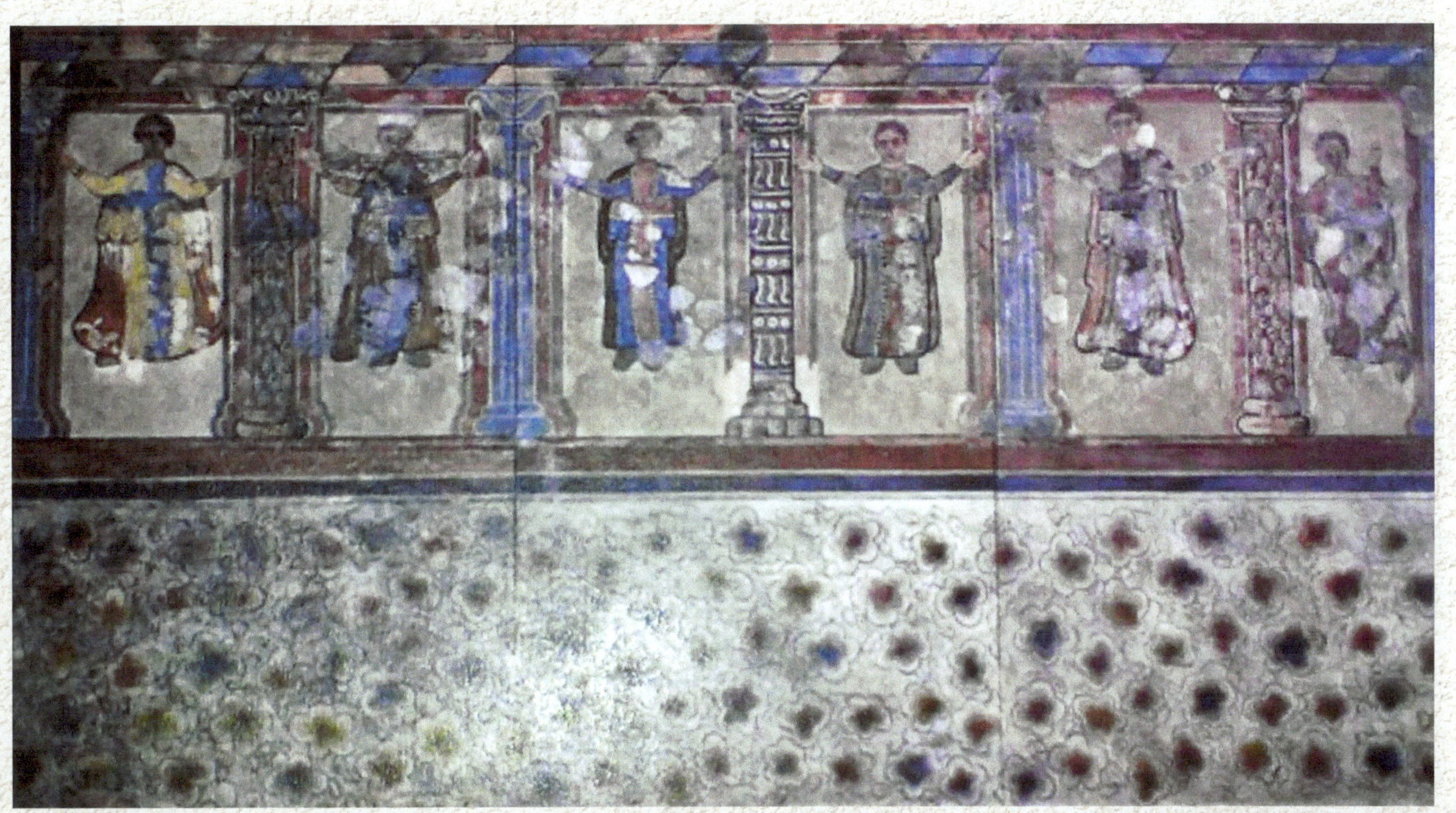

Possibly the villa owner and his family

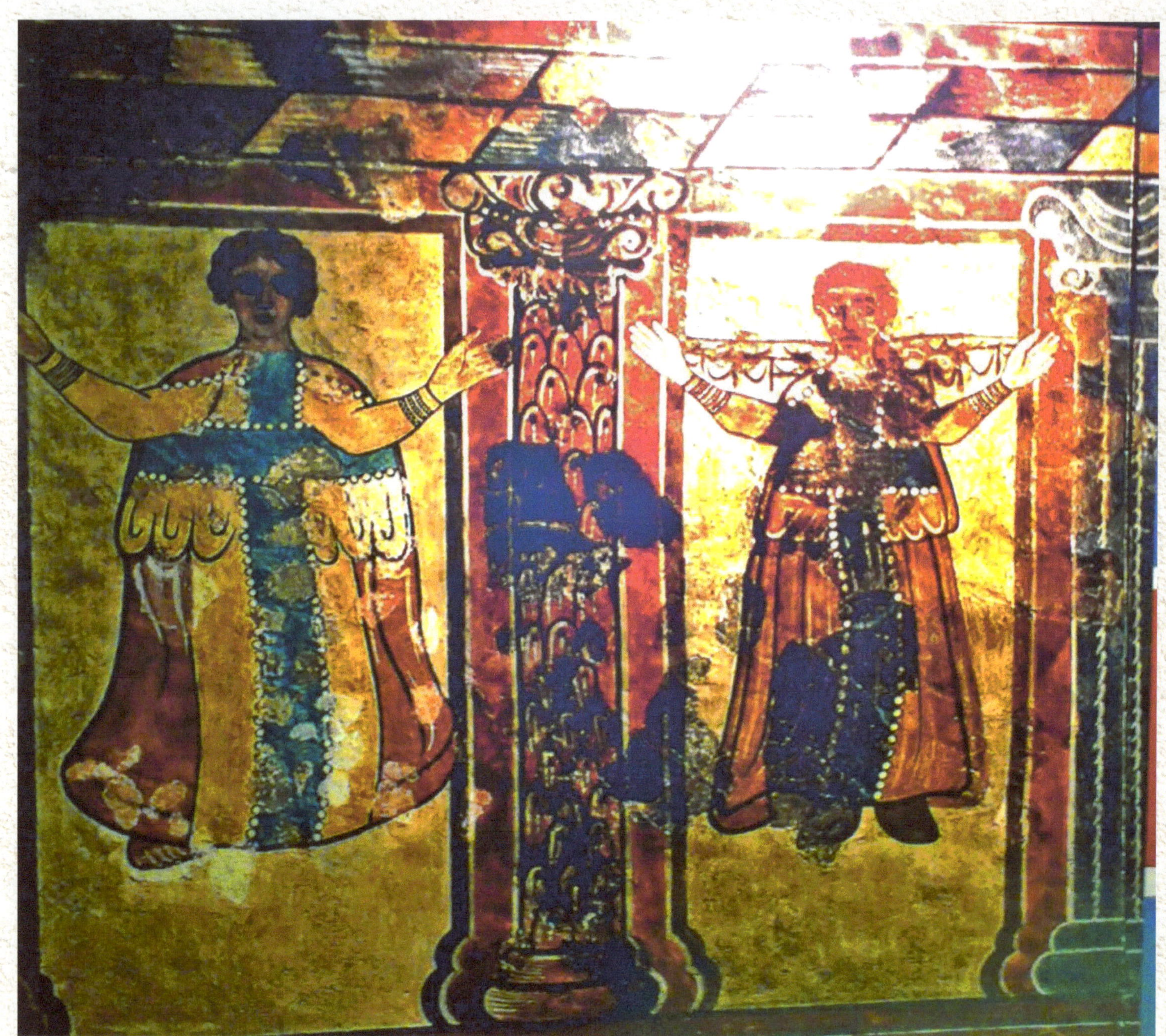

Reconstruction showing the curtain behind the second figure

CONCLUSION

The Lullingstone Roman Villa seems to have been inhabited from the late 1st Century AD to its demise by fire in the early 5th Century AD. Much of what is visible to the visitor today relates to the last hundred years of its life, although the 12 years of excavations have supplied sufficient evidence to be able to reconstruct the development of the villa during its 300 years, or so, of its domestic life. Four hundred and thirty five coins were found, some from each century of occupation, with the 4th Century coins being the most numerous.

The Western Roman Empire in 312 AD came under the rule of a single emperor, Constantine the Great. His defeat of Maxenties, at the battle of Milviane Bridge, overthrowing the 'Tetrarchy' system of rule by four emperors, freed Britain from financial stringency and economic stress. Within this peaceful background prosperity blossomed. In the early 4th Century AD, a huge granary, 24 metres by 10 metres, was constructed between the villa and the river. This would have stored wheat/barley ready for transportation by river and road, via Watling Street, and then perhaps to London and onward to the continent. This period of time was a golden renaissance for the Lullingstone villa. With the proprietor's growing wealth the middle of the villa was radically altered, the mosaic floors were constructed and the décor updated with a range of fresh, splendid colours.

Under the rule and guidance of the new Emperor, Christianity became the dominant religion of the Roman Empire. In 313 AD Constantine and Licinius issued the Edict of Milan, legalising Christian worship. This then, in all probability, stimulated the growth of Christianity in England and, in due course, the rooms above the deep room of the villa were converted to a house chapel dedicated to Christian worship. By 380 AD the high tide of prosperity was beginning to ebb for the villa's inhabitants. Civil strife within the Empire, caused by the disastrous ambitions of prominent Romans casting and throwing their Legions against each other, left the borders of the Empire more vulnerable to be pierced by the barbarian tribes. In Britain the daily living was filled with the air of uncertainty and consequently the villa started to be scaled down in size and amenities. The kitchens went out of use, the baths were filled in and the granary was down-graded to just a barn. With the borders of Britain weakened by the loss of man-power, the penetrating waves of Saxon settlers now became a flood. It is possible that the villa's working life as a farm ceased and it became a place of pagan and Christian worship for the local community. By the late 4th Century 14 pagan and 14 Christian ceremonial days coincided with each other, which indicates that both pagan and Christian worship could have been practised at the same time without conflict. Perhaps the people of the surrounding community would have assembled in the rooms containing the mosaics before attending the services to their chosen worship. Although no more families grew up in this tranquil and beautiful valley within this villa, Christianity began to prosper. Pagan gods were for the present, Christianity was the future. How could any pagan god compete with a God that offered up to its worshippers everlasting life?

Chapter III
Chedworth Roman Villa

In this chapter about Chedworth Roman Villa, I will try and evaluate its evolution and interpret the footprints of its past, as left by many generations of its inhabitants.

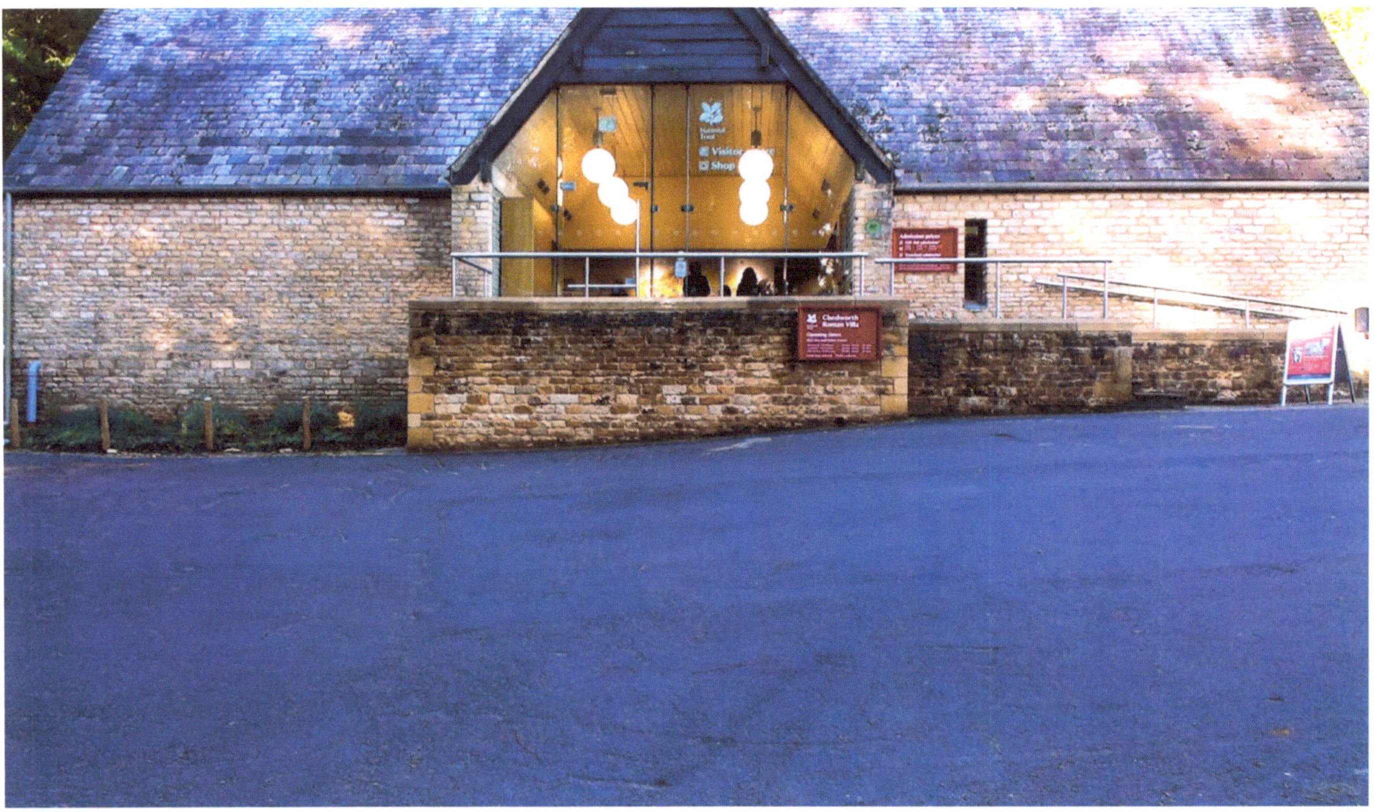

Entrance to the villa

OVERVIEW

The village name of Chedworth, in all probability, was conceived by the tongue of the west Saxons. The word 'worth' relates to an enclosure or an enclosed settlement by a wall of wooden stakes. In the 9th century the area was listed as Cedda's Homestead, and in the Doomsday Book the settlement was recorded as Cedeorde. The much later village of Chedworth lined a street over a mile long and was formerly three distinct settlements, upper, middle and lower Chedworth.

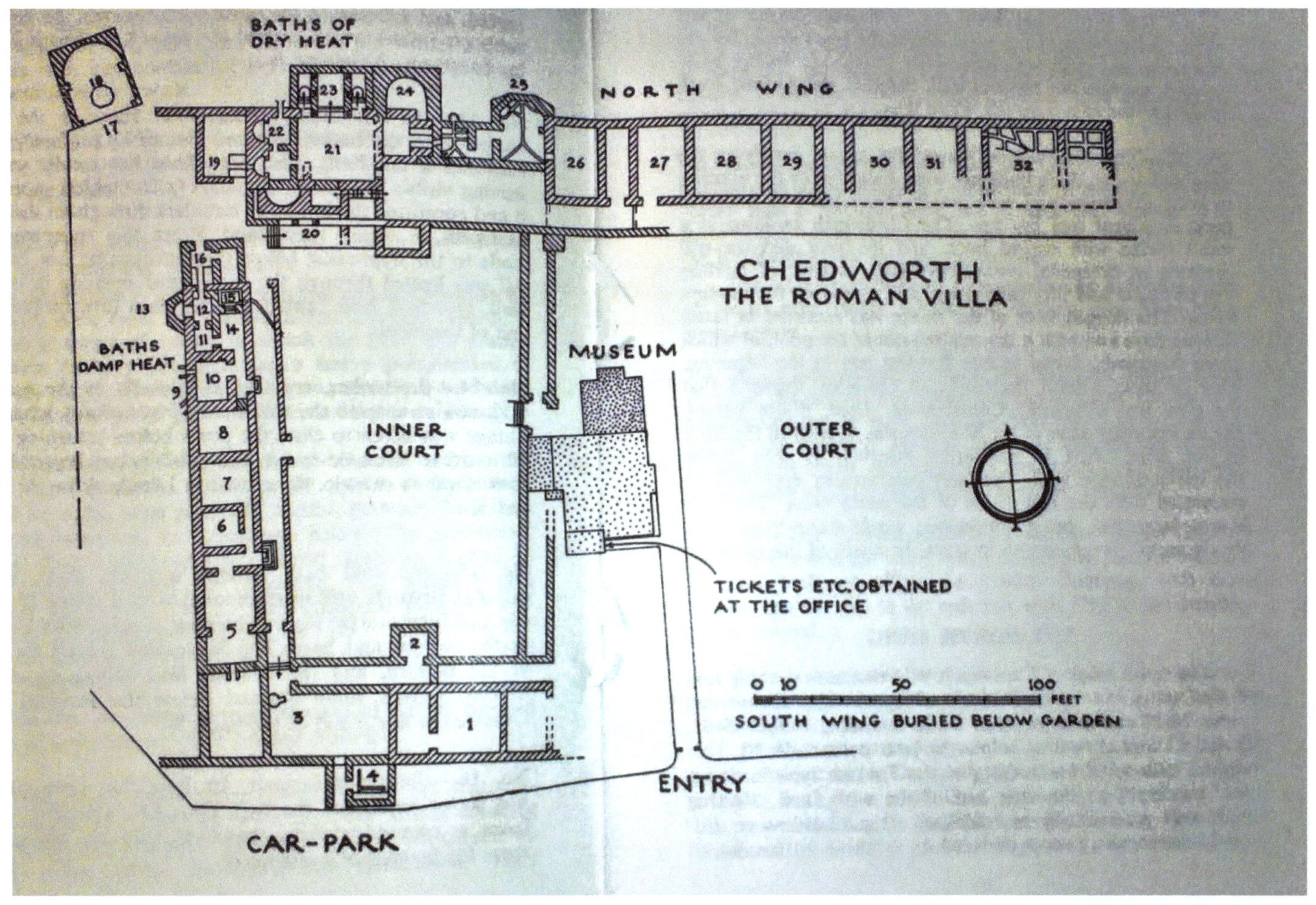

Ground plan of the villa

The villa nestles contentedly within the Cotswolds, in the county of Gloucestershire. It is imposed on the landscape 500 feet above sea level at a point where three gullies meet to form the head of a single valley. This valley falls gently to the east towards the River Coln. This useful waterway rises up from the womb of Mother Earth at Brockhampton and flows south-southeast to marry with the River Thames, south west of the village of Lechlade.

The north and the west wings of the villa were constructed on artificial terraces, partly recessed into the hillside, while the south wing rests at a lower level nearer the valley floor. The villa is sheltered from the weather by the protection of the surrounding wooded hillsides, but these slopes denied the villa of much of the warmth of the sun. The advantages for the villa were a steady and regular water supply served by a spring. This is coupled with the availability of good building stone (oolitic limestone).

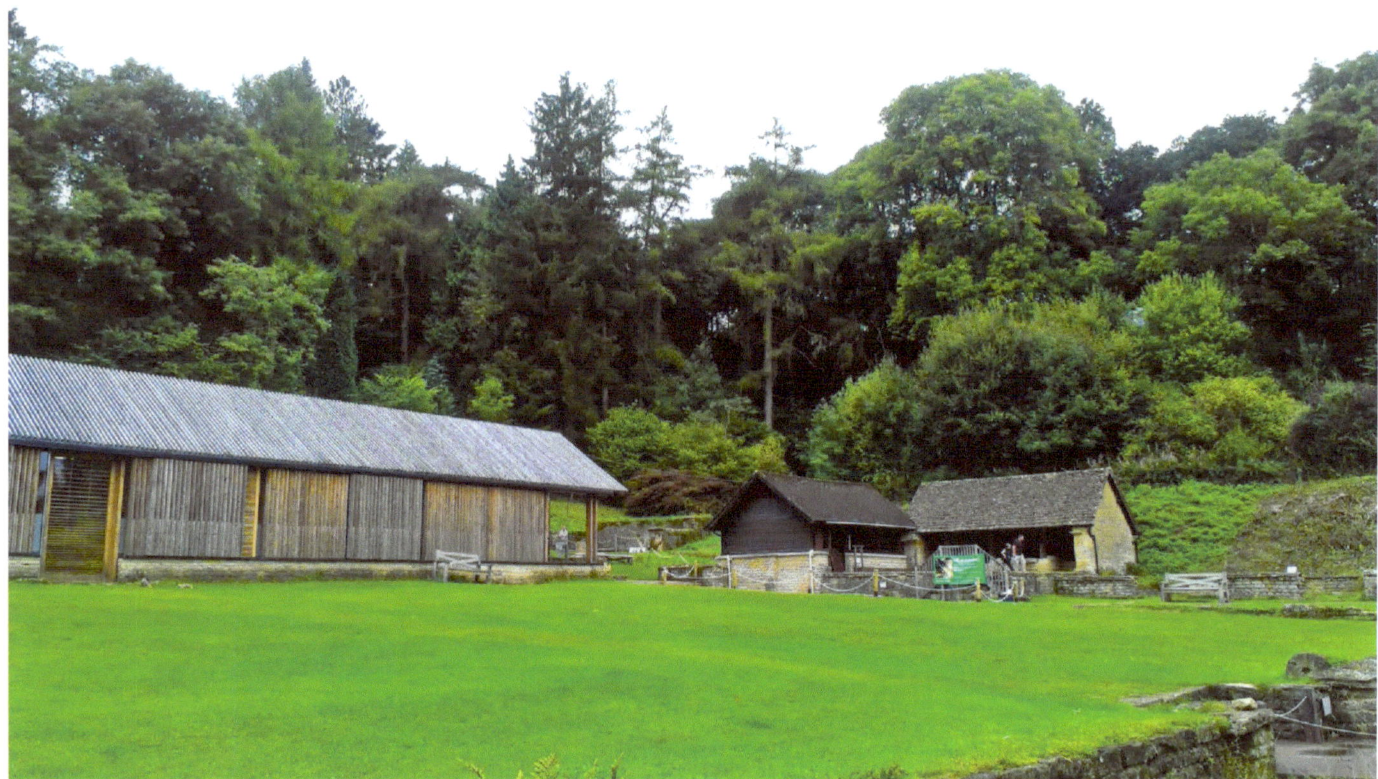

View of part of the West-wing and the North-wing bath-house.

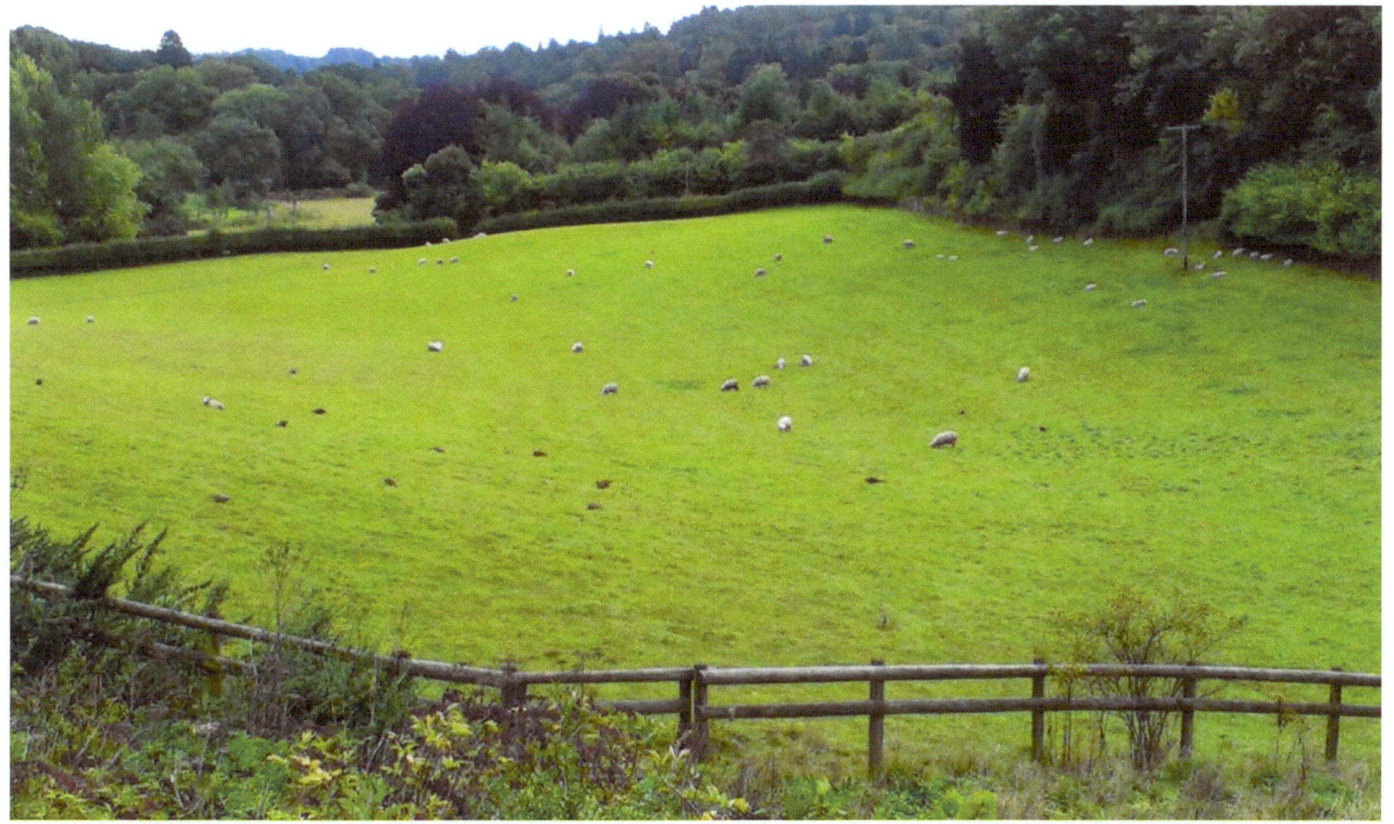

Views from the villa looking East

The indigenous people made good use of the fertile valleys within the Cotswolds, many being farmers and highly skilled craftsmen. The Romans recognised these people as a Celtic tribe known as the Dobunni. They minted their own coins and were pagans. The focus of their worship fell upon the natural world, with deities associated with the landscape. An example being Cuda, a mother goddess associated with the Cotswold Hills, and its rivers and springs; and Sulis Minerva, the water goddess, at the town now known as Bath. Other cults embraced the social actions of hunting and mining.

THE ROMAN VILLA

Many, many long years ago, in 1864, a gamekeeper on the land of the Earl of Eldon was digging on an embankment, searching for his missing ferret, presumably lost while out hunting rabbits in the area.

He was a man with a keen eye and an inquisitive mind and, as he searched, he began to uncover a trail of clues which opened the creaky doors into the hazy past of this villa. He observed fragments of Roman paving, much fallen stonework and shards of pottery. Most of the discovered material related to Room 32 of the north wing of the villa. The news of these finds reached the ear of a Mr James Farrier, a Scottish antiquarian. The Earl of Eldon, being this man's nephew, subsequently paid for the forthcoming excavations. Mr Farrier no doubt utilised some of the Estate's male employees and, following the archaeological excavation techniques of that era, had revealed by 1867 most of that which is on view today. The Earl also provided the funds for the museum and for the roofing structures of the site when the original excavations came to an end. In 1924 the site was bought for the National Trust by means of subscriptions raised mainly by the Bristol and Gloucester Archaeological Society, by the sustained efforts of Mr St Clair Baddeley, a local archaeologist. From 1958 until 1965 Sir Ian Richmond conducted a series of excavations within the site. Then, from 1979 to 1983, Mr R Goodburn led a series of further excavations. Sadly neither of these investigations were fully published. In the year 2000 the Cotswold Archaeological Trust re-examined some of the reburied mosaics in order to help with the plans for the new proposed cover-building. In 2010 the exciting news surfaced that £3 million was to be invested on a major project to improve the protection for the fragile Roman remains and to upgrade the visitor facilities. This project was made possible by the generous donations of the following: £700,000 grant from the Heritage Lottery Fund; £150,000 from the Gloucestershire Environmental Trust, with landfill tax contributions donated by Cory Environmental; £100,000 from the Garfield Weston Foundation; other donations from the Somerfield Charitable Trust, the Roman Research Trust, The Cotswold AONB Sustainable Development Fund and the Kinsurdy Trust. Further donations came from a number of National Trust supporter groups and individual donors who have sponsored protective winter covers (socks) which prevent damage to the Roman pillars which support the underfloor heating system during the winter months. Included in this project design were five weeks which were allocated to excavate and conserve two areas of the 4th Century mosaics. Parts of these mosaics were last seen and devoured by human eyes over 150 years ago, when they were reburied after the Victorian excavations. Some of these mosaics, when the present excavation is finished, will be housed for public viewing in a proper environmentally controlled building which will protect them from deterioration from frost, damp and direct sunlight. This project will be recorded in an academic monograph to be published in 2014.

THE OCCUPATION OF THE VILLA

It seemed that the first Romano-British establishment on this site was constructed on virgin ground, but a chance find in August 2001 revealed an infant burial which was scientifically dated to be from 360 BC. This suggests that an Iron Age settlement of unknown size may have been on this site during that period of time.

In all probability, the first Romano-British villa was an unpretentious one with the aspect of utility being the main requirements. Archaeology offers up the suggestion that the original villa was laid out in the first half of the 2nd Century AD and originated as a range of three separate buildings, on the north, west and south sides of the valley. The main house, being on the west side, was constructed without a bathhouse. The south wing was a half-timbered building and on the north side there was a small bath suite on the site of the later bath suites. Close by there was a water cistern where the nymphaeum was later built. These early ranges contained no mosaics or verandas but, for this period of time, the size of Chedworth was considerable. It was a disastrous fire in the late 2nd Century AD that sparked off the updating and improvements at this villa. The main house and the south range were destroyed but when the ashes were swept away they were immediately rebuilt. In addition the baths were then enlarged and more rooms were added to the north range. There was still no evidence of mosaic floors being constructed during this period of rebuild.

In the late 3rd Century and early part of the 4th Century AD, the villa was lavishly remodelled. The villa complex would have been at its most elaborate and the remains now on view mostly date from that period of time. A new bath-suite was constructed at the northern end of the western range and the north-west baths were refurbished. The north range was extended with the addition of more rooms and each range was fronted by long, covered, colonnaded porticos. A new cross gallery created an upper courtyard which separated the residential area from a larger, lower courtyard further down the slope to the east. More recent excavations have revealed that the south wing seemed to be a mirror-image of the north wing. The south wing's corridor/portico had its own shallow, channelled heating system (hypocaust), as did one of the rooms within this wing.

The entrance to the villa would have been from the east by a road/track way, from close to the modern river crossing and then through the middle of the adjoining field. Unlike Fishbourne Roman Palace, no formal garden, bedding trenches, pathways or fountains have been revealed by the excavations. It seems that the inner courtyard, just as it is today, was grassed over.

THE RISE OF THE COTSWOLDS VILLAS

To understand the rise and fall of the Romano-British villas like Chedworth, we have to stop for a moment, dwell and take an enlightening stroll back into history. It seems that the local inhabitants, the Dobunni tribe and its factions, chose to welcome rather than repulse the advancing Roman legions as they sought to impose Romanisation within this part of England. Today the main town within this area is Cirencester. It is approximately 93 miles west-northwest of London and lies on the lower dip slopes of the Cotswold, an outcrop of oolitic limestone, close to the River Churn, a tributary of the River Thames. The Romans built a fort here in AD 47 where the Fosse Way crossed the River Churn. The fort helped to defend the provincial frontier. The Dobunni tribe were based at a settlement three miles to the north, known as Bagendon. They were encouraged to relocate to create a civil settlement near the fort. When the Roman frontier moved further north, following the conquest of Wales, the fort was levelled in approximately AD 70, but the town/settlement persisted and flourished bearing the name of Corinium Dobunnorum. The local civic leaders were essentially the native aristocracy who were most influenced by the Roman culture. The population of this settlement continued to grow and by the 2nd Century it was the second largest town in Britain. By the 4th Century, Corinium Dobunnorum (Cirencester) was possibly a provincial capital. The town began to show the trappings of wealth with many town houses displaying numerous mosaic floors of high quality and elegantly painted interiors. Many of these mosaics and fragments of painted wall plaster can be seen in the Cirencester museum. The continued rise in population expanded the growth of the villas (farms) within the Cotswolds valleys. In the 3rd/4th Century villa estates clustered quite thickly around this neighbourhood, with perhaps each villa controlling hundreds of acres of state encouraged farm and forest land. Alternatively, some of the villas could have been owned by entrepreneurs who invested their wealth in farmland. Sheep farming in these valleys was no doubt profitable, as the wool from these breeds was highly prized on the continent. With the local deposits of fullers earth (a sedimentary clay), a material used to absorb lanolin and other greasy impurities from the fleeces, this would have fuelled a local industry, such as dyeing, fulling and cloth weaving. The distribution of the crops/cereals and produce from these valleys was well served by an abundance of roads/highways. Three miles down the Coln valley lay the Fosse Way, the main road to Exeter and Lincoln. Akeman and Ermine Street could also have been used to distribute these wares. Akeman Street joined Cirencester to St Albans (Verulamium) via the Roman town of Alchester.

THE TOUR AND DISCUSSION OF THE VILLA AND ITS MOSAICS

As I turn left off the thickly tree-lined A249 and head towards Chedworth Roman Villa, the scenery changes dramatically. On both sides of the narrow highway green rolling hills and steep wooded valleys are viewed, seemingly filled with sheep, their heads bowed as they busily nibble away at grass. The sun breaks free from a bank of dark cloud and, as I open my car window, the feeling of tranquillity abounds, it gushes in and absorbs from me the stress of the 120 mile car journey. The next three miles disappear within a blinking of an eye as the entrance of the villa looms up and peers down at me from above. As I park the car to my left is a steep wooded embankment and to my right, just visible between the gaps in the foliage, the valley ebbs away to the east. I climb the awaiting stairs and enter into a warmly illuminated lobby. The villa staff, dressed in clean cut, black outfits, are delightful and informative. I recommend that the visitor arms themselves with a guide book as this enhances the understanding of the visual layout of the villa and its mosaics. To the left, within the lobby, is a small café serving fresh hot drinks, sandwiches and cakes that beg to be eaten. Interestingly, the water supply to the café is from the same spring that provided the villa with water during the 4th Century AD. The right hand side of the lobby contains numerous historical books and delicately, visually presented gifts to purchase.

Also, the right hand side of the shop contains the door which transports the visitor from the 21stcentury back to the 4th Century AD. Immediately, a model of the villa is set before you and it is from this place that the hourly tours of the villa begin. Before entering the new cover building to view the west wing and its mosaics I stop, take a glance to my right and view the valley which falls away from the north to the south and from the west to the east. The calm and the tranquillity of the Cotswolds wraps itself around my being like a welcome blanket. There is no noise pollution from either road or sky, just the rustle of the breeze as it travels through the wooded embankment behind me. It was with rising anticipation that I strode up the stairs and through the entrance of the new building containing the West Wing.

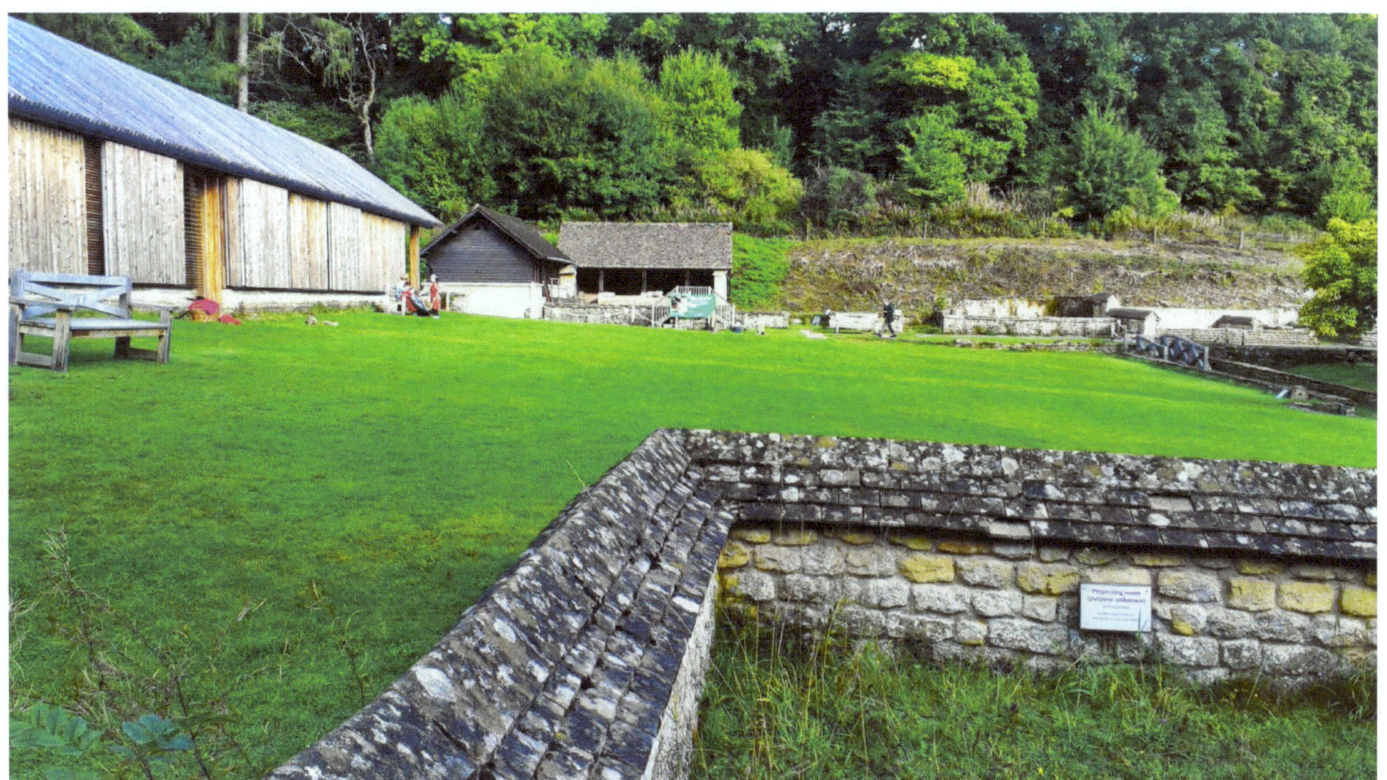

Views from the villa looking East

During 2010 the remaining parts of the mosaic corridor were exposed from the ground after more than a millennium of burial. The corridor, 116 feet six inches long and eight feet five inches wide, revealed that the complete pavement was a series of rectangular panels of intersecting circles alternating with square panels of guilloche mat.

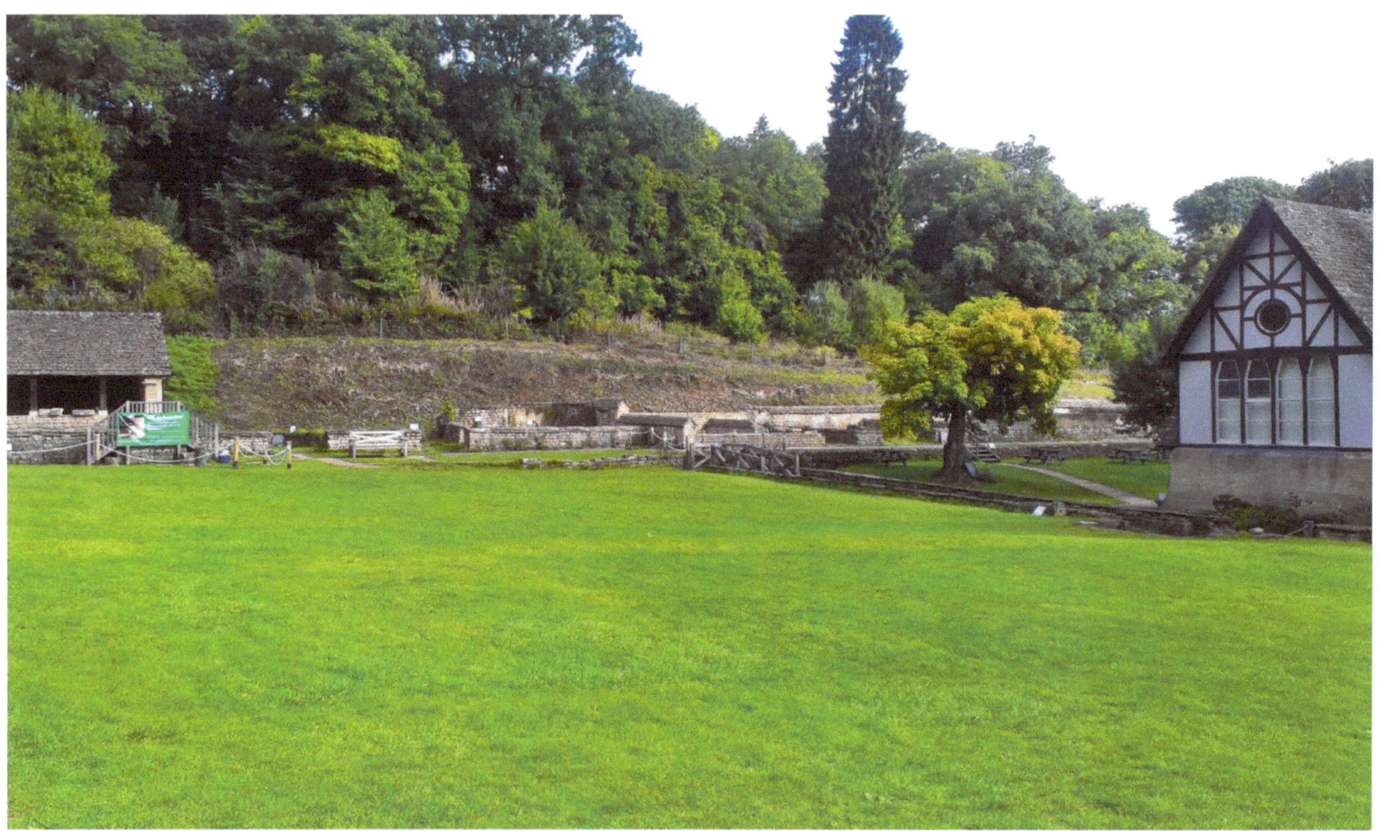

View of part of the West-wing and the North-wing bath-house.

The tesserae composing this 4th Century mosaic pavement are of the colours red, white and dark and pale blue/grey. It seems that the red tesserae are made of brick/tile, the white of local limestone and the dark blue/grey are from a rock called lias shale, found in the county of Dorset. The circular panels seduce and engage the eye seemingly more so than the square panels of guilloche, as the interlocking circles create concave-edged squares. Each square, at their centre, contains a solid red square alternating with a square of blue/grey. Opposite this corridor were a number of rooms adorned with mosaic floors, the finest creation being constructed for the dining room/triclinium (room 5). This 4th Century room was 29 feet by 19 feet in size and was heated by a hypocaust. The mosaic in this pleasant room contained tesserae of numerous colours – white, red, dark blue/grey, brown, grey, yellow ochre and some of a purplish brown. Some of these coloured tesserae could possibly be from the sandstones found on the eastern side of the Forest of Dean. This magnificent entertaining room was probably entered into via the mosaic-paved passage (5B) by the use of a flight of steps, located in the corridor.

This mosaic is of exceptionally high quality and laid by hands of much experience. A continuous swastika meander border captures within it two large panels of design. The inner panel, perhaps the main dining area, is of a square geometric design. My attention is drawn to the small, square, central motif (swastika-pelta) and as my eyes explore it my perspective is deceived. At first my interpretation is of a ball, safely and securely held within an inner square. But with continuous study, I perceive four pointed leaves protruding from a Solomon knot and their finely pointed leaves rest gently on the east, west, north and south of the inner boundary. I think we should accept that this mosaic panel would have contained the seating arrangements of the dining area, so that the participants could view and discuss the figured scenes set within the other mosaic panel. It seems possible that the small central motif, within the seating area, would still have been visible, and the never-ending, continuous design of the Solomon knot could symbolise the faith/hope that this high standard of living would also be never-ending. (This same design was also noted in a tessellated pavement in the Roman town of Bath.)

Sitting comfortably within this panel are long rectangles to the east and to the west. Both reveal, from jewelled rimmed bowls, continuous acanthus scrolls. Beyond these, looking inwards, a large geometric square contains an absorbing design of squares of guilloche pattern penetrated by four rectangles of guilloche pattern. Note the varying complexity of the swastika meander which binds this inner panel together. The neatness of the way the tesserae are laid is a pointer to the skill and patience of the art of mosaic making, for they seem to go unnoticed when viewing the whole bigger picture of the design.

As I view the northern panel of this mosaic, I see in my mind's eye a servant after, perhaps, a fun-filled and riotous evening of entertainment, swabbing, washing and cleaning this floor and then guiding the waste water towards what looks like a tile drain in the south east corner of the floor.

The gentle covering of fresh water would have enhanced the colours of the tesserae and, for a short period of time, the figures within this mosaic would have glowed with pride. Perhaps then, prior to the dinner party, the mosaic could have been buffed up with a polish to hold this more visual effect during the evening. The ravages of time have denied us the most northern compartments, and the centre-piece, of this mosaic. It is possible that the centre held a medallion of Bacchus (the God of wine). This, perhaps, would be most fitting, as the guests' inhibitions would have become more liberated as the wine flowed, with the guests' drinking goblets regularly topped up by the attentive servants. Fortunately, large parts of three trapezoidal panels in the south of this mosaic can help with its interpretation.

These panels possibly contain Bacchic scenes of satyrs and maenads, who were mythological beings, who were always represented as part of the entourage of Bacchus. Their main role seemed to be to take part in wild and frenzied, drunken activities associated with the worship of Bacchus. The central, southern trapezoidal panel could relate to a mythological story of the first meeting of Ariadne (the daughter of Minos, King of Crete) and Bacchus. Ariadne had been abandoned by Theseus (the mythical founder king of Athens and the son of Aegeus and Poseidon) on the Greek island of Naxos. Bacchus, on first sight of Ariadne, falls passionately in love with her. This central panel would have been the most visual for the diners, who would have been seated around the southern mosaic panel. This depiction seems to show perhaps their first meeting. Ariadne is clad with a cloak/mantle draped over her left side and legs. She seems to be supporting herself with her left hand and looks coyly at Bacchus. Bacchus, with his cloak billowing out behind him in the breeze, looks longingly towards Ariadne and seems poised and ready to seduce her, aided by gentle and soothing sounds from the tambourine held within his left hand. In his right hand (lost) he grips a thyrsus, a symbol of prosperity, fertility and of pleasure of the highest order. Her seduction is imminent. In the right hand panel Ariadne swoons across the lap of Bacchus. Her left hand entering his tunic feels his heart racing and pounding with passion. Ariadne, startled by this, as the open palm of her left hand suggests, drops from it what seems like a shepherd's crook. Bacchus pins the crook to the floor with his right foot thus informing her to leave it be as the seduction proceeds. The thyrsus seems to have been discarded as it stands alone but still within reach if needed. Also, a pan-flute can be seen lying in the bottom right hand corner. Perhaps this instrument was used to help with the seduction. If we turn our attention to the left hand panel, both the tambourine, in the right hand corner, and the thyrsus, lying prone across the floor, have been discarded. Bacchus, like the depiction of him in the right hand panel, seems to be cloaked in a leopard skin (Bacchus' chariot was drawn by two leopards or cheetahs), but here he also wears a wreath upon his head, perhaps an ivy wreath which would have been most sacred to him. Ariadne and Bacchus seem to be ready to exchange a kiss. Ariadne's right arm hangs casually around Bacchus' shoulder as he grips her left arm at the wrist and while her fingers hold fast to control her billowing cloak.

The mosaisist shows versatility in the use of colours, for while the females' are of a purplish brown in their outlining, these colours are used again but as infill for the male figures. The creamy grey colours used for the vines enliven the white background of the three panels. Also noted is how these panels are framed, alternately with a single band of guilloche and a dark blue wavy scroll.

In the four corners of this mosaic panel, in triangular compartments, depictions of the four seasons of the year joyously engage the eye. In the south west corner, below the trapezoidal panel depicting Bacchus wearing a wreath upon his head, spring skips gaily within his setting, with his draped waistband hanging limply on his left side, while on his right it seems uplifted by the breeze. The cupid with the swallow perching upon the hand of his outstretched right arm, seem to exchange a welcoming and warming gaze. In cupid's left hand is, perhaps, a basket containing spring bulbs or flowers. Creamy/grey foliage accompanies two heart-shaped leaves in this scene; perhaps these hearts symbolise the joy of the pending longer days of summer. In the north-west corner awaits summer. The cupid seems to have just fluttered down as a wing is noticed behind his left shoulder. In his right hand he grips a garland of flowers and in his left, held tightly within his arm, is a basket possibly full of flowers from which blooms appear to be falling.

These are noticed by his left knee, as they fall gently towards the ground. In the top right and left we perhaps view healthy-looking ears of corn. In the north east corner just a glimpse of autumn remains. His legs seem crossed and round his waist, like spring, he is draped by an uplifted stole. As with spring and summer he hugs a basket and from this a heart-shaped leaf seems to have sprouted. Once again a creamy/grey infill of foliage is noticed. In the south east corner winter, with his left foot protruding the inner frame, seems ready to run away. Perhaps in the top right and top left hand corners we view ears of corn with their tips blighted. Dangling from his right hand is a dead hare and he grasps in his left hand a leafless twig. Does the twig symbolise the starkness of winter? And does the hare symbolise that the weak and vulnerable will perish? Alternatively, is the twig representing firewood, so that the hare can be cooked and eaten? In this scene the cupid is well prepared for the icy cold winds and frosty days of winter. He wears thick leggings and perhaps boots. He sports a hooded cloak (birrus, which was made in Britain) from which the whites of his eyes peer out. He seems to be wearing, close to his body, a tunic which would act as a vest, for over the top of this is a much thicker tunic.

Unfortunately very little of the original wall-plaster from this villa has survived. But, no doubt, the walls of this dining room would have been decorated to complement the mosaic floor and in some of the coloured panels, possibly of red, orange, green and yellow, vines would have been depicted with deep red, drooping grapes in abundance.

Next to view is the mosaic floor in Room 5B, which has been dated to the late 4th Century when this room was constructed to be an antechamber/lobby. Perhaps this room was for the gathering and reception of the guests prior to their entry into the main dining room (Room 5). The mosaic on view here is the remaining part of a continuous pelta design. Each pelta is tipped with a blue/grey cross and contained within them is an infill of red. All are bound together with thin travelling, wavy bands of blue/grey tesserae. The design is held in place by a continuous right angled broken meander of Z-pattern and this, in turn, by a surround design of red-stepped triangles. The colours of the tesserae within this mosaic are white, red, dark blue/grey, pale blue/grey and a creamy/grey. It seems that pure limestone was used for the white and the blue/grey could be from Liassic limestone with an iron content.

As we move further north down this west wing, we engage with Room 6. This room was heated by a channelled hypocaust which consisted of masonry piers, instead of the usual pilae, supporting the mosaic floor. Sadly, the passing of time has claimed the central panel, but parts of the borders of the north and south ends have survived. There is an outer border of Cotswold stone which completely surrounds this square room. The inner square border is constructed of red tile, and looking inwards, a dark blue/grey swastika-meander rests within a setting of creamy-grey tesserae. Halfway along this north and south meander small rectangular boxes are noticed; each contain a guilloche design constructed of red and creamy/white tesserae. The central panel (missing) is framed by a continuous three strand guilloche constructed of red, yellow and white tesserae.

The next treasure that awaits us is in the small west range bath-house, Room 10. The bath-house was one of the main symbols of Roman civilisation and consequently the mosaics within them would have been of high visual quality. Room 10 was the changing room (apodyterium) and measured 4.45 metres (14 feet six inches) by 3.9 metres (12 feet nine inches). In antiquity the walls would have been lined with benches and the bathers' clothing and belongings would have been stored in cubicles or on shelves, but perhaps here, due to the small size of the changing room, they would have been stored in a nearby room. It is also open to speculation as to who looked after the bathers' items of worth during their absence. Some would have had their own privately owned slave; if not, possibly a slave could be hired at the baths (capsarius).

But …. Alternatively, if the villa was owned by one family and the baths only used by themselves and their guests, their bathing requirements would have been utilised by in-house servants. I feel that the final design of the mosaic floor within the apodyterium would have been constructed only after much thought and discussion by the proprietor in conjunction with his team of mosaicists. The mosaics within the baths were perhaps second only to the floors of the dining room in their importance, for, like the dining area, visitors would have spent considerable lengths of time within them. While the dining room mosaics, containing depictions from Greek mythology and of the four seasons of the year, would have stimulated interest and conversation, here in Room 10 the bathers' attention would have been more eye-focused on the mosaic pattern which contains many interesting and similar, but subtly varying motif designs. This mosaic is constructed within and around a saltire (diagonal cross) design. At its centre is a roundel containing a cantharus which binds the four arms of the cross together. A 'jewelled' band surrounds the lip of the cantharus and two heart-shaped leaves with stalks reside around its lost pedestal. Within each arm of the diagonal cross are pelta-urns with volutes which have varying depth of design and colours. Beyond these pairs of lozenges are noticed, each containing within them varying designs of heart-shaped motifs. A square of simple, three-strand guilloche composed of creamy/grey, red and yellow tesserae, which divert on each of its four sides to form triangles, frames the internal design. The outer border of the mosaic is of a swastika meander and contains within it varying sizes of rectangular, boxed guilloche. White 'eyes' exist in all of the guilloche constructed in this mosaic.

In 1978 his mosaic was lifted and re-laid for conservation purposes and as we view it, in the present, it becomes obvious that in antiquity there were several areas of repair. It is noticeable that compared to the quality of the craftsmanship of the original mosaic, the repairs seem to be substandard. In the north east corner the angles of the lozenges are now rounded compared to the original elsewhere which were perpendicular. In the east and the south borders substandard repairs are visible. Also, sadly, within the central roundel, containing a depiction of a cantharus, creamy/grey tesserae were used instead of the original colour, white. Thankfully, enough of the original design remains which would have stimulated enjoyable debate between the visitors and users of this apodyterium. There are a number of subtle differences of construction and of colour within the areas of the pelta-urns with volutes, also within the heart shaped motifs that reside just beyond these, but within the lozenges. Also notice the difference of bulk and colour of the heart shape designs within the triangles on the east and west side of this mosaic. Within the triangle on the east side a bird, perhaps a pigeon, which is outlined in white tesserae, dwells alone. It seems to be showing interest towards a small red flower within a curving piece of foliage. I assume that its mate would have resided in the west triangle where its depiction would have held subtle differences.

I have suggested that it is a pigeon as this bird was a symbol of a mother goddess associated with the Cotswolds hills and its springs and rivers.

The next mosaic floor is found in Room 11, the warm room (tepidarium), which contains a floor consisting of geometric designs. For the bathers, the sequence of use of the rooms would have been as follows – changing room (apodyterium), warm room (tepidarium), hot room (caldarium), then from the hot room through the warm room to the cold room (frigidarium), then returning to the changing room. The mosaic in the warm room is constructed with the combination of just three different colours of tesserae. The outer border of coarse red tesserae leads the eye to a continuing border of white tesserae. Beyond this a double fillet of dark blue/grey surrounds the central rectangular panel.

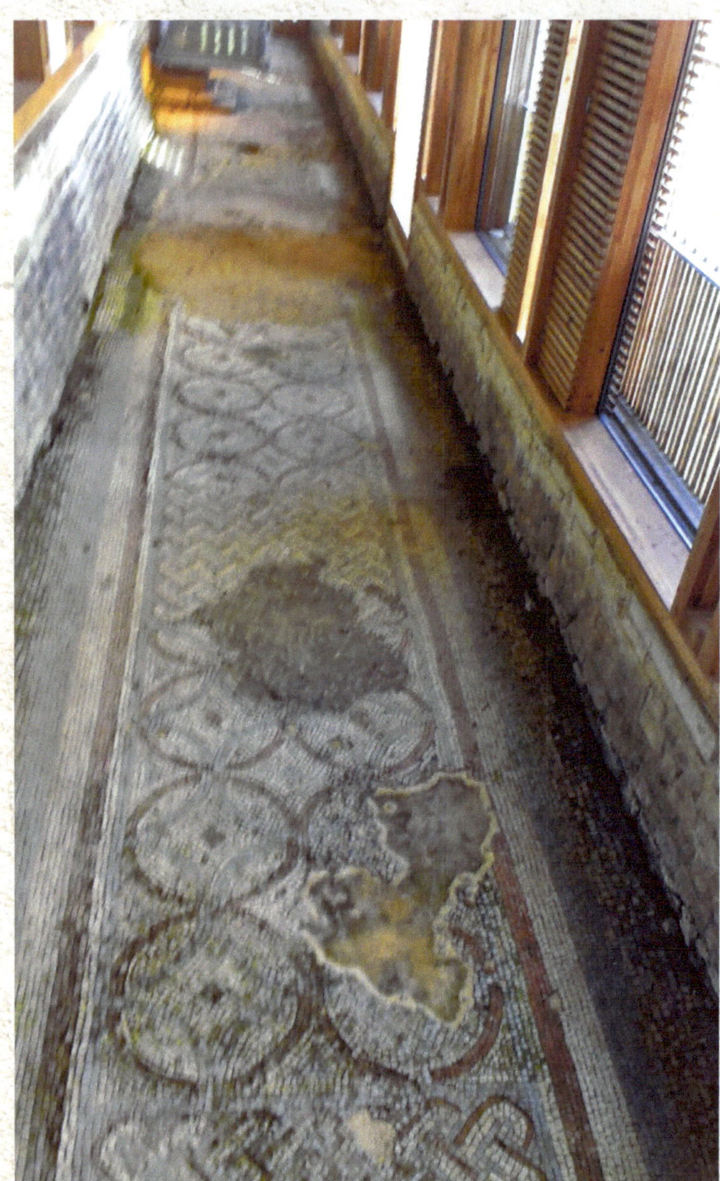

View of the West-wing porticus.

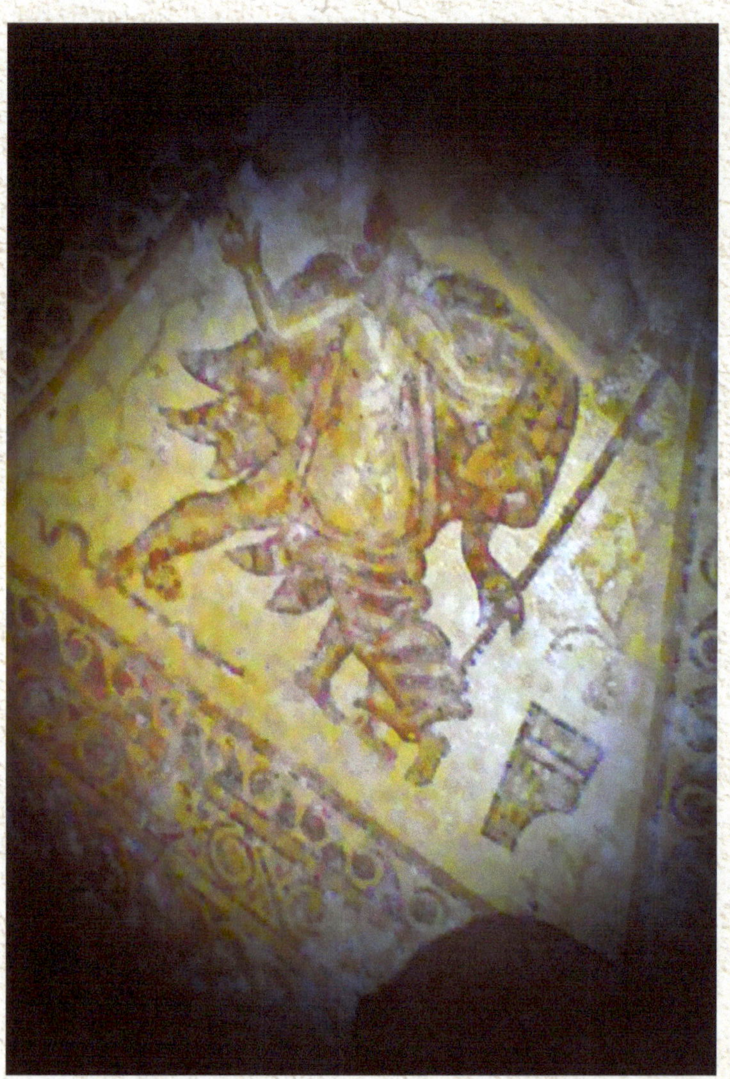

Ariadne and Bacchus.

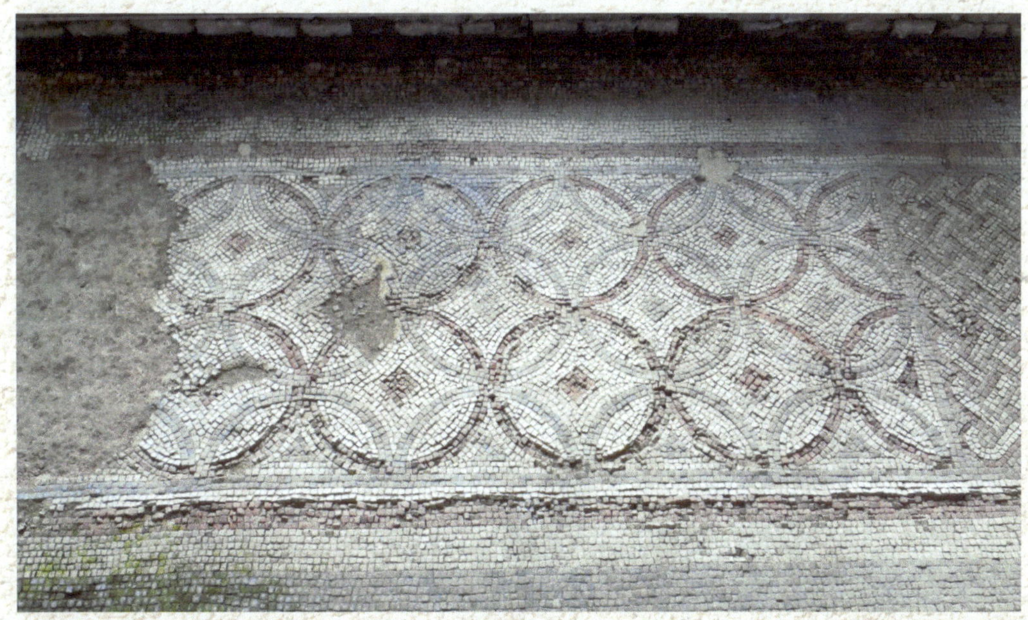

Another view of the West-wing porticus.

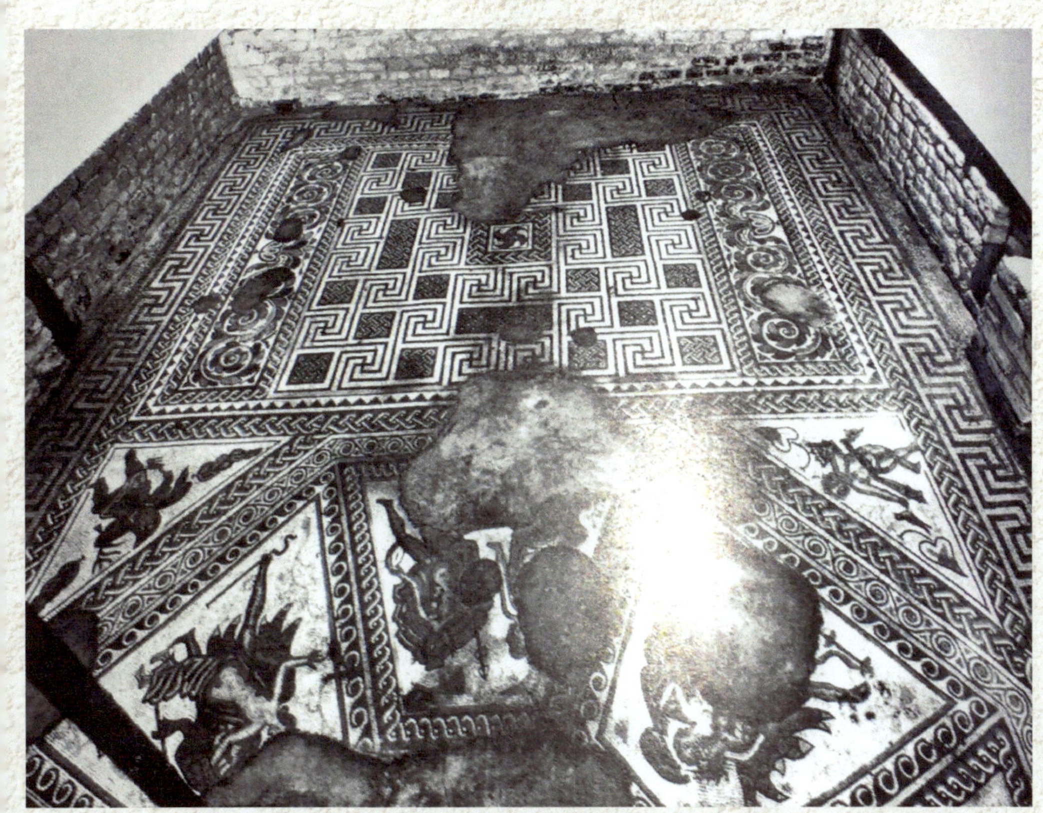

View of the dining room 'triclinium', from the North. Crown Copyright

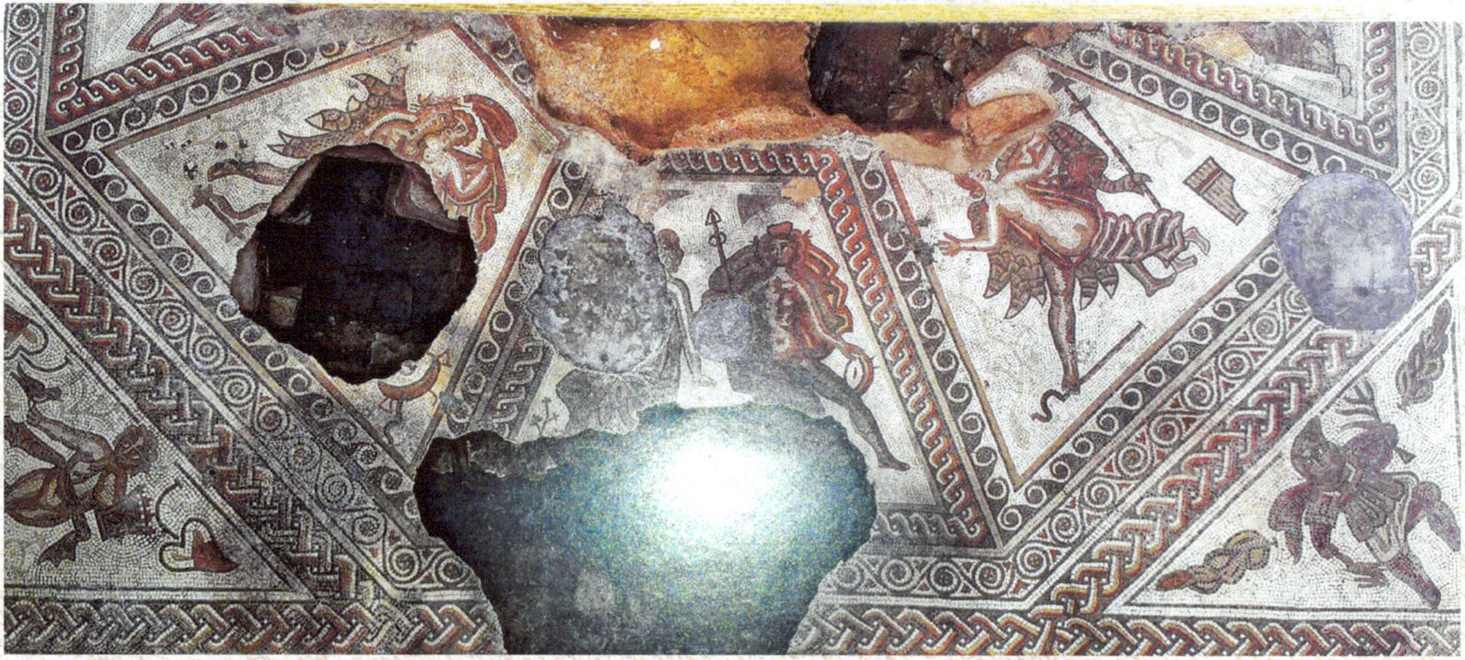

Trapezoidal Panels of Ariadne and Bacchus

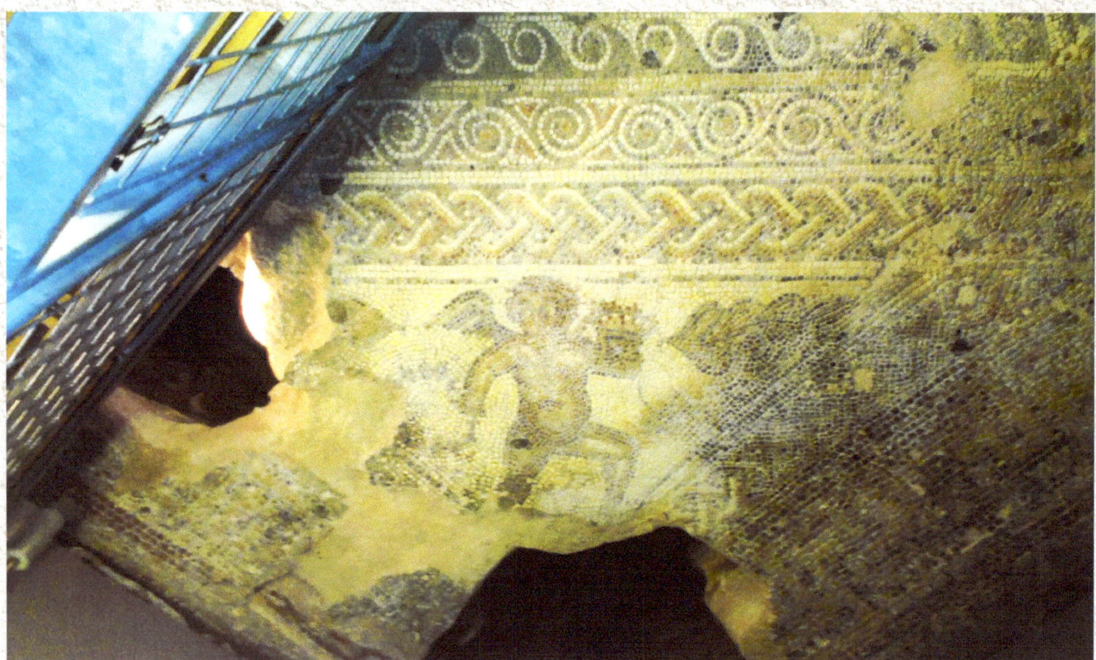

Cupid depicting Summer

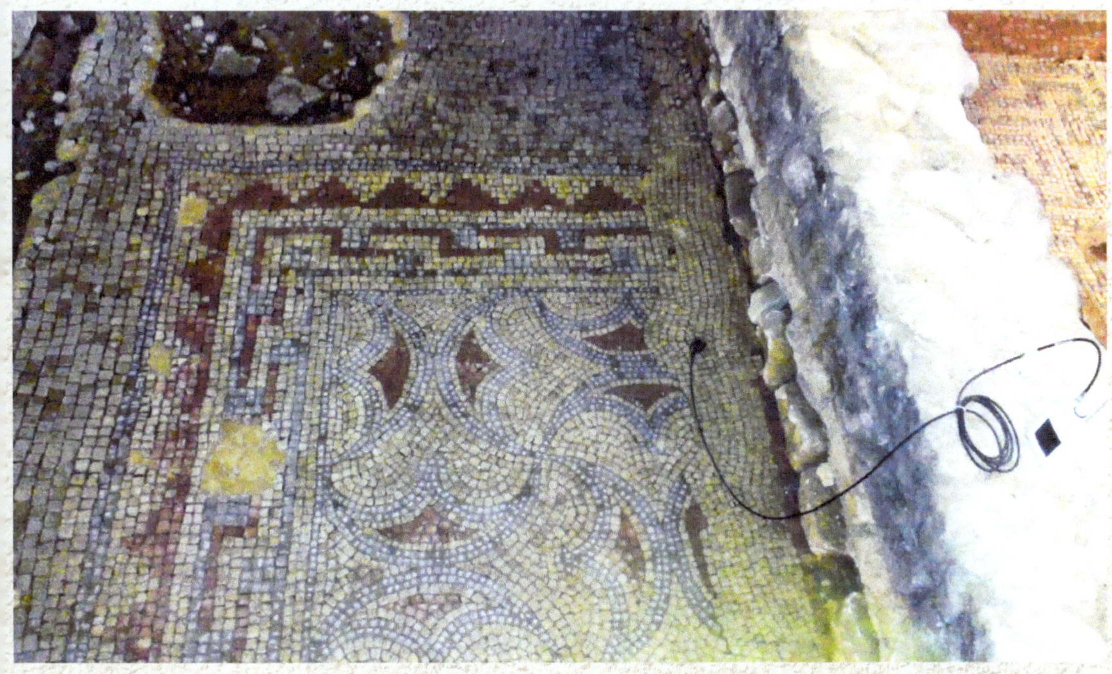

Mosaic, Room 5B

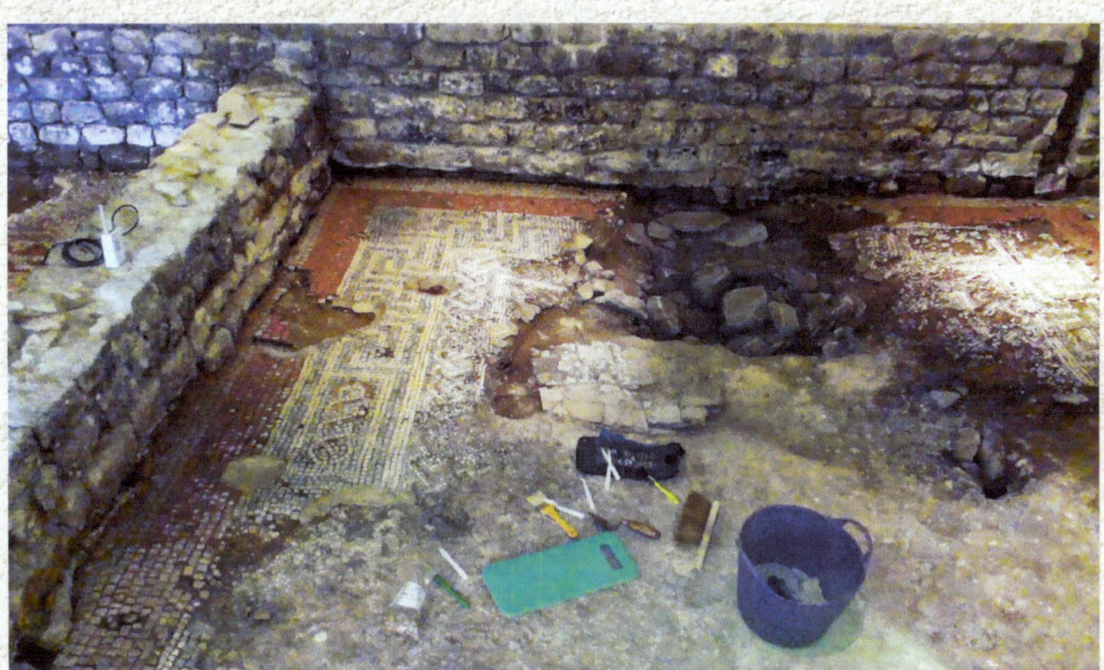

Room 6

Apodyterium from the East.Crown Copyright

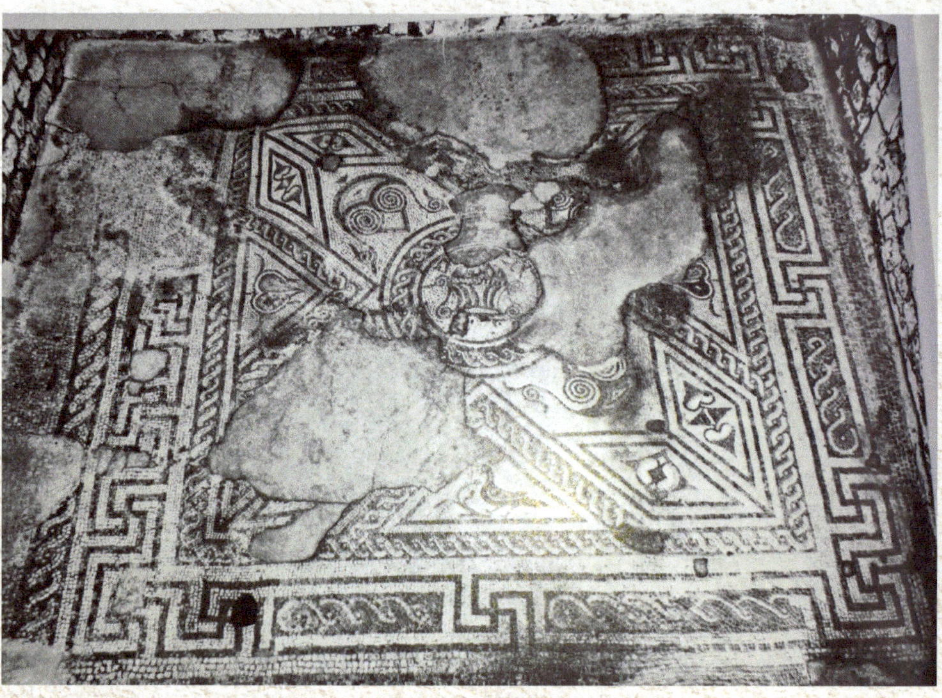

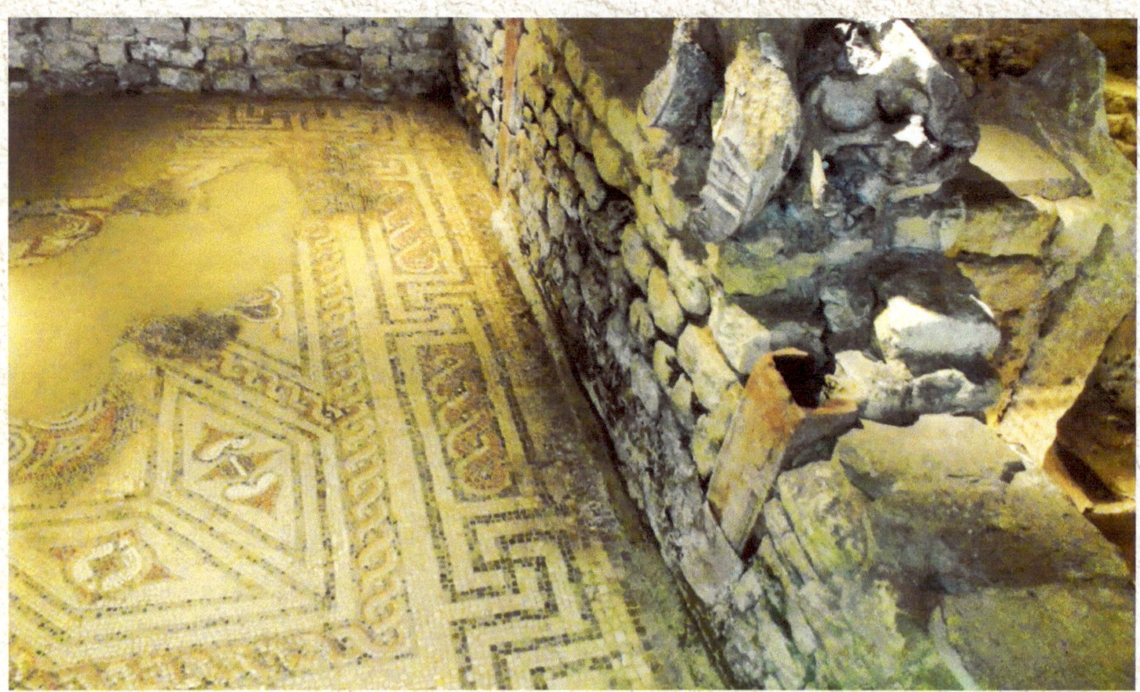

Changing room / apodyterium

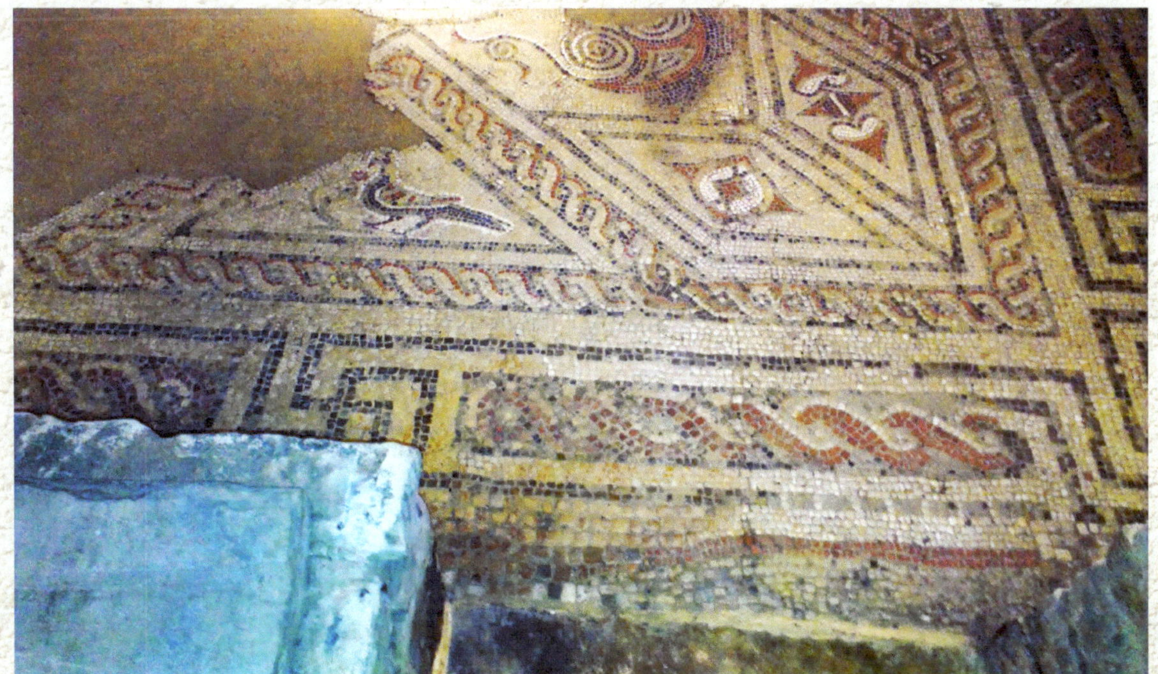

More apodyterium

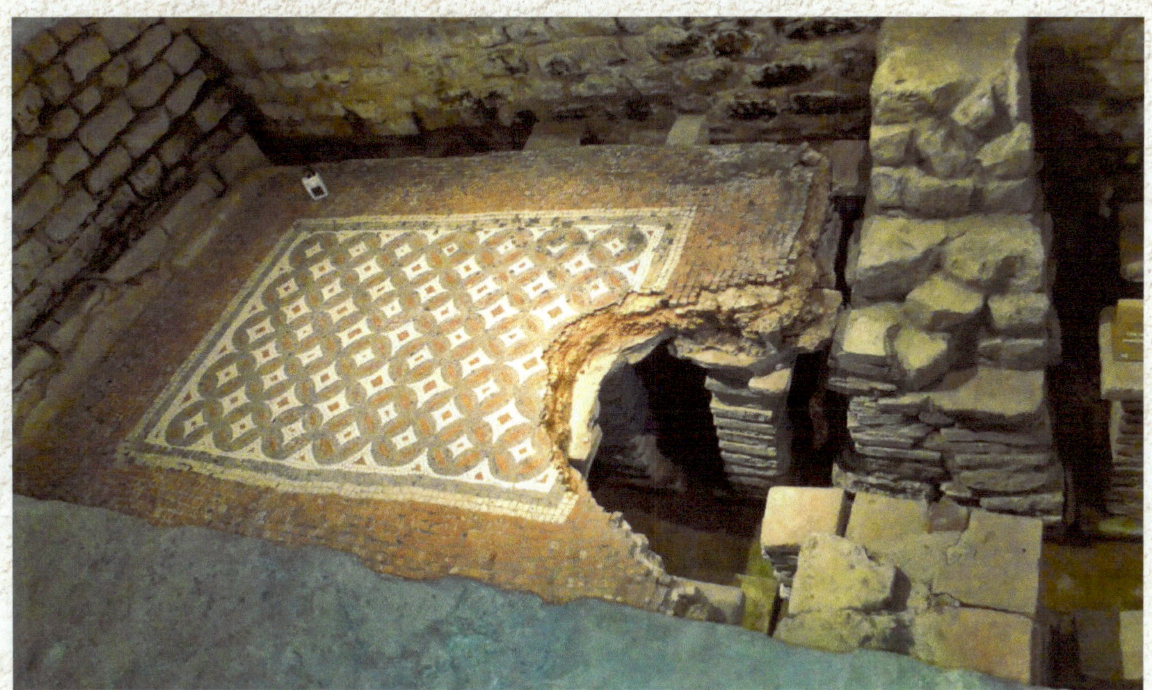

Room 11

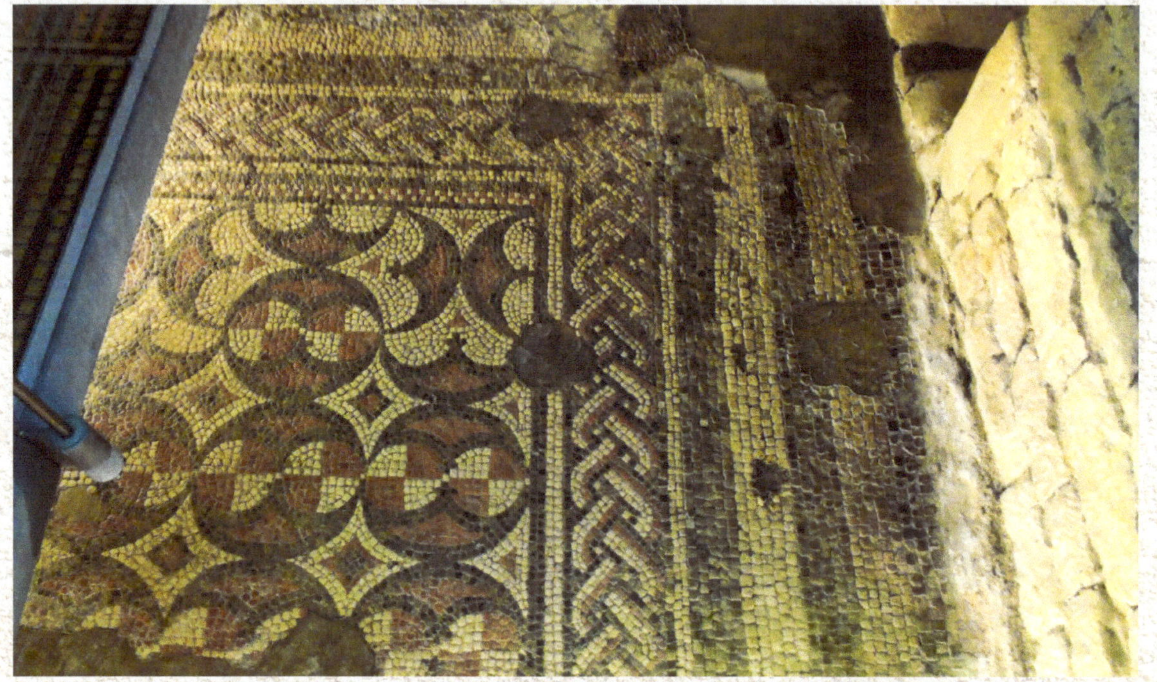

Mosaic in room 14

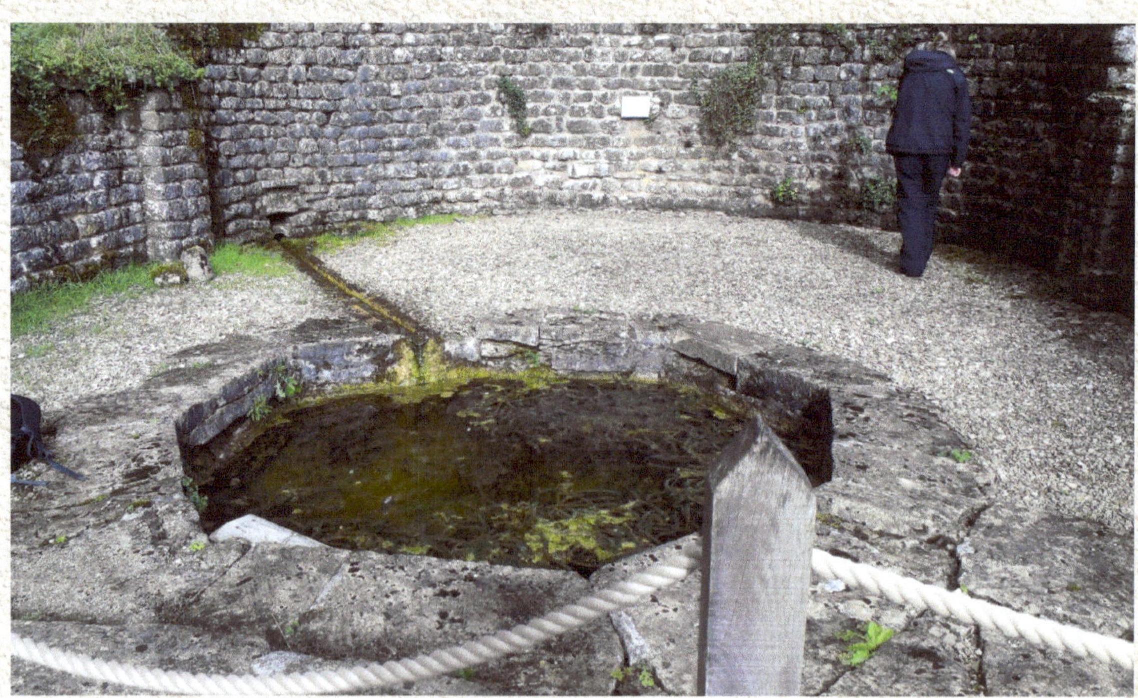

The Nymphaeum

Mosaic of the North-wing bath house

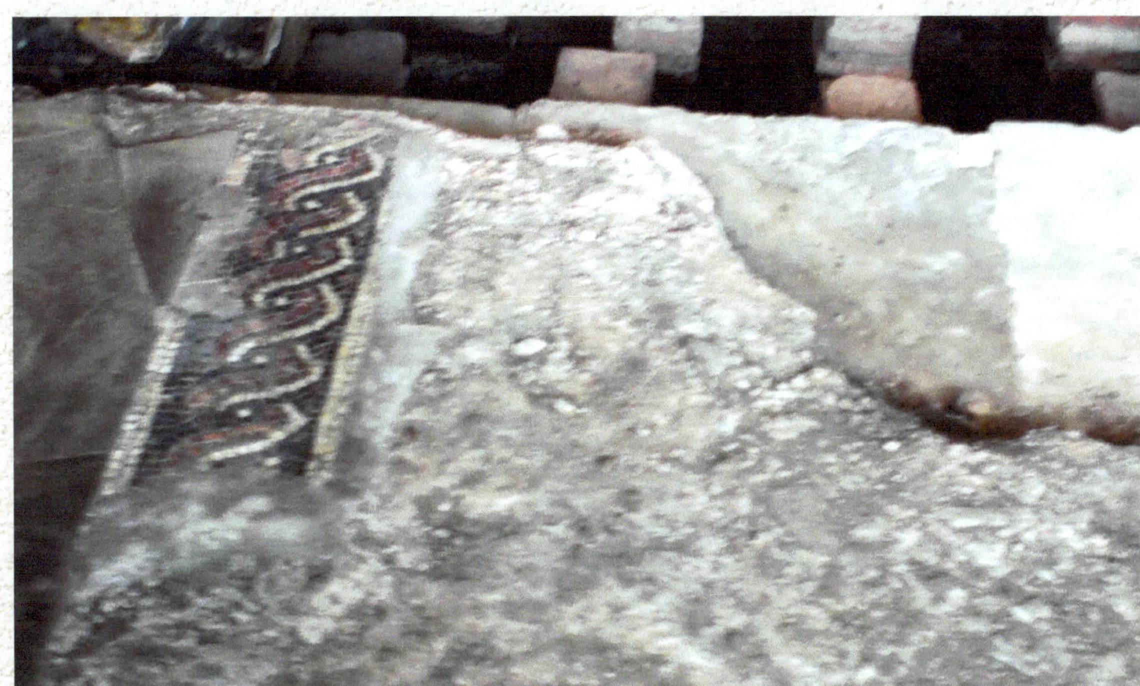

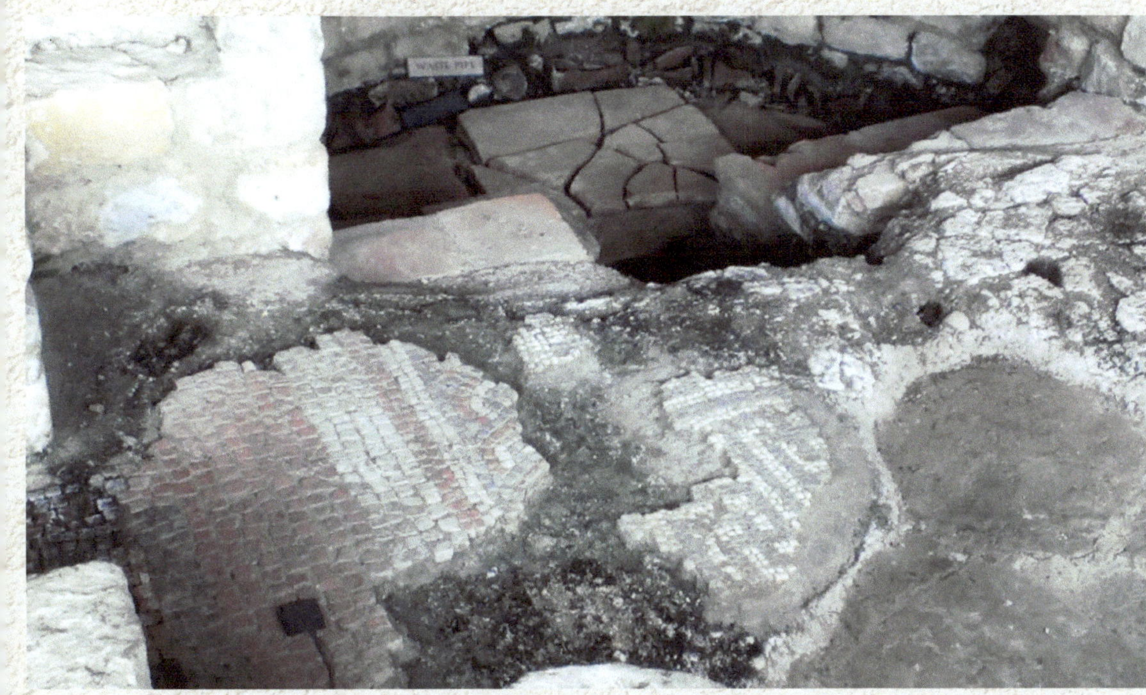

Mosaic of the North-wing bath house

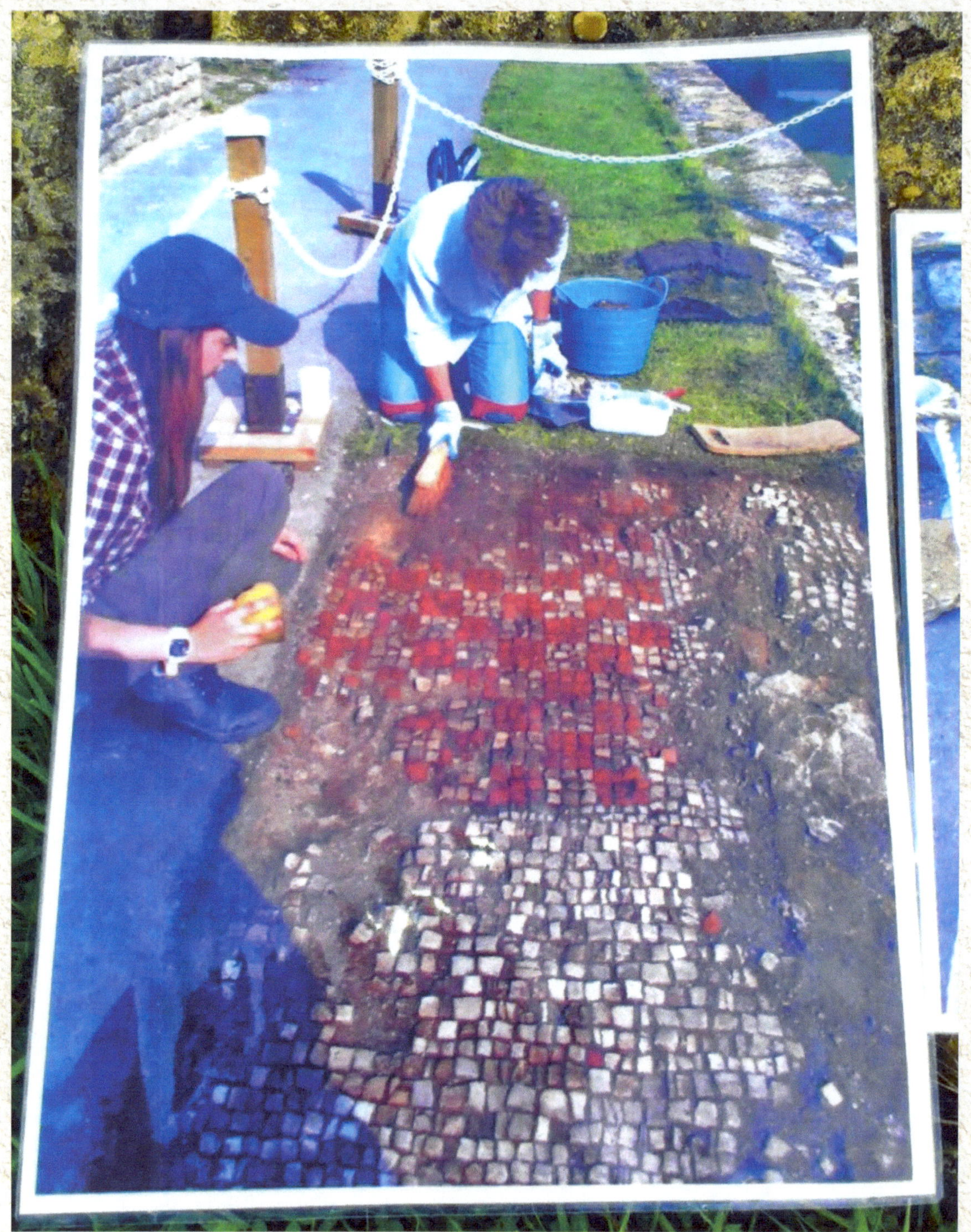

Part of the North-Wing Veranda

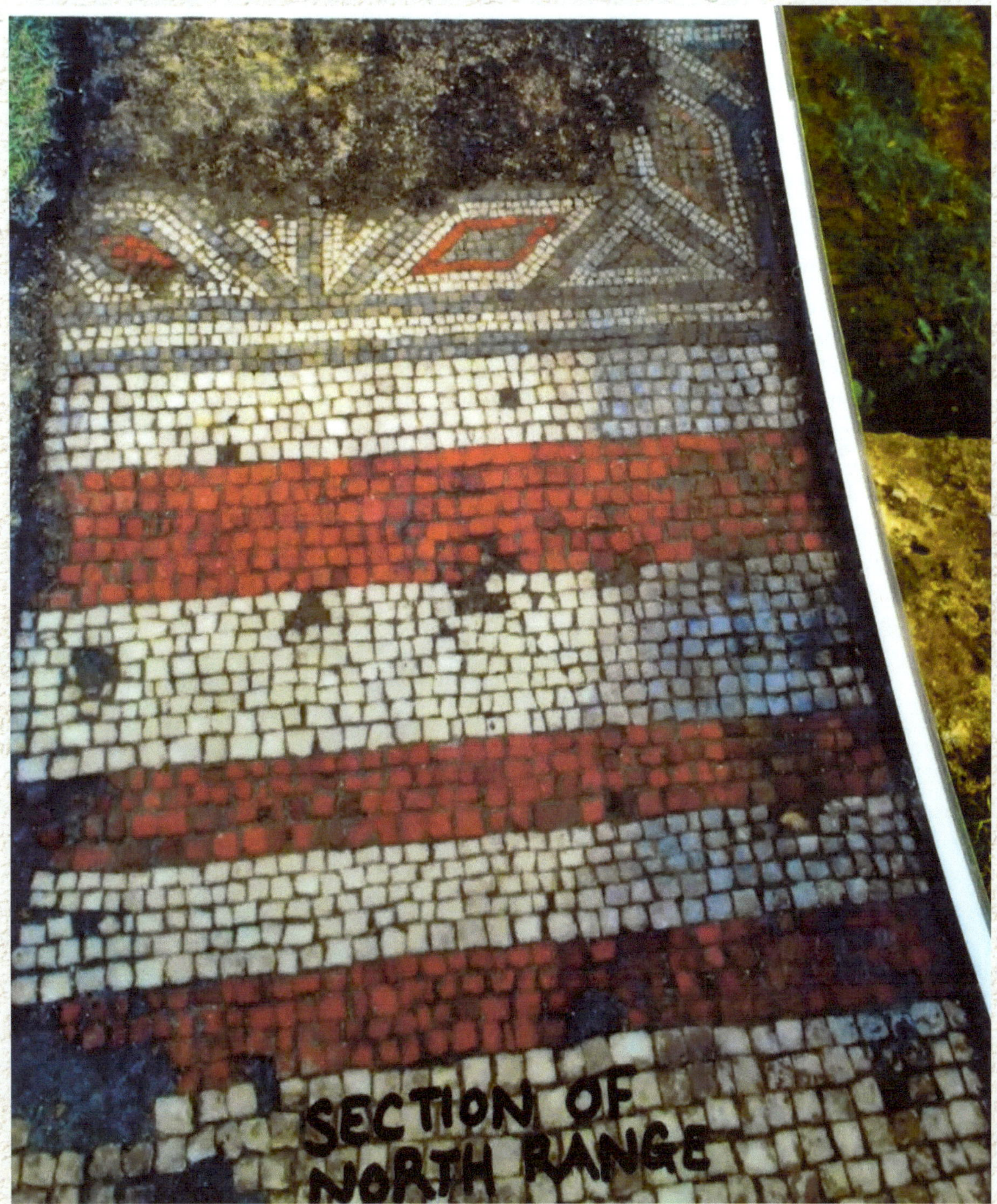

Part of the North-Wing Veranda

The rectangular panel is of a patterned design of dark blue/grey intersecting circles. These circles create white concave-sided squares which contain red at their centres. The whole of this design is set on a white background. If we look long and hard enough some of the circles can also relate to a joined up petal design. This visually engaging and intriguing design could possibly have stimulated debate amongst the bathers as they whiled away their time.

The pavement of Room 12 has succumbed to the ravages of time, but its pillars have been preserved for our modern eye to view. Gladly, the frigidarium (Room 14), with the cold plunge bath at the rear, retains part of its mosaic floor. Again we see a design composed within a rectangle which, like Room 11, only contains tesserae of red, white and dark blue/grey. A pattern of opposed pelta/styalised shields are used to form two circles with opposite quadrants in red and/or white. Between the pelta circles, concave-sided squares are noticed and within them are smaller concave squares. Some are shaded in red and the alternates with a dark blue grey. At the southern end of the panel the pelta design, in the south west and south east corners, shows a different arrangement which adds visual variety to the overall design.

All the pelta show dark blue/grey crosses at their central points and those at the southern end have small red triangles just beyond the crosses. The southern end shows a small red and white chequer border contained within a dark blue/grey frame. In all probability, this end design and its border would have been replicated at the northern end of this mosaic floor. The mosaic is surrounded by a series of coloured borders. There is a large one of a creamy/grey and within this there are two bands of red. Beyond the second red band a white border runs alongside another border of dark blue/grey. The dark blue/grey border outlines a three-strand guilloche, one being of red and two of white.

As I leave the west wing of this villa and progress out of the cover building to view the remains of the north wing baths and to observe and dwell upon the mysteries of the nymphaeum, I cast my mind's eye back to the west wing bath-house. The rooms, possibly, were constructed of stuccoed walls depicting trees, birds and other pastoral images. The ceilings may have been adorned with a sky-blue colour dressed with white, fluffy clouds. Other ceilings, perhaps, were full of stars and celestial imagery – all this to add to and compound the human emotion of relaxation, peace and tranquillity.

The nymphaeum housed the spring which supplied the early villa with its life-blood, water. It rests, detached from the villa, in the north-west corner, just below the woodland. The water would have percolated gently down from the bed of Fullers earth beneath the wood, to be captured in an octagonal basin capable of retaining 1500 gallons. This early shrine, perhaps without a roof and open to the elements, would have been curved at the back. A short distance from and at the centre of the semi-circular apse, would have stood a stone altar and forward from that the octagonal pool was set within a stone-flagged floor. The altar would have held a stone carved British/Romanised water goddess, standing proudly and presiding over her spring and peacefully returning the gaze of her worshippers. The elevated position of the shrine would have made it visually noticeable as the villa's inhabitants and visitors went about their daily business. An upward glance would have been a constant reminder that all who resided here did so only with the continued blessing of the Mother Earth goddess and of her chosen water deity. In this villa's later life, this spring would have been just one of its numerous water supplies. The shrine would possibly have been refurbished at a later date with a roof and would have held more architectural detail and pictorial coloured stucco.

From the nymphaeum my mind and attention is now drawn to the south-facing, 100 metre (300 feet) long north wing. This wing still holds numerous secrets of its past, but careful archaeology and interpretation have afforded us much to digest. For instance, Room 30 was the kitchen and from a midden (rubbish pit), which was against the east wall of this room, bones of domestic fowl, small birds, duck, sheep, oxen and pig were retrieved which give an indication of the wide range of meats available to the villa's diners. Outside and just to the north beyond this room another midden hoarding sherds of pottery, dated from the 2nd Century AD to the 4th Century AD, were excavated. Perhaps some relate to accidents that occurred within the kitchen as meals were being prepared or cleared away. It seems that Room 27, with its plain concrete floor, was utilised as a workshop because a small clay crucible, used for small scale smelting/casting, was excavated from here. Both of these rooms have doorways opening on to mosaic-paved verandah.

Mosaic floors were recorded in the following rooms, Room 22, 24, 25A, 28, 31A and 32, plus the whole length of the northern porticus and the passage connecting Rooms 10-14 with the verandah in the west wing. Perhaps the most visually impacting section of the north wing now is the remains of its baths – in its final phase, the whole suite was used for sauna bathing. On view are the fragments of two mosaic floors. On one floor a simple guilloche can be seen with bands of red, white and perhaps yellow all set in a dark blue/grey background and outlined in white. The centre is much damaged and repaired with opus signinum (pink mortar). The white 'eyes' within the guilloche help to give it more visual impact. The other mosaic design, also extremely damaged, reveals the remnants of a swastika-meander. On the left side, as we view it, lines in white, red and a dark blue/grey are perhaps part of a square design of which many would have been contained within the overall swastika-meander. On the far left a red border of large, coarse tesserae bond onto four rows of coarse, white tesserae and this in turn leads on to a double row of smaller red tesserae followed by a double row of white tesserae.

Of the mosaic floor in Room 24, just two pieces remain and these can be viewed within the villa's museum. On this, my latest visit, a number of photographs were laid out of the mosaics that were excavated from the north range and then reburied after they were drawn and recorded by students from the University of Birmingham. One of the photos relates to Room 25A of the north wing. At the top of the photo, part of the inner fragmented design of the mosaic can be seen. It seems to be based upon a square and triangle design; the in-fills of these are of red and dark blue/grey. These inner designs are enclosed in a double fillet of dark blue/grey and of white. Outside the immediate design alternate borders of bands of red and creamy/grey (Cotswold stone) are visible. The other photo probably relates to part of the northern porticus, where two students, one with a damp sponge and the other with a small hand brush, are busy cleaning the mosaic. The mosaic is a chequerboard pattern of red and white squares and joins another section of, seemingly, plain white tesserae. Possibly more information about these two mosaics will be revealed in the academic monograph to be published in 2014-2015. Rooms 31, 31A and 32 seem to be a dining area and, in reality, the north wing is a close replica of the west wing.

As for the south wing, a small excavation across the lower part of it in 1997 suggests that this wing was constructed of a range of rooms fronted by a heated corridor. So, perhaps, this wing also provided residential accommodation. Interestingly, archaeology suggests that the latrines (Room 4) went out of use in the early 4th Century. I can only imagine that perhaps that bigger and grander latrines were constructed somewhere further east within this wing. The rest of the wing remains an apparition for, although more was glimpsed by magnetometry and resistivity surveys, there is evidence that the wing runs east for at least 20 metres beyond the National Trust boundary.

I recommend that visitors spend time visiting the museum which was constructed immediately after the Victorian excavations. It was built by James Farrier and the floor consists of red and black tiles with a central 'E' for Eldon (who financed this museum and the excavations). Within the museum are numerous interesting reminders of the villa's past, including some of a personal nature relating to the villa's inhabitants/visitors.

CONCLUSION

My mind is embedded within a constant swirling mist as I seek answers as to how all this opulence at Chedworth was funded. At the time of writing this chapter, religion seems to be taking centre stage as the oxygen that fuelled and sustained the villa's finances during its final years. But only, I feel, because as yet archaeology has not revealed a sustainable alternative. Profits from sheep farming are a possibility, as British wool was a sought-after commodity within the Empire for its quality and would have generated much wealth. However, how many heads of sheep were farmed here is impossible to estimate as the boundaries of the villa estate are unknown. Perhaps they were natural boundaries determined by escarpments and stream valleys.

RELIGION

Only one half of a mile south east of the villa the remains of a Romano-British temple was discovered. It was constructed on an artificial platform 35 yards from and 50 feet above the flood plain of the River Coln. The platform is estimated to have been 50 feet square with a colonnaded portico and cella set on a podium of huge hewn limestone blocks. Around the platform area drums of stone columns one and a half feet in diameter, a fragment of a capital and pieces of moulded stone architrave were retrieved. This then was a luxury temple of classical architecture. A number of coins dated from the middle of the 2nd Century to the 4th Century AD were excavated from here and a number of small finds from this temple can be viewed in the museum.

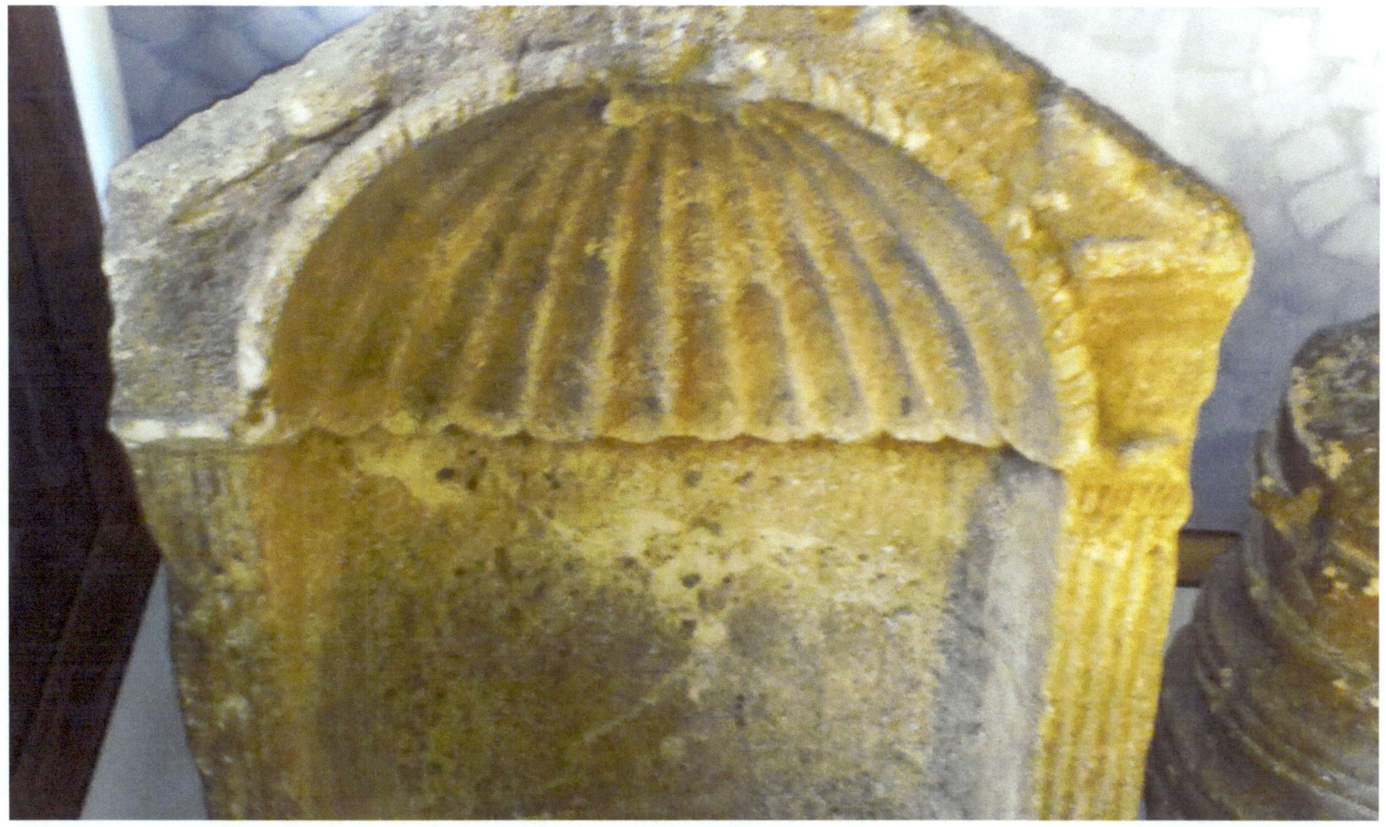

An Altar

Perhaps, like the local, oval amphitheatre, which could accommodate up to 8,000 people and offer up various forms of entertainment, the villa was for public use for the people's religious practices and festivals, with the benefit of accommodation and baths for relaxation. The villa may have been in the control of the town's administration and its upkeep paid for by taxation and the various rental and hire charges. The archaeology suggests that both paganism and Christian worship were practised within the villa's complex, although it is not possible just through archaeology to interpret whether both were practised in union or one religion prevailed over the other in certain periods of history. A number of pagan reliefs depicting certain gods were excavated at Chedworth, including one set in oolitic limestone of a hunter-god. Also two altars were found, both depicting the god of Mars Lenus; one is crudely sculptured compared to the other one. A larger and uninscribed altar was excavated from the nymphaeum and other statues found on site can be viewed in the museum. The latest find seems to be a pewter libation cup recovered from the north wing in 1998. The fingerprints of Christianity are fewer and less clear than those of paganism, although for a period of time they were set in stone for all to view on one of the coping stones from the octagonal pool, at the nymphaeum. The coping stone had been incised with a symbol of an X (chi) and P (rho). These two letters are the first two letters of Christos/Christ in Greek. This may suggest that the waters of the spring were purified for Christian use and therefore the presiding water spirit was driven out. Interestingly, the coping stones from the octagonal pool, including the one that was incised, were recycled as building material to construct the steps of the west bathhouse at some later date within the villa's history. This then could indicate that the traditional religions have re-established themselves. Perhaps then a clearer picture may appear if we now turn our attention to the religious preferences of certain Roman emperors during the period from 300 AD to 410 AD, when the Roman legions were officially removed from this island.

Under the Roman Emperor Constantine the Great (306-337 AD) Christianity was legalised in 313 AD when the Edict of Milan was issued, but this also granted tolerance to all religions, including Christianity. Therefore this edict also reaffirmed the importance of religious worship to the welfare of the state and empire. The Emperor Julian (361-363 AD), who was the last emperor of the Constantinian dynasty, the Empire's first Christian dynasty, tried to revive the traditional Roman practices at the cost of Christianity. The Emperor Jovian (363-364 AD) re-established Christianity by revoking the edicts of Julian against Christians. The next emperor, Valentinian (364-375 AD), was a Christian and permitted liberal religious freedom to all of his subjects. Theodosius (379-395), who was the last emperor to rule over both the eastern and the western halves of the Roman Empire, promoted Christianity within the Empire and he declared the 'catholic church' as the legitimate imperial religion. In 391 AD pagan temples were closed and pagan worship was forbidden.

At what depth the chosen religious preferences of the emperors were absorbed by the local populous in

Britannia is open to debate. Although it does seem that Theodosius was extremely aggressive to enforce his chosen beliefs, it is possible that the Roman administration in Cirencester were advised to pursue his commands and consequently paganism at Chedworth went into a steep decline.

More daylight may be shed upon the fate of Chedworth Roman Villa if we take a look at the coins which were excavated here and compare their dates against those found elsewhere, in other Cotswold villas and in Cirencester. Coins ceased to come into Britain in any quantity after 400 AD, but it is difficult to assess when they eventually became redundant as a currency for trading. In Cirencester and some of the villas in the surrounding valleys coins were excavated dating to the reign of Arcadius (383-408 AD), but at Chedworth, only one coin datable to after 383 AD was found. Possibly, Chedworth villa went out of general public use and therefore the volume of people who visited dried up when paganism was declared unlawful. Perhaps the villa reverted to just a subsistence level of farming carried out by its remaining inhabitants.

Over the passing of the years the villa fell into general decay. Good building stone would have been stolen and used elsewhere. During the initial excavations a lime kiln, built from the materials of the ruined walls was excavated from the steep hillside behind the north wing. It was, no doubt, an active agent in the destruction of the remains. Once the stealing of any wanted, reusable material had ceased, the lime-kiln and the dismembered remains of the villa would have been abandoned to the elements. Hill-wash and the occasional landslide would have engulfed the remains and laid a fertile bed of earth for bushes and trees to propagate and eventually the villa's remains would have been set free from prying human eyes.

THE FUTURE

There are at least 22 known villas within a 10 mile radius of Chedworth, but a number of these have only been glimpsed through archaeology – although the remains at Worthington have revealed mosaic floors of quality. More of these villas' secrets could possibly be revealed to the living by the use of modern satellite technology. Since the declassification in 1995, by the US military, corona satellite images can be used for archaeological investigations. They produced high resolution stereo images which preserve pictures of archaeological sites and landscapes which have been destroyed or obscured by modern development. But the application of corona imagery, in archaeological research, needs to be conducted by specialists because of the challenges involved in correcting spatial distortions produced by the satellite's unusual panoramic cameras. At the moment it seems that the best exponent of this technology, which allows us to see the invisible, is Dr Sarah Parack, an archaeologist and Egyptologist at the University of Alabama, in Birmingham, USA. The use of this revolutionary satellite technology, along with her passion for history, have driven her to unveil and open the doors back into antiquity at Portus, the long lost harbour of Rome.

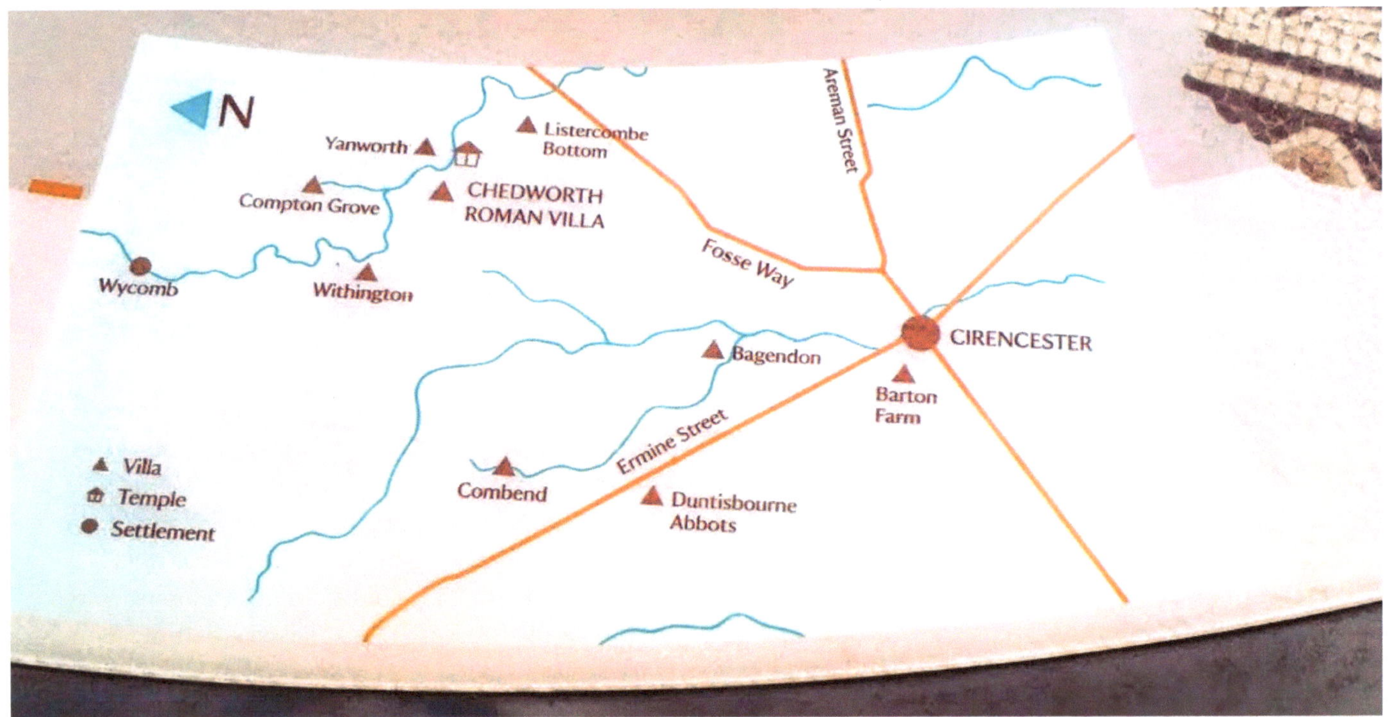

The local villas

In these times of austerity the funding to use this technology in the Cotswolds valleys would have to come, no doubt, from a private source. Perhaps from a benefactor, like Ivan Margary was to Fishbourne Roman Palace, someone with a hunger to understand more of our ancestors' past. Personally, I hope that a benefactor steps forth from the shadows sooner rather than later as my candle of life burns low and its flame has begun to flicker. Whether the Cotswold valleys are hushed with snow or bathed in sunshine, or in shadow, the natural beauty of the ebbing and flowing of the seasons has made me realise that being born in Britannia is indeed a blessing.

Footnote: At the end of Summer 2014 National Trust archaeologists discovered a new mosaic between the 4th Century villa's North Bath and a range of rooms further to the east. The remains of a tessellated floor covering an area 18 metres by 6.75 metres were found. The mosaic was decorated with intricate geometric patterns bounded by bands of red and white stripes. The mosaic has extensive patches of damage but is still clearly a single surface covering the entire floor of a single room. This was probably a grand reception room. The mosaic has been recorded and has been reburied for its own protection.

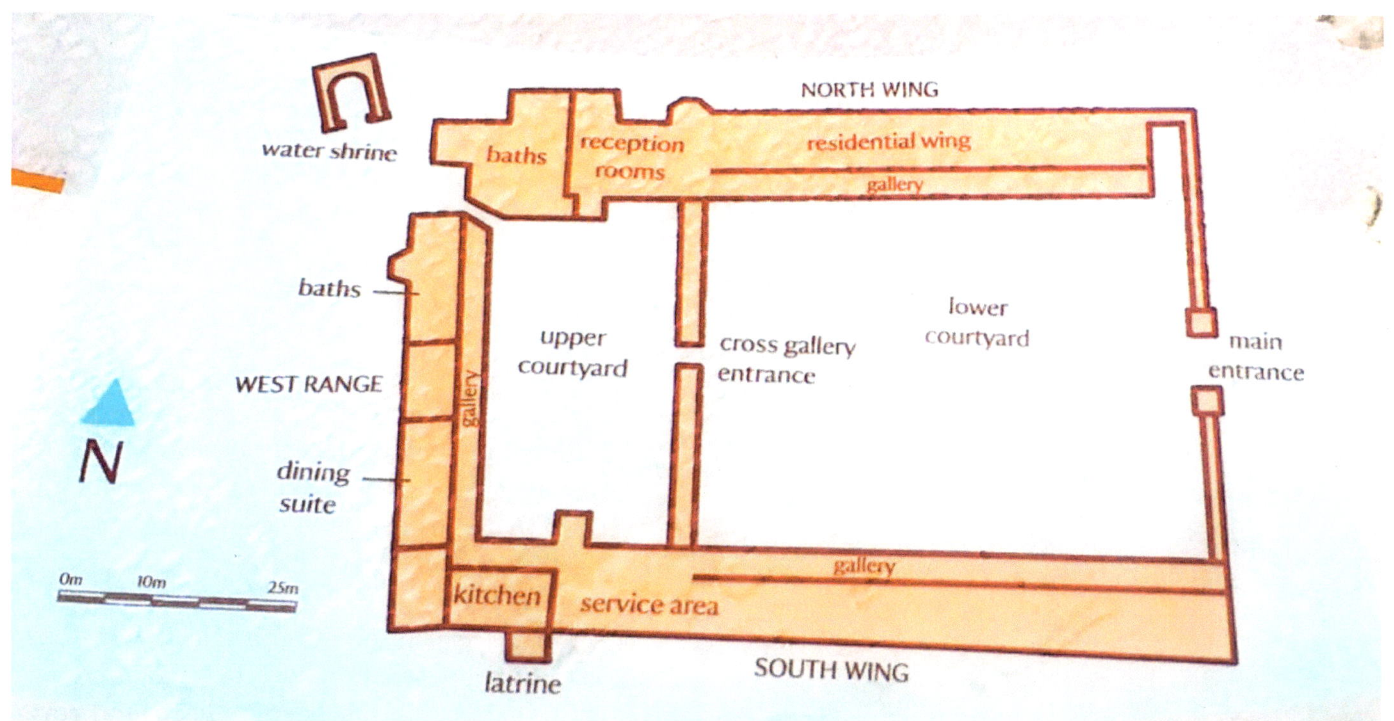

The complete plan of the villa

Chapter IV
Brading Roman Villa

AN OVERVIEW

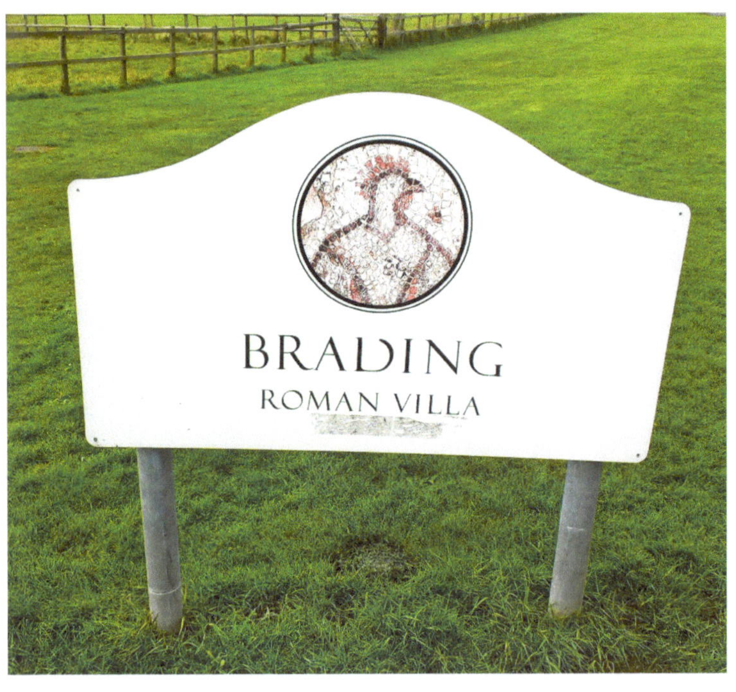

Brading Roman Villa is situated a few hundred metres south of Brading Down on the Isle of Wight, the local section of the chalk ridge that runs across the island from the Needles, in the west, to Culver Cliff, in the east. As the Villa is sited at the foot of Brading Down, it is sheltered from the North winds. The Villa faces east and overlooks an alluvial plain that once formed a small harbour, known as Brading Haven, at the mouth of the East Yar River. The harbour is now silted up and the Villa is now 1.5 kilometres from the coast. Perhaps to make the Villa more prominent at some time in its inhabited lifetime, the outside would have been painted white or even multi-coloured. This, set against the dark background of the then woods, would have advertised the wealth and status of its owners.

The Isle of Wight landmass, at one point in its evolutionary history, would have still been attached to Europe and South East England. About 10,000 years ago the great ice sheets of the last ice-age melted, causing a substantial rise in sea level. Because of this, around 7,000 years ago, the island was separated from the mainland. The Isle of Wight is now located about five miles off the coast of the county of Hampshire and separated from Britain by a strait called the Solent. It is a diamond-shaped island of 147 square miles and is about 26 miles across.

The Roman occupation of this island, then known as Vectis, began in 44 AD when the 2nd Roman Legion, commanded by the future Emperor Vespasian conquered and subdued the local tribes. How difficult, how long it took and at what cost to human lives is sadly not recorded by the early historians. The ancient name of Brerdynge, from which Brading is derived, perhaps meant 'the people living by the ridge of the downs' and dates from about 683 AD. Brading Roman Villa is one of four Roman villas on the island to have contained mosaic floors, where a known floor plan exists. The other three were at Carisbrooke, Combley and Newport. Also, there have been tantalising discoveries of tesserae on the island that suggest that more villas with mosaic floors existed.

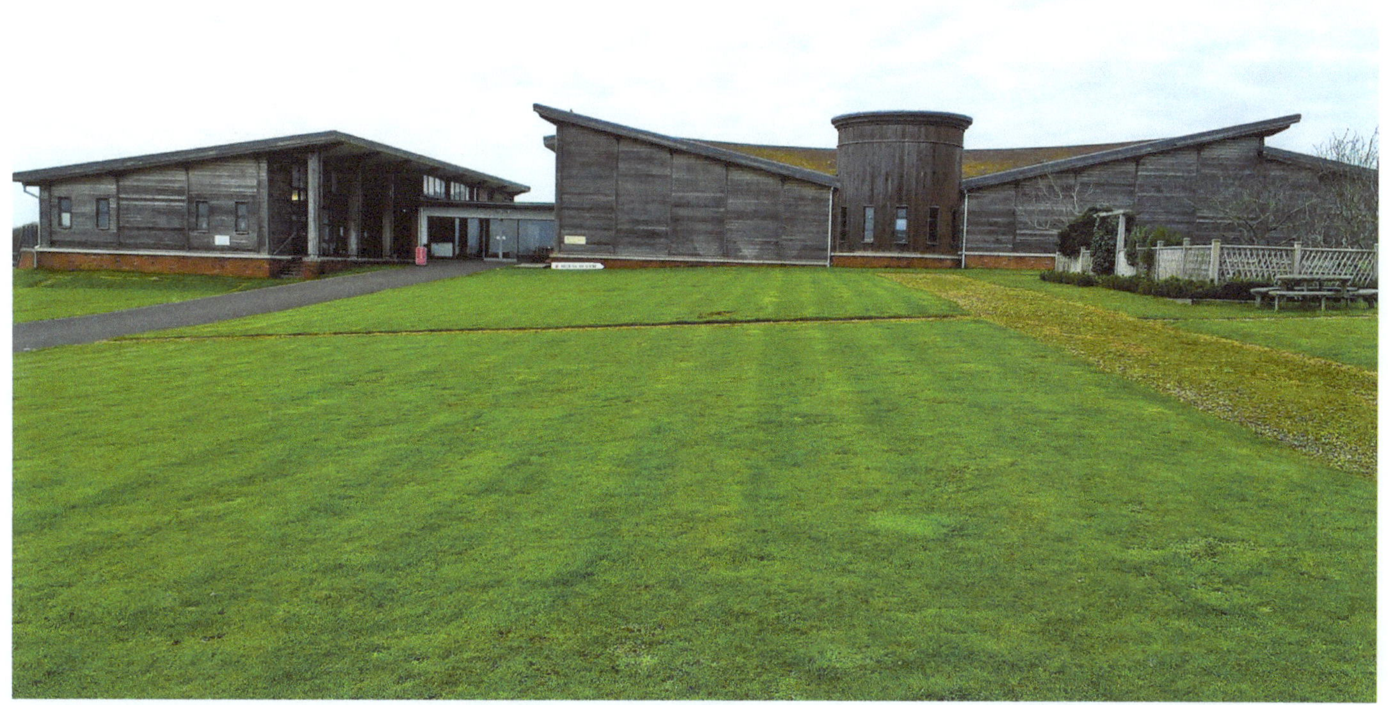

Villa cover-building

The Brading Roman Villa began its resurrection in 1879 and instrumental in this was a resident of Yarbridge, a merchant seaman by the name of Captain Thorp. At this point, it may be of interest to the reader, if I quote the discovery from the journal of this gentleman… '1st May 1879. During my researches

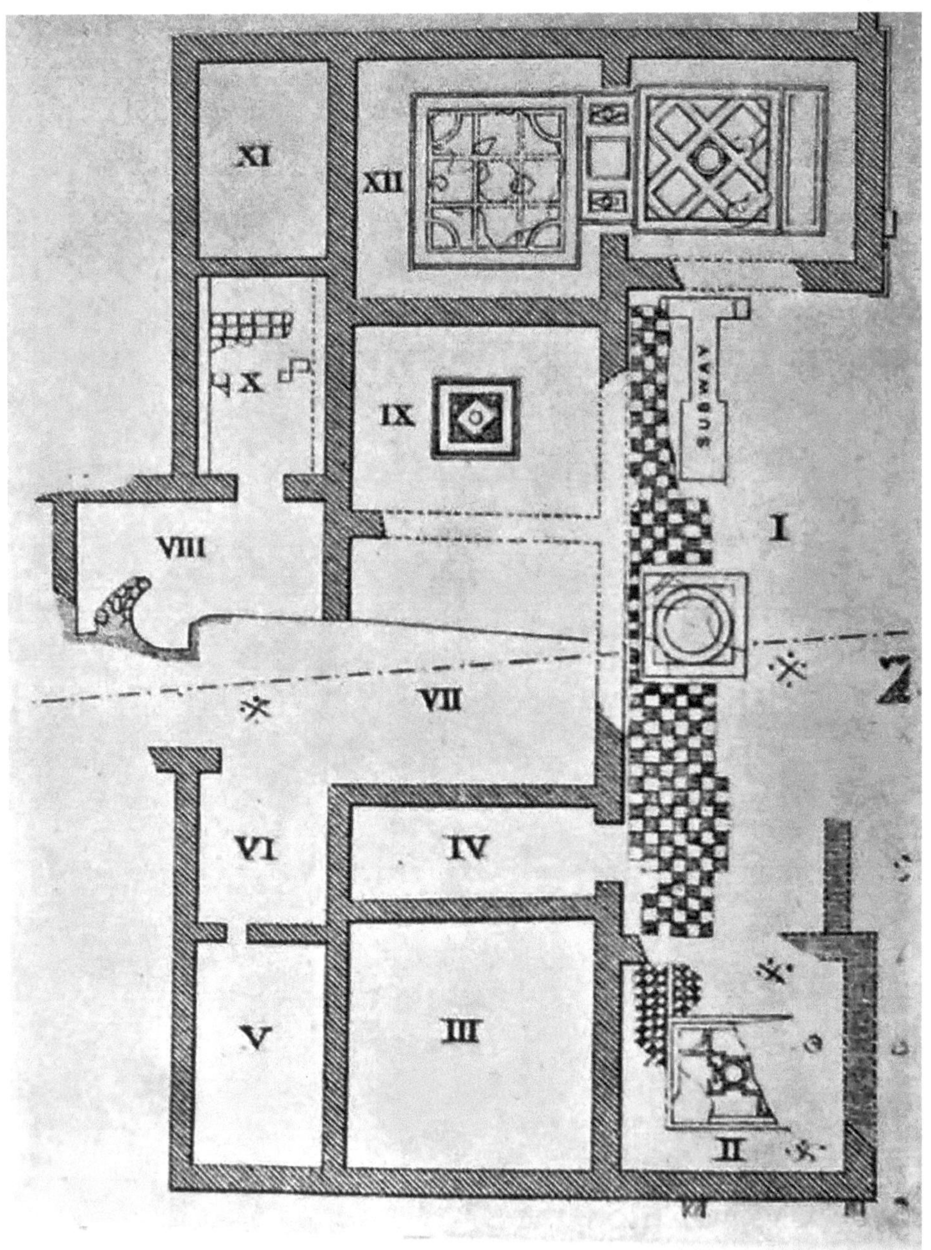

The Ground-Plan of the Villa

on Morton Farm, after probing many square yards of land, I hit upon broken Roman pottery in quantity on one spot near a hedge which divides Lady Oglander's land from that of Morton Farm. Continuing my work, I found more tesserae in a loose state, but upon further search I found some in parts lay solid and evidently a pavement extending for some distance east and west. After making my work on the surface of the land all safe, I took bearings of the exact spot, and where I meditated to excavate at some future time.' …'March 22nd 1880. The land, now being free of crops, and with the sanction of the owner of the property, I exposed to view the first portion of the Roman pavement I had discovered on 1st May 1879 on Morton Farm.' Captain Thorp continued his excavation work with a farmer, Mr Munns, until they had uncovered the mosaic containing the Orpheus design. The site of the villa at this time was owned by two different families. The southern half of the villa, where the Orpheus mosaic was found, belonged to Mr Munns. The northern half

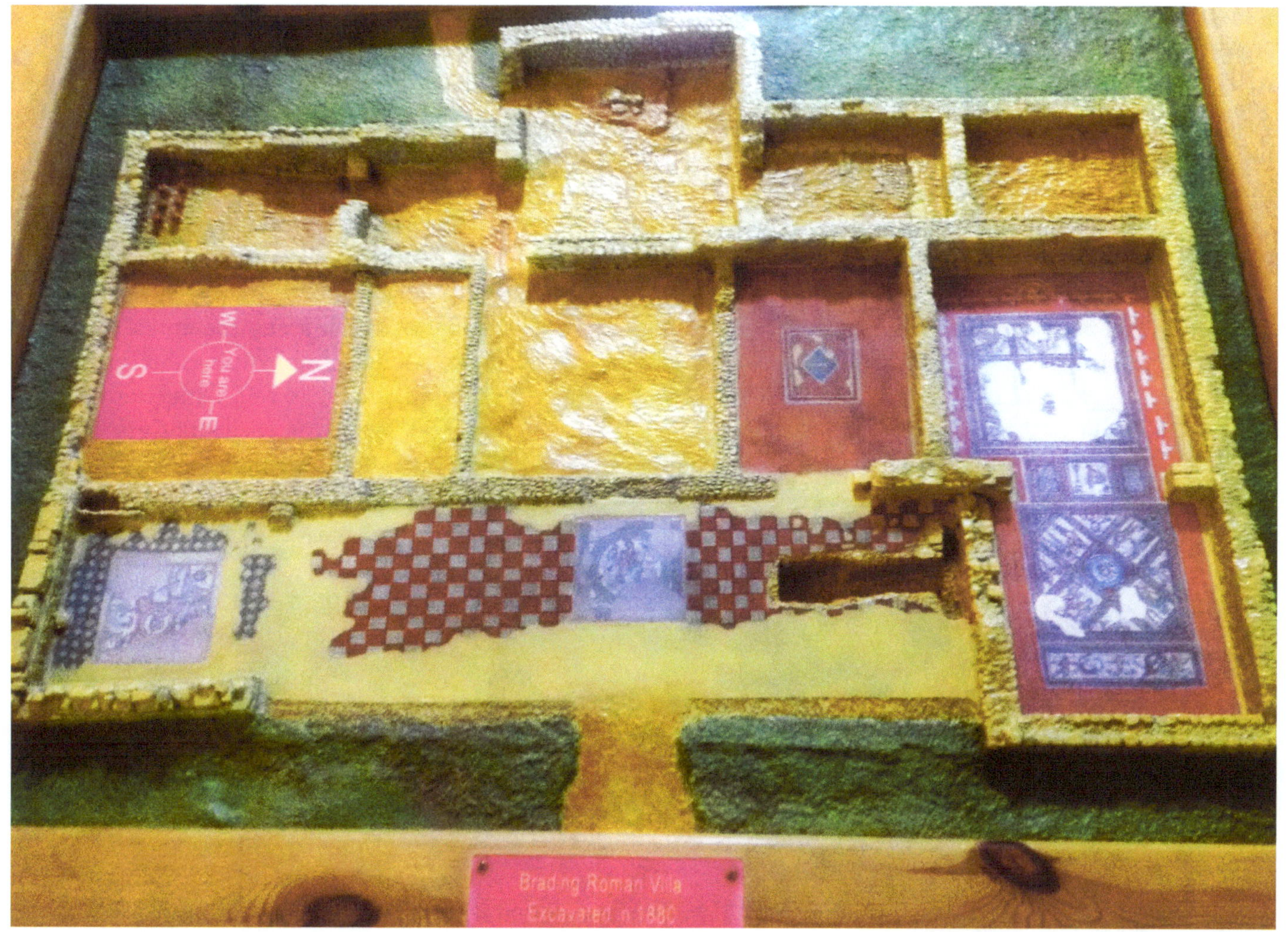

Model of the villa

was owned by Lady Oglander, of the Nunwell Estate. Lady Oglander then progressed to purchase the field belonging to Mr Munns, so the whole site could then be under one ownership. Excavations continued over the next 15 years under Mr John Oglander FSA, initially with the guidance of the Antiquarians JE Price and FG Hilton Price. The mosaics for many years were enclosed within a large steel-framed agricultural structure, clad in corrugated iron. This was financed by Lady Louisa Oglander. An average of 20,000 visitors a year paid three pence per head to view the three rooms containing the figured mosaic panels.

Sadly, with the passing of time, the steel-framed structure began to show its age. Therefore a structural survey of the building, organised by the newly formed (1994) Oglander Roman Trust, which was a new registered charity, revealed that the iron stanchions were rusting at ground level. Under the Trust's driving determination and aided and supported with advice from English Heritage, the fruits of their work stand before you: an innovative new cover building. It has a grass sedum roof with a D-shaped ground plan. The building nestles unobtrusively, but eye-catchingly within the surrounding environment. To our modern-day eye, I feel it is just as impressive as the Roman Villa would have seemed to our ancestors, who viewed it all those hundreds of years ago.

As I enter this unusual building, I feel inside me a huge wave of anticipation, then it engulfs my mind and senses like a crashing tsunami. I know that waiting for my eyes to feast upon are many individual panels, joined together to form two main floors, for each panel has its own individual story to tell. I stop and draw breath and find that I have landed in a welcoming and spacious lobby. The lobby area is thoughtfully laid out with a number of interesting books, glass objects, jewellery and gifts to view, handle and purchase. I highly recommend that the visitor purchases a guide book when paying the entrance fee. It is the most informative guide book that I have seen for many years. Contained in its XLVII pages is an introduction to Greek/ Roman mythology and this knowledge will enhance your understanding of what you are about to view. Also within it is a section for the younger visitor.

If we then turn to our right we enter through large, automatic glass doors, the building containing the mosaic floors. The sense of space inside creates a comforting and relaxing atmosphere. Looking up we notice the glue-laminated roof which trusses over the Villa in a single span. There is also a ramped walkway which allows two levels of viewing. All around the inside walls are artefacts, informative boards and maps which help to create, within the imagination, an insight to everyday living in this establishment and the surrounding estate.

Before we look at the three mosaic floors, I should perhaps mention what is known of the stone types that make up the tesserae. The white tesserae are derived from the local chalk formation on the downs, overlooking the villa. Analysis has shown that the black/grey tesserae are from the black stone beds of the Kimmeridge clay of Dorset. Many orange and red shades of tesserae are present but these are man-made ceramic tesserae, almost certainly from the local clays. Purbeck marble, which is a limestone from Dorset, can present the green/blue colours. Some of this limestone is noticeable in the Medusa head within the mosaic in Room 12. Other colour shades have not yet been successfully analysed to determine their origins, but they could possibly come from the local sandstone deposits.

THE MOSAIC FLOORS

The first mosaic to be revealed in 1880 was Room 3 which contains a strange looking 'cock-headed man', therefore it is fitting that we start the tour of the villa within this room. Within this room there is an effigy of Captain Thorp, one of the first people to discover this villa, kneeling over and viewing the mosaic. This mosaic was lifted in the 1980s for conservation purposes and a supporting floor of concrete was laid underneath it. Of this colourful mosaic, only five of the original nine panels survive. This is a shame, for this denies us a chance to interpret the overall meaning of this floor. Nevertheless, the remaining five panels have themselves created many interesting and debateable interpretations. The central medallion and the one surviving corner quadrant contain a bust, both possibly depicting Bacchus. This is possibly confirmed by the single row of black tesserae across the right shoulder which depicts a staff/thyrsus. Bacchus was the God of wine and revelry and he travelled to all the four corners of the then known world which included Greece, Asia Minor, Ethiopia and India. Bacchus, who travelled in a chariot, was accompanied by men known as satyrs and women known as maenads. Therefore, it could be that all four quadrants of this mosaic contained the bust of satyrs. In one of the many stories of Bacchus/Dionysus, we are told that when his wife Ariadne died he had her crown, which was decorated with five stars, put into the Heavens as the constellation Corona. The staff/thyrsus, which is shown over his shoulder, was also a powerful wand and one of the benefits of this wand was that Bacchus could use it to destroy those who opposed his cult and the freedom this represented.

Below the central Bacchus medallion a gladiatorial scene can be viewed. To the left is a retiarius dressed in a protective tunic with extra padded material on his left arm. The retiarius has presumably already dispatched his net towards his rival, possibly a secutor, in the hope of entangling him. The retiarius shown here is striking his opponent's hooded head with a trident and will possibly be following this up with a thrust from his knife.

The panel to the left of the Bacchus medallion contains a scene with a running fox, a tree and part of a building. As I continue to view it, what begins to drip into my mind, is the fable 'The Fox and the Grapes' written by Aesop, the Greek slave storyteller. In the fable we are told that a fox stumbles upon some grapes, just ripening on a vine, which has been trained over a lofty branch. Wishing to quench his thirst, the fox takes a run and a jump at the hanging bunch of grapes. After a number of unsuccessful attempts, unable to reach them he gives up and runs off declaring 'I am sure they would have been sour anyway'. The moral of this fable is that 'it is easy to despise what you cannot get', (now known as 'sour grapes'). Possibly, at the end of the branches, in the mosaic, we are viewing bunches of grapes and not leaves. If we now turn our attention to the building in the mosaic, it is noticeable that part of it is protruding out next to the fox's head. I interpret this as a chute into which grapes were thrown before the juice was pressed out of them. Therefore the building could have been a wine-press/torculum. If the reader refers to page 266 of volume 3 of the book Roman Mosaics of Britain Part 1, by David Neal and Stephen Cosh, this chute can be clearly seen. I think that the overall message of this mosaic is that Bacchus is declaring that grapes are better suited for wine making than they are for eating.

The next panel to view is the one to the right of the Bacchus medallion. Within it can be seen a 'cock-headed man', a building with steps leading up to its door and to the right of this building two leopards with wings are noticed. I am confused by this and wonder if the mosaicist was trying to depict griffins. The griffins were part-lion and part-eagle, the lion being king of the beasts and the eagle being king of the birds. In antiquity griffins were revered as being powerful and majestic creatures. Within this scene they symbolise the guardians of the arena. The cock-headed man is dressed like a lanista, recognisable by his tunic, he was a trainer of animals to be used in the arena. The lanista is possibly wearing a mask of a cock, symbolising the high regard that he had for the fighting cock. The cock was a fearless and courageous combatant. Greek history tells us that even lions, king of the beasts, were wary of the cock. At a given time the lanista would begin to ascend the steps and the audience would fall silent in expectation. He would enter the henhouse/ gallinaria through the door depicted here in black tesserae. Inside, fighting cocks would have been kept in a darkened environment in individual cages. After a few moments, the lanista would reappear on the top step, holding aloft two fighting cocks. One in his left hand, the other in his right. The cocks would be individually marked so they could be easily recognised. At this sight the crowd would erupt with excitement and expectancy. As the lanista descended the steps a frenzy of betting would take place within the crowd. Cock fighting goes back many thousands of years and Greek history tells us that the commander of the Greek Army, General Themistocles, organised cock fighting for his troops to view on the night before a battle against the invading Persians. The point the General was making to his troops, through watching the cock fighting, would be that the cock would continue fighting until he killed his opponent or he himself was killed. This was the sort of courage that Themistocles demanded from his troops when the battle descended into hand-to-hand combat. Even in Roman times, Julius Caesar was a fan of cockfighting. This room could also have been a place of worship, known as Christian Gnosticism. One of the symbols used by the sect on amulets is that of a fowl-headed man and therefore the building in the mosaic could represent a temple. Overall, I feel that this floor is a wonderful piece of craftsmanship and design. As the panels consist of a combination of squares and rectangles, it adds more interest to the viewing eye. The use of red and grey colours with an outer band of black in the borders of the panels, helps to highlight the content of the individual panels. It is refreshing to see this type of border rather than the usual borders of guilloche. The colours used in the tesserae, although now faded over the course of time, would have looked impacting when freshly laid. The tesserae are neatly constructed and include a number of colours consisting of red, white, black, yellow and a grey/blue.

We now make our way to view Room VI, which contains a mosaic panel depicting Orpheus. This mosaic lies within the original entrance hall of the villa. The hall had a simple but hard-wearing red and grey floor laid in a chequerboard design. The walls of the original hall were richly decorated with illustrations which included a parrot-like bird and a green basket of purple plums. The central medallion of this floor is enclosed in a circle of guilloche; this in turn is sealed on both sides (inner and outer) by a black and white circle of tesserae. If we now view outwards we notice that this itself sits in a box of black and white tesserae with lost designs within its spandrels of the four corners. The whole design is then framed in a continuing box of interlocking guilloche. The coloured tesserae on view within this mosaic would have included black, white, red, grey, a blue/pale grey and buff, which was possibly mudstone. Orpheus was the son of Apollo and the Muse of epic poetry, Calliope. Orpheus himself was a legendary musician, poet and prophet in Ancient Greek religion and myth. Major stories about him are centred on his ability to charm all living things with his music when playing the lyre. There are many engrossing stories about him including that Zeus ended his life by striking Orpheus with lightning for having revealed the mysteries of the Gods to men. When he died the Gods placed his lyre in the Heavens as the constellation Lyra. Within this mosaic we view Orpheus seated and wearing a red Phrygian cap, which depicts freedom, and is clothed in a tunic and a red cloak. His playing of the lyre has attracted an audience of animals. Although some have been lost over the course of time, some are still visible. On the left, as we view it, a monkey/ape and possibly a peacock can be seen. To the right, as we view it, there is a fox and, intriguingly, a local bird, recognised by its red beak and red legs to be a chough.

Beyond this mosaic we can view Room IX. This room measures 19 feet and nine inches square and contains a geometric mosaic pavement. This, in all probability, was a dining room and would have been adorned with attractive painted wall-plaster. The viewer's attention is immediately drawn to the centre of this mosaic where an 'eye' seems to be returning one's gaze. I interpret the 'eye' as being regarded in antiquity as an amulet/talisman, used as a symbol to ward off evil influences and, therefore, protecting the room and those who used it. The 'eye', composed of black/grey tesserae' is enclosed in a circle of white. This, in turn, rests in a larger circle of red /orange tesserae. This itself is composed in a blue/grey square (set as a diamond) and is protected by a surrounding white border. As we continue to look outwards a red/orange square is noticed, which is surrounded by a large blue/grey square. Many of the coloured tesserae in this geometric mosaic are difficult to interpret as a result of burning. This could have been caused when the villa's inhabited life was ended due to a destructive fire.

If we now continue down the villa we can view Room XII, a bipartic (two parts) room linked together by a central rectangular panel. This whole rectangle is filled with interlocking guilloche, containing a square and either side of the square, two smaller upright rectangles. Within the square a bearded figure of a seated, partly clothed man can be seen. With increasing interest, to the figure's right, a globe and above this a sun-dial (?), which is resting on a column, can be noticed. To the figure's left we see a cup containing a twig (?) or a feather (?) or a spoon (?), resting on the outer rim. As I view this panel, I feel that the draw-bridge of my mind is slowly lowering and I begin to feel more intimate with this seated, partly clad, muscular and bearded male. The figure holds a rod in his right hand, which is pointing to the globe and the tesserae within the globe are arranged to define the four quarters of the Earth. The dial upon the column is depicting 12 compartments representing the 12 signs of the zodiac. The astrologer is, therefore, about to cast a horoscope. The vase/cup could have possibly contained wine. The wine would have been scattered before the horoscope was cast, as an insurance against bad luck. Also, we notice that the instruments are placed on the astrologer's right hand side, which holds another belief that omens appearing on this side were lucky. Those coming from the left would have held the opposite. This belief of the right being of good and the left being of bad luck, is borne out when guests entering a dining room are requested to enter by the right foot first.

Alternatively, we are viewing an astronomer surrounded by the tools of his trade. The two small upright rectangles are identical, both containing diamond-shaped lozenges and their centres seem to be depicting an eye. Each eye seems to have a single row of tesserae, pointing outwards, in a north, east, south and west direction. If we relate this to the central bearded figure, symbolically this could read that one eye would have been cast towards the Earth and the other eye cast towards the heavens. As I continue to view the seated figure, I wonder which person from antiquity this figure is depicting. The two names I find sparring together in my mind are Hipparchus, a scientific astronomer and observer, and Aratus. Aratus describes the constellations and believed in education and teaching and is best known for his poetry about the constellations and weather signs.

Above the central panel we can view two squares of guilloche, one seated within the other. All the coloured tesserae within the guilloche in this mosaic are of red, white and a blue/grey and these are outlined in black. Four squares have been constructed in the corners separated by rectangles, but sadly only one of the rectangles now survives. The centre of this mosaic has perished almost completely. The missing centre has fuelled a number of theories and debates by interested academics. Some of their theories/readings are drawn from other Romano British mosaics and from mosaics from distant lands. The female busts in the corners are representing the four seasons, although Autumn in the north-west corner is lost. In the South-west corner is Summer, her head decked with roses or poppies. In the south-east corner is Spring decorated with a wreath of fresh flowers. In the north-east corner sits the bust of Winter, warmly clad in a hooded cloak and over her left shoulder is a branch with a dead bird dangling from it by its legs. Perhaps the dead bird signifies that winter takes its toll on the weak and vulnerable. Just beyond and to the west of the remaining rectangular panel, in the bordering red tesserae and sitting in an additional decoration of white fret pattern, is a swastika.

The swastika (sanskrit svastika 'all is well'), an equilateral cross, with its four arms bent at 90 degrees, is in all probability a symbol of good luck. This relates to the four seasons as depicted in the four corners of the mosaic below. Each of the seasons, spring, summer and autumn requires its own relative weather to guarantee a successful harvest. This then ensures the financial security of the villa and provides a store of food for the inhabitants of the villa and its estate to combat the long dark cold days of winter. It has been well recorded that the only surviving rectangular panel depicted the lovers, Perseus and Andromeda. Perseus was the son of Zeus and Danae. Andromeda was the daughter of Cepheus, an Aethiopian king, and Cassiopeia was his queen. The story that this panel seems to be depicting is Perseus rescuing Andromeda from being sacrificed by Neptune to a sea monster (not shown in this panel). When the monster appeared from the waves, Perseus showed it the head of the gorgon Medusa and the monster was turned to stone. Perseus and Andromeda were subsequently married, and on their deaths took their place in the heavens as constellations. Very little of the other panels survive. In the panel to the north we can view a fragmented torso of a man; to the east, but now barely visible, is the peak of a pitched, red tiled roof of a building.

If we now look to the east we can view a mosaic floor with its central medallion containing the head of Medusa. She is surrounded by four panels, each depicting a man and a woman. Directly to the north, east, south and west are smaller, triangular panels containing individual figures. All the eight panels are edged on the inside with black tesserae, with the figures resting in a buff background. In the four corners below the panels containing the two figures, sits an eye-catching design of black and white triangles. A continuing guilloche encloses all of the two-figured designs and the central medallion. A thicker, deeper guilloche contains the whole mosaic floor. The mosaicist has excelled with his skill of the blending and use of the colours and we can view buff, black, white, red, shades of brown, shades of pink, yellows, purples and blues. Within the four two-figure panels a number of stories from Greek/Roman mythology await us. If we look at the panel in the northeast corner, the one which has been the most damaged in the course of time, we can read perhaps two stories. The first is of Achilles, son of the nymph Thetis and Peleus, king of Myrmidons. Thetis, wishing to keep her son safe from the war sends Achilles, in the disguise of a girl, to the court of Lycomedes, king of Skyros. Odysseus learns from the prophet Calchas that the Achaeans would only be able to capture Troy with the aid of Achilles. Therefore Odysseus goes to the court of Lycomedes dressed as a woman, so he can blend in with the women of the court, knowing that Achilles would be amongst them.

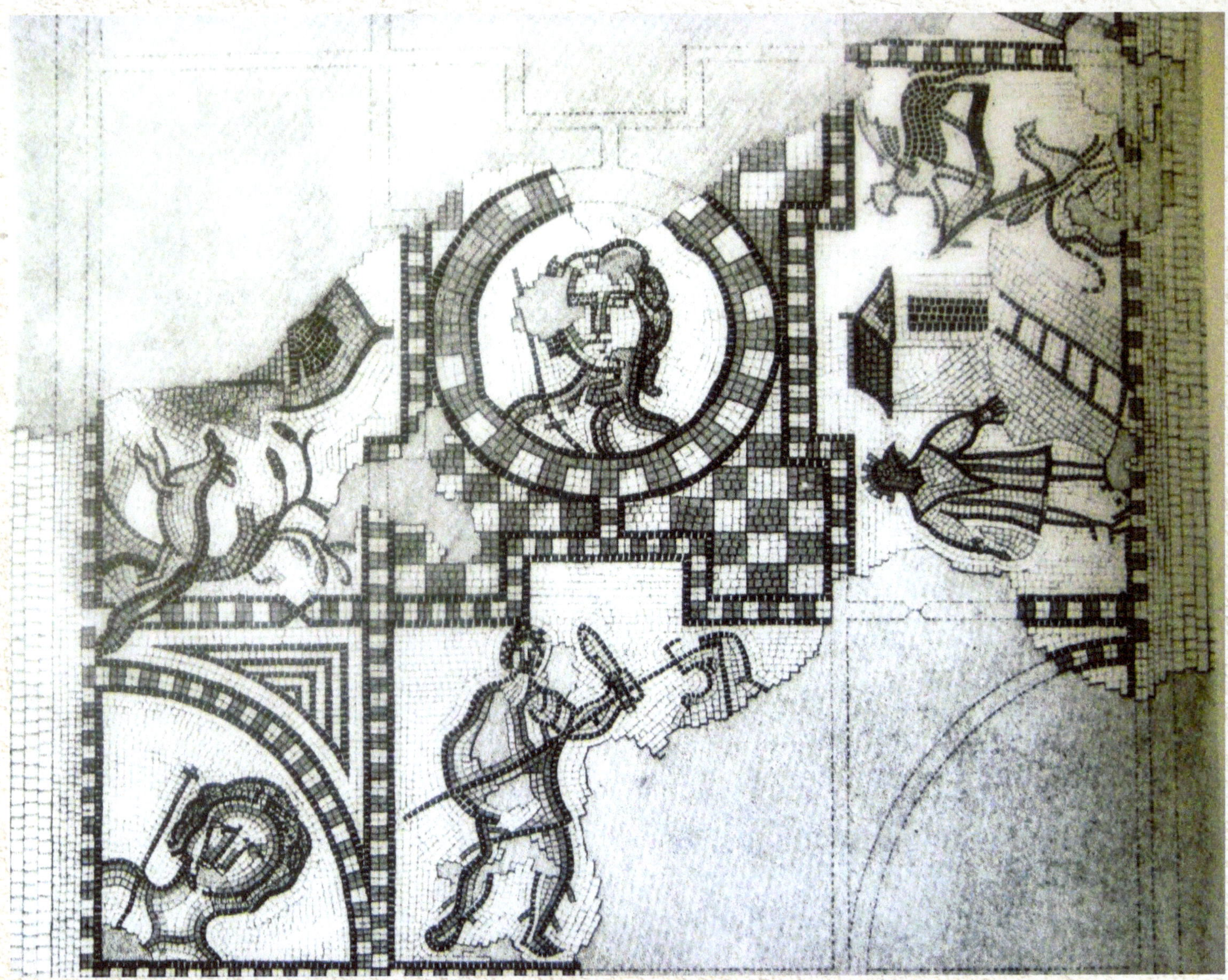

Gladiatorial scene
Drawing by Margaret Rule and Keith Sturgess 1974

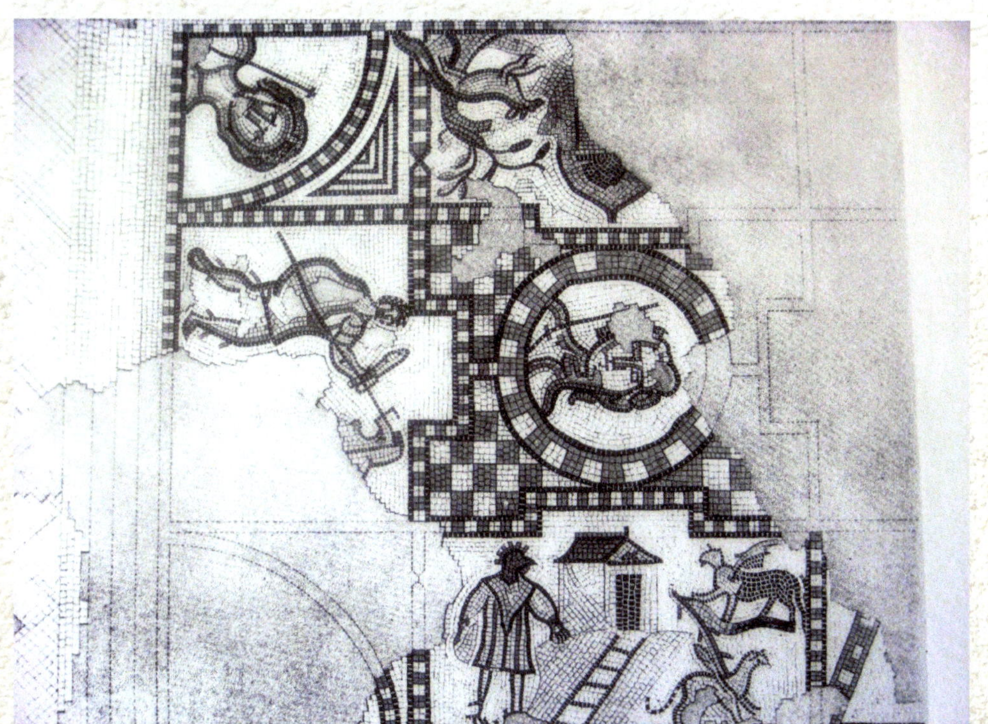

The cock-headed man
Drawing by Margaret Rule and Keith Sturgess 1974

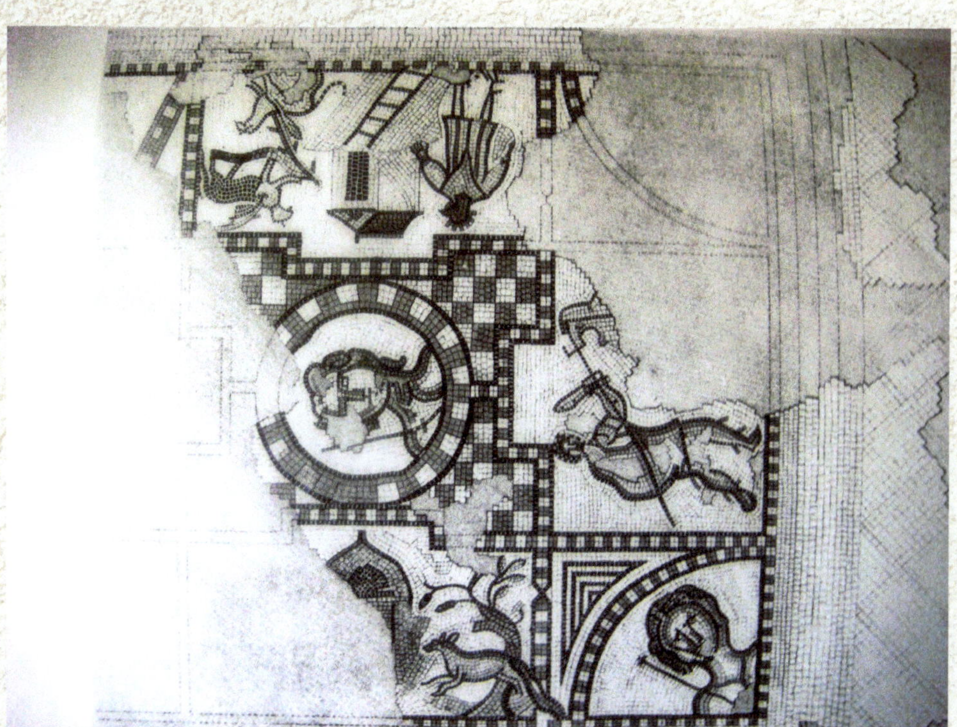

The running fox
Drawing by Margaret Rule and Keith Sturgess 1974

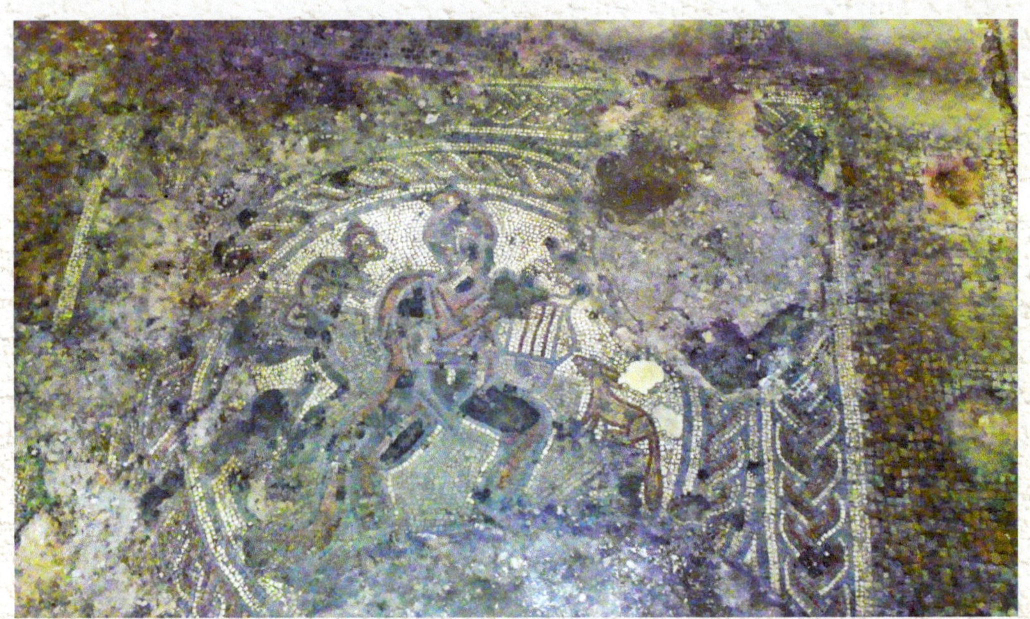

Room 6 Orpheus

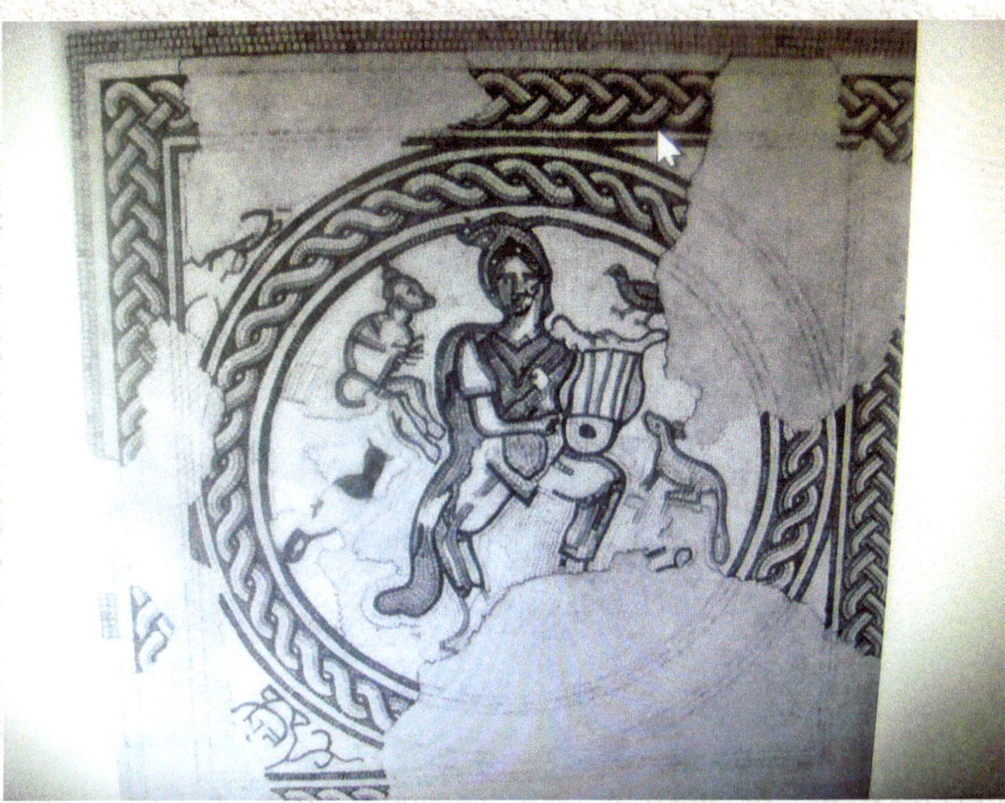

Room 6 Orpheus
Drawing by Margaret Rule and Keith Sturgess 1974

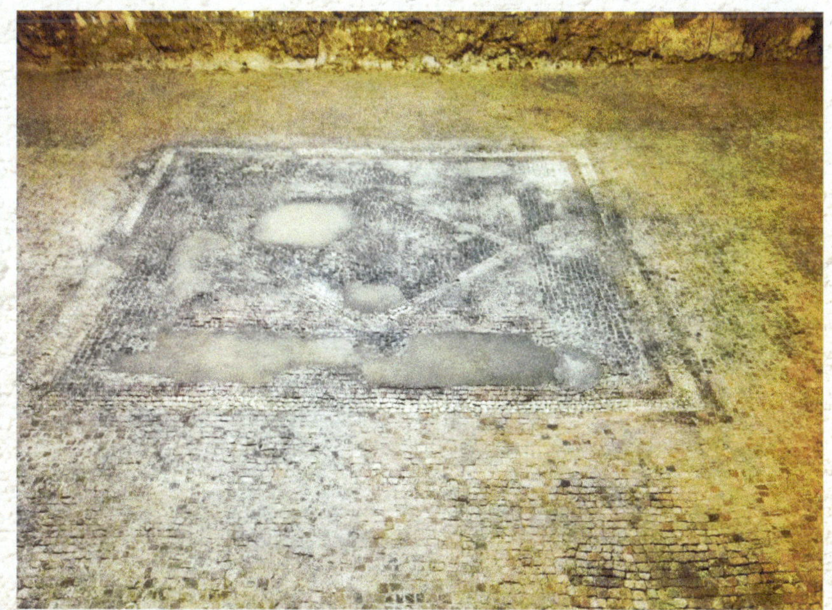

Room 9

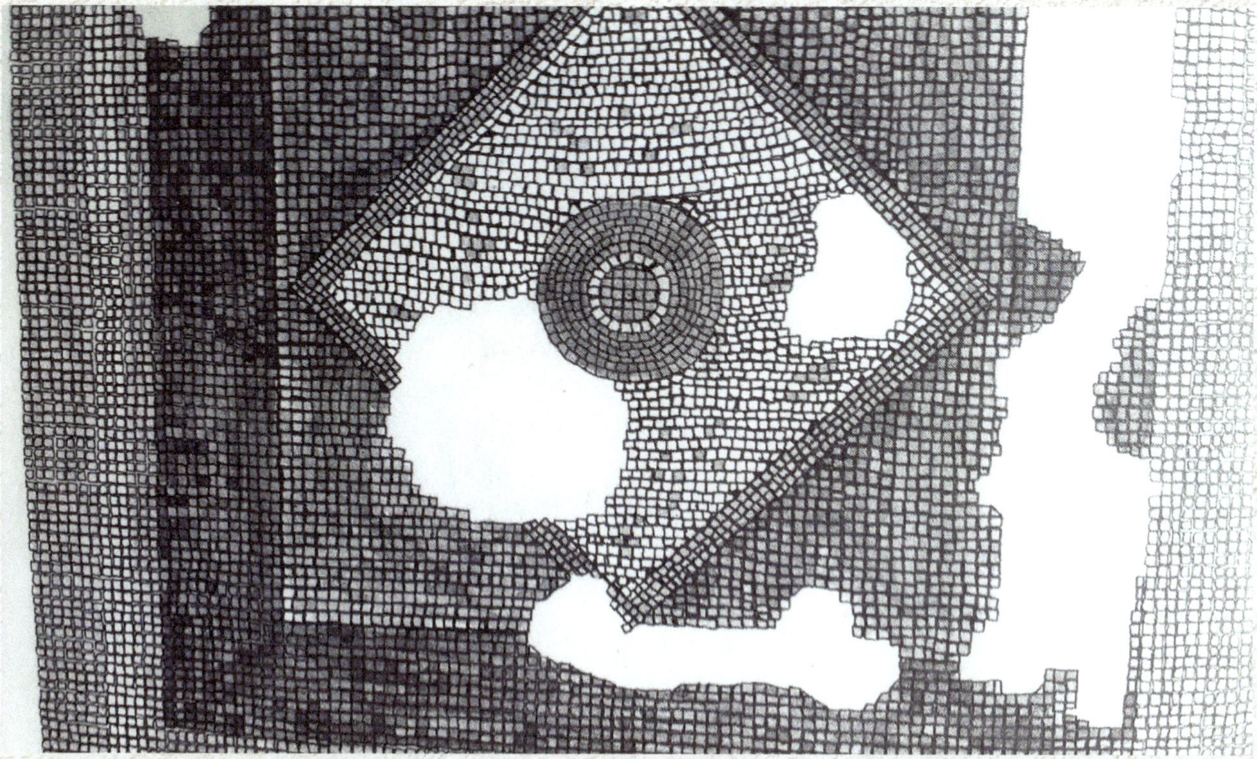

Central view of room 9, Drawing by Margaret Rule and Keith Sturgess 1974

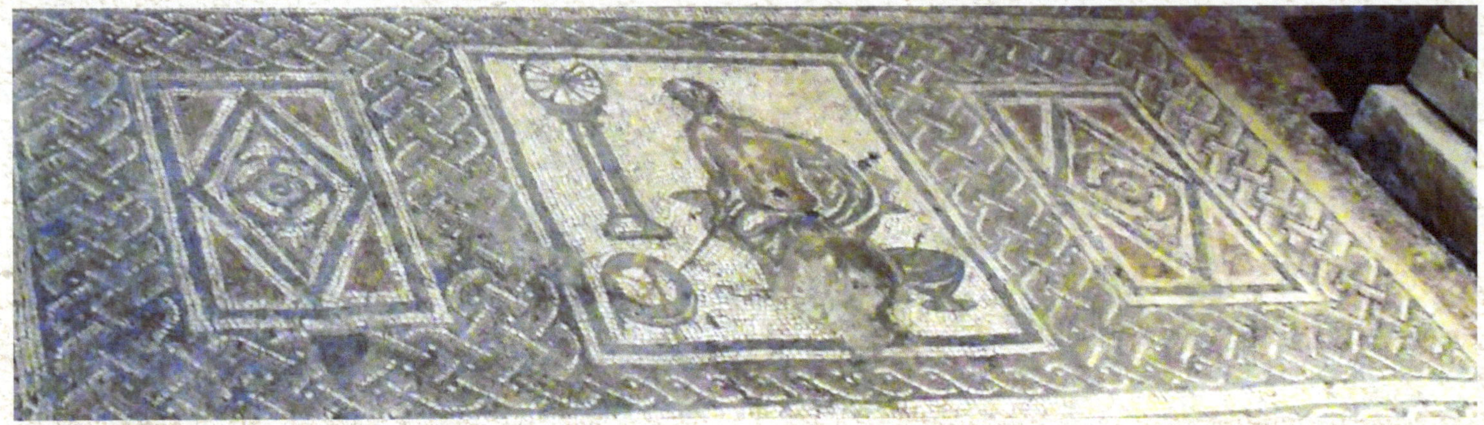

Astrologer/ Astronomer

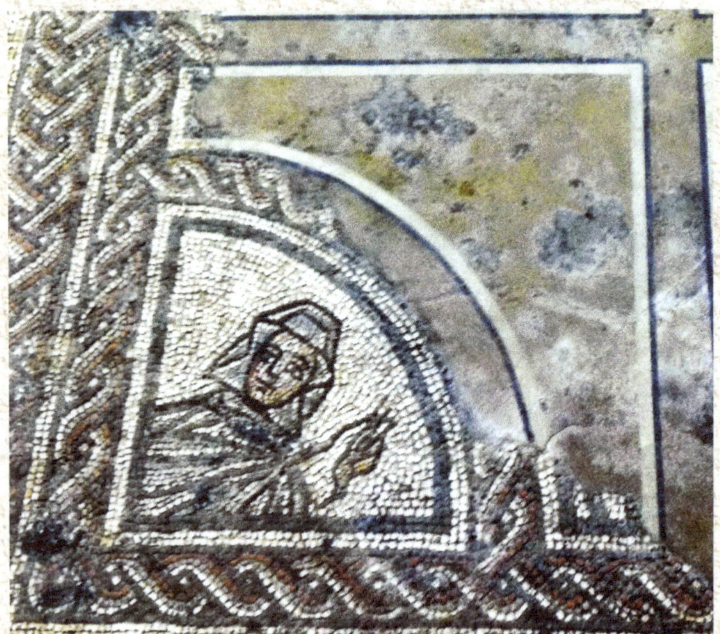

Winter-Room 12

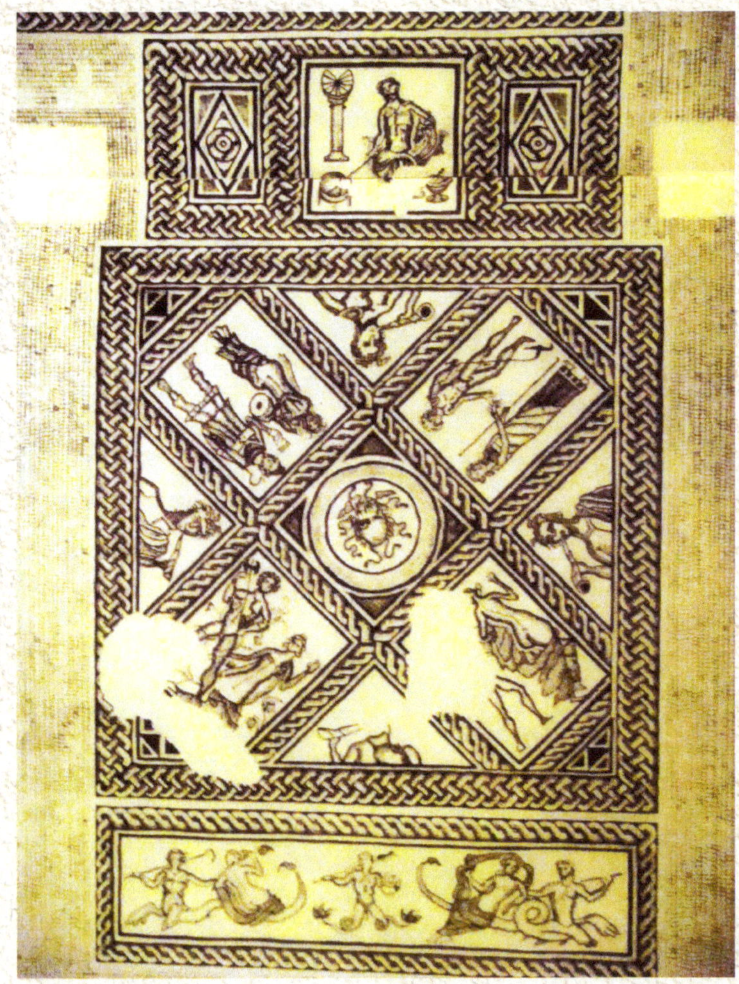

The Medusa Mosaic with two rectangular panels
Drawing by Margaret Rule and Keith Sturgess 1974

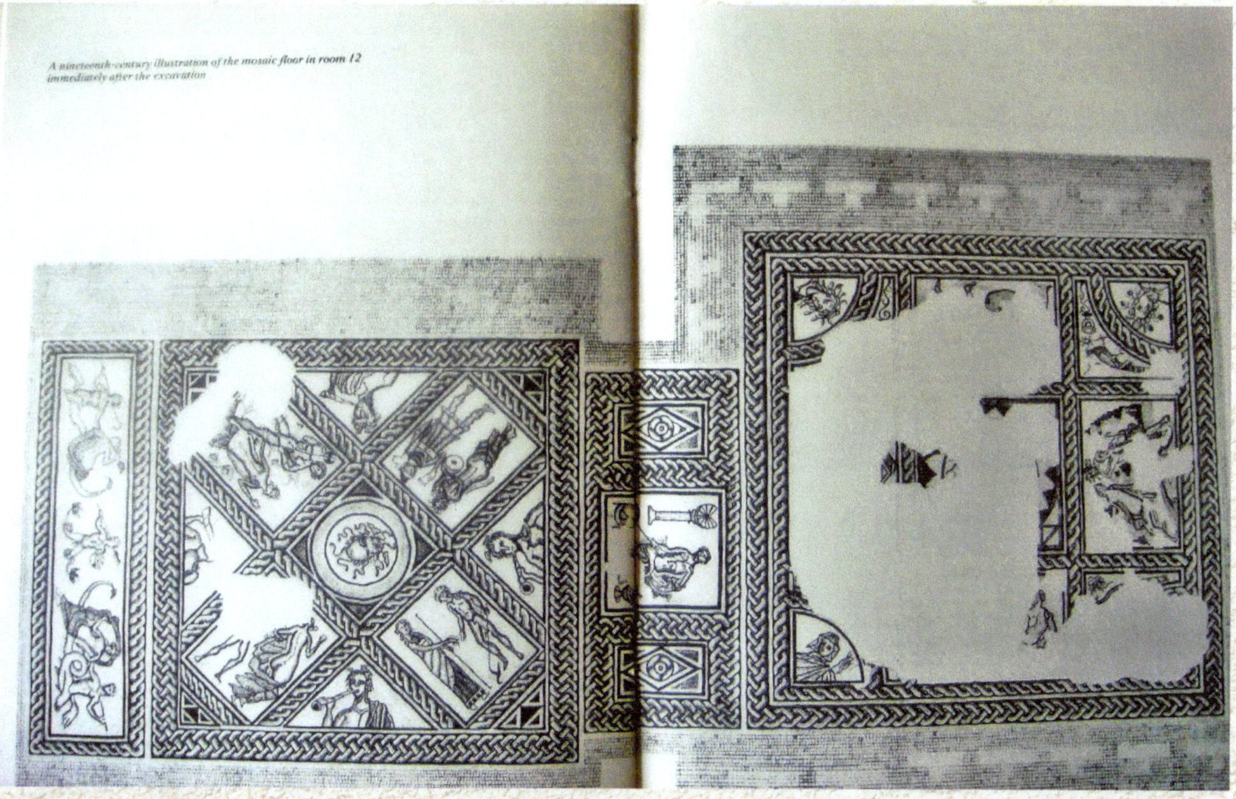

A nineteenth-century illustration of the mosaic floor in room 12 immediately after the excavation

The two parts of Room 12, Drawing by Margaret Rule and Keith Sturgess 1974

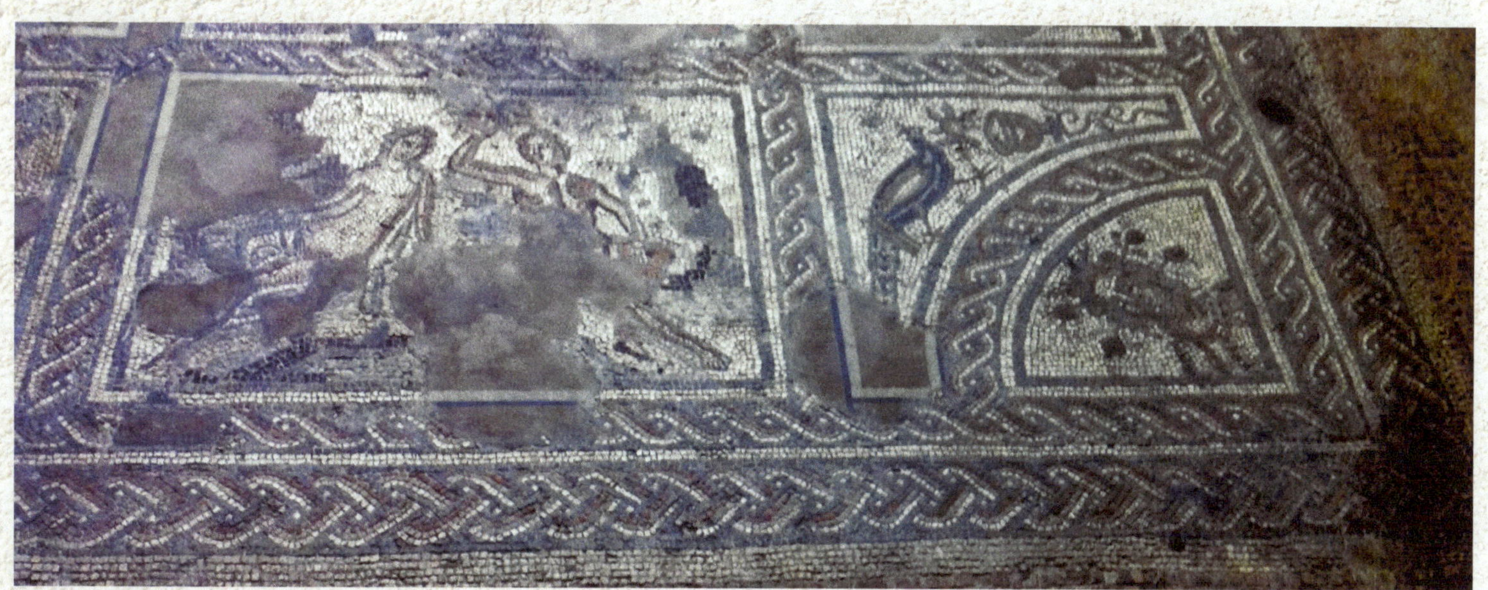

The Perseus and Andromeda panel

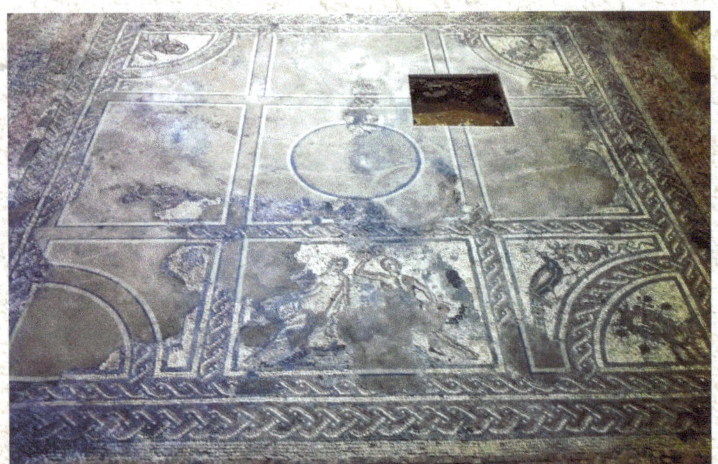

The Four Seasons

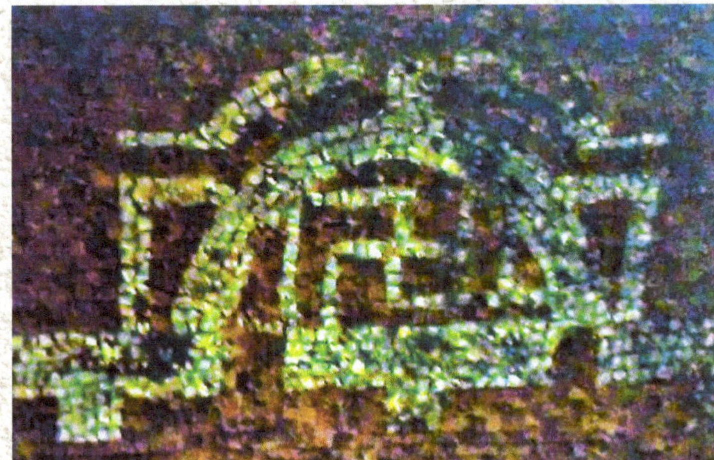

The Swastika

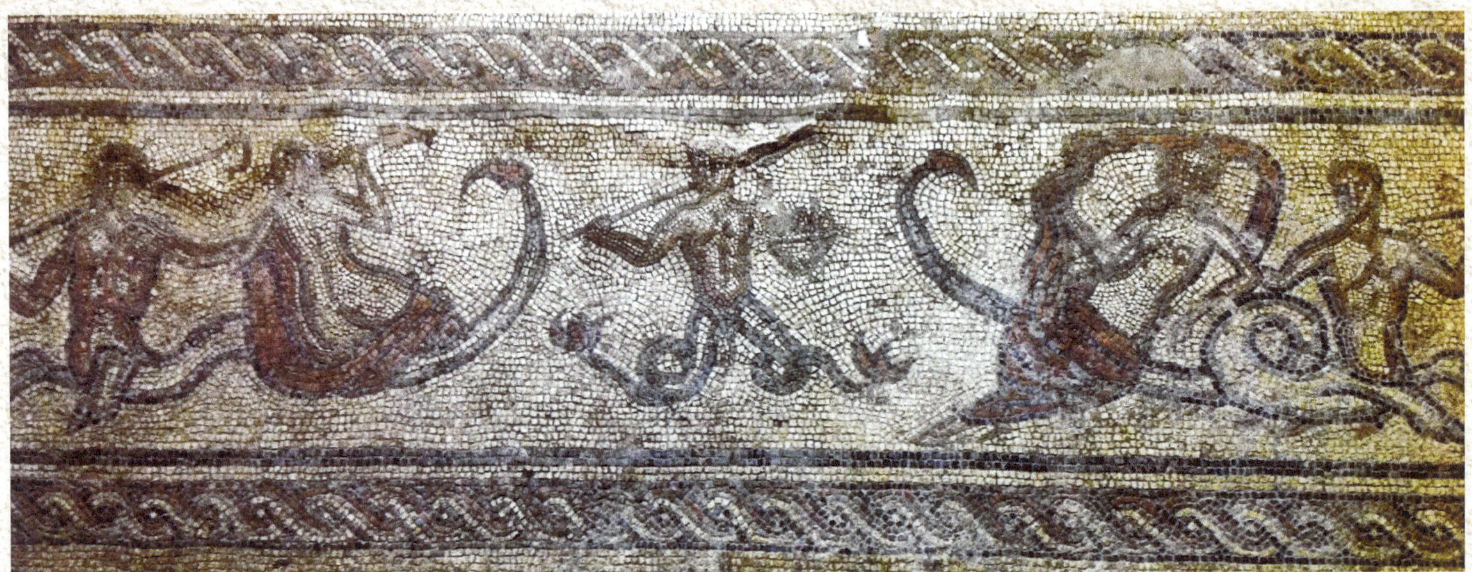

Merman-Tritons and Nymphs

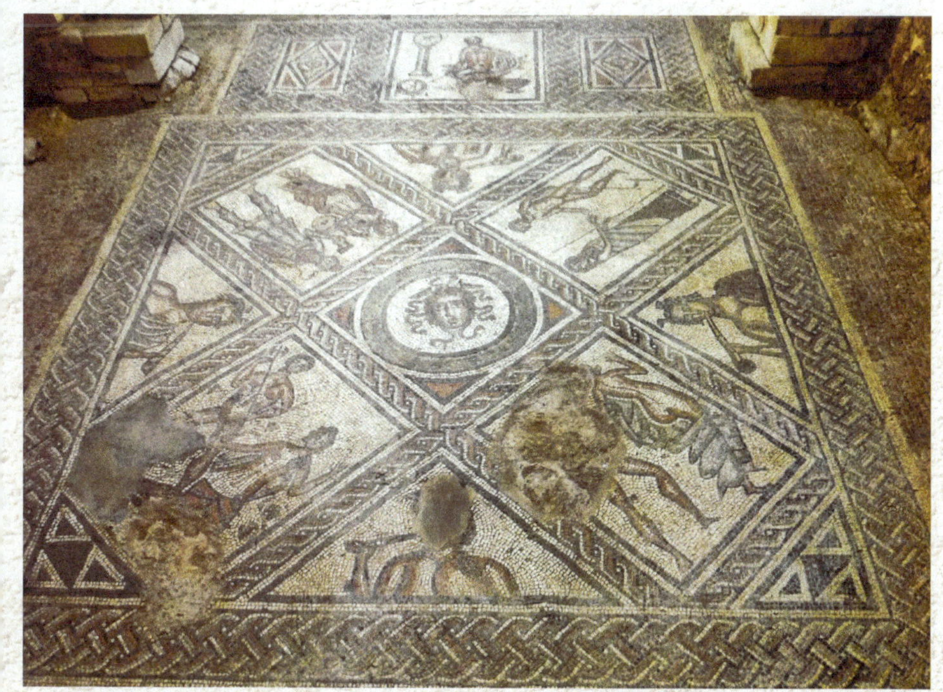

Medusa Mosaic

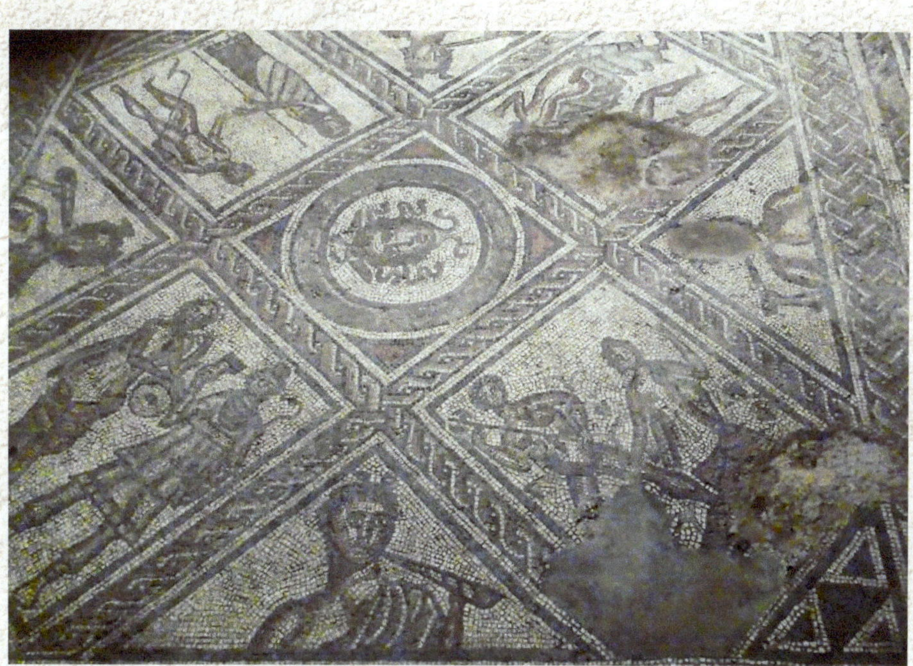

Medusa Mosaic

Odysseus arranges for a trumpet alarm to be sounded; all the women flee in panic, except one, who turns out to be Achilles. He throws off his disguise ready to defend the women of the court. Odysseus thereupon persuades Achilles to help capture Troy. Interestingly, a similar but more complete panel of this scene is depicted in a mosaic at Cologne, Germany. Alternatively within this panel we could be viewing Apollo chasing Daphne, a daughter of the river God, Peneus. Daphne is fleeing Apollo's advances of love, as Cupid has shot Daphne with an arrow tipped with lead to repel love. At the same time, Apollo has been pierced by the love arrow, the tip of which contains gold. This was Cupid's revenge towards Apollo, after Apollo had scolded him for playing with real arrows rather than his toy arrows.

If we now view the panel in the northwest corner this depicts Ceres and Triptolemus. Ceres, the Goddess of agriculture and civilisation, wears a long red dress and a white cloak which is wrapped around her. She holds a staff in her left hand and with her right hand offers Triptolemus an ear of wheat. Triptolemus is seen here naked and holds out his right hand to accept the wheat, while in his left hand he holds a plough. Ceres gave birth to a daughter named Persephone, the Goddess of vegetation. Persephone was abducted by Pluto who made off with her to the underworld. Ceres, searching for her daughter, arrives in Eleusis and in the house of Celeus; she comes upon the sick son of Metanira, named Triptolemus. Ceres, disguised as an old woman during the search, kisses the sickly boy and gives him vitality from her divine lips. The people complain to Jupiter of famine as Ceres has been neglecting her duties during the search for her daughter. Jupiter, assessing the situation, intervenes and rescues Persephone from the Underworld and reunites her with her mother. Consequently, Triptolemus, now a fit and healthy young man and the foster son of Ceres, is engaged by Ceres and taught the secrets of agriculture. She grants Triptolemus a chariot drawn by winged dragons. In it he travelled the world teaching people how to plough, sow and reap.

Next to view is the panel in the southwest corner. The male figure to the right, in the guise of a shepherd, wears a Phrygian cap, baggy trousers and a short tunic. He carries a crook in his left hand and pan-pipes in his right. The female figure seems to be wearing reeds in her hair and in her right hand she seems to be tilting an upturned vase. The possible reeds in her hair indicate that she depicts a water nymph. Unfortunately it is difficult to confirm this as the upturned vase (if it is a vase) shows no depiction of liquid dripping from its rim. I wonder if the mosaicist has missed out in error in not illustrating this. The two figures could depict Attis and Sagaritis, the water nymph of the Turkish river Sangarius. One version of the story is as follows – Attis was a worshipper of the Goddess Cybele and she tells him to guard her temple and not to marry. Unfortunately, Attis falls in love with the water nymph Sagaritis. Cybele, in a fit of jealousy, causes Sagaritis' death; Attis, distraught, flees to Mount Dindynus, where he kills himself. Another version involving Attis and the Goddess Cybele unfolds as follows – Attis is the child of Nana, a daughter of the river-God, Sangarius. Nana abandoned the baby Attis and he was brought up by a he-goat. As Attis grew into a young man he became very handsome and god-like and Cybele fell in love with him. Attis was to marry the daughter of Midas, king of Pessinos. Before the wedding ceremony was complete Cybele appeared and in the storm of her jealous passion she drove Attis mad and he killed himself. As Cybele's storm of jealousy subsided, she became distraught at what she had done. She repented and with the help of the God Jupiter, Attis was resurrected. Attis became the Phrygian god of growth and fertility.

Alternatively, this panel could depict Paris and Oenone. Paris was a prince of Troy and Oenone was a mountain nymph. They fell in love and had a son called Corythus. Oenone was a mountain nymph on Mount Ida, in Phrygia. Paris was the son of the king Prian and the queen Hecuba. Paris fell in love with Oenone when he was a shepherd on the slopes of Mount Ida. He abandons her for Helen of Sparta. Out of revenge Oenone sends their son Corythus to guide the Greeks to Troy. Paris, not recognising his own son, kills him. Later, Paris, mortally wounded, returns to Oenone begging her to heal him with her herbal arts. With scorn, Oenone tells him to return to the bed of Helen. Paris dies on the slopes of Mount Ida where they had met. Oenone, overcome with remorse, throws herself onto Paris' burning funeral pyre.

If we now observe the panel in the southeast corner we see the male figure, Lycurgus, king of Thrace, nude, holding in both hands a double-headed axe. He seems to be threatening the kneeling Ambrosia, one of the nymphs accompanying the God of wine, Bacchus. The story goes that Lycurgus is incensed that Bacchus is travelling through his kingdom instructing men in the art of wine-making. As his fury builds Lycurgus attacks the maenads, who were mortal women with many powers and the female followers of Bacchus. The maenads scatter. Ambrosia seems trapped and in panic begs Mother Earth to rescue her. In response, Ambrosia is transformed into a vine. The vine begins to entwine Lycurgus who is eventually strangled to death by it. There is an alternative ending to this story where Lycurgus is driven mad and hacks in a frenzied and indiscriminate way at the approaching vine, eventually hacking himself to death.

If we now turn our attention to the four single-figured panels we can view four individual young men with cloaks draped over their left shoulders. Each figure seems to be blowing into a conch shell symbolising the wind from that direction – north, east, south and west. The parents of the winds were Aeolus, son of Poseidon who married Eos, a daughter of the Titans Hyperion and Thea. Four of their sons became the following winds. Boreas became the north wind, the bringer of cold winter air. Notus was the south wind, bringer of storms in late summer and autumn. Notus, for some reason I cannot explain, is depicted in the panel facing in the opposite direction to his three brothers. A third brother, Zephyrus, was the west wind, bringer of light spring and early summer breezes, and Euros was the east wind, bringer of warmth and rain.

The whole mosaic is bound together by the central medallion depicting the head of Medusa from which eight serpents/snakes project. The head rests in the middle of a circular band of blue-grey Purbeck stone. The Medusa, in all probability, was a protected amulet to guard against evil influences and, therefore, protects all those mortals who use the room. The room possibly could have been divided at any time by a thick and luxurious curtain drawn across the central rectangular panel.

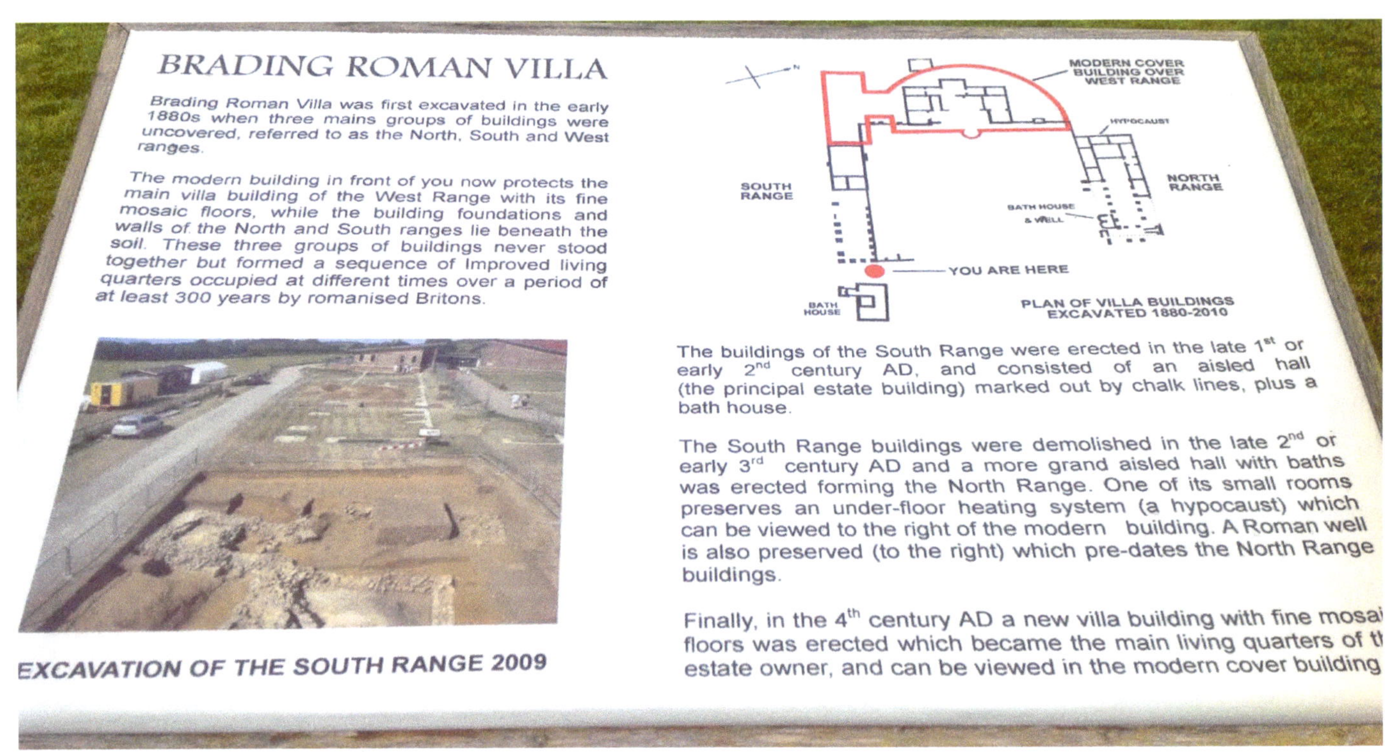

Excavation of the south range

To the east we can view the final rectangular panel of this floor which rests in its own frame of guilloche. It depicts a scene from the sea containing figures of Nereids and Tritons. The Tritons (males) are represented as humans down to their waists; beyond that they have tails of fishes/dolphins and were the demigods of the sea. The Nereids (females), seen here lounging on the tails of the Tritons, were the goddesses of the sea. In their care was the rich food bounty of the sea. The Triton in the centre of this panel seems to be holding in his right hand an oar (?) and in his left hand a plate of seafood (?). The Triton to the south seems to be holding a shepherd's crook in his right hand; his left hand seems to be embracing the Nereid. The Triton to the north also embraces a Nereid and in his left hand is, possibly, a sea shell which when blown into would be used to calm or raise the waves. In trying to read this mosaic panel a question comes into my mind: why are a shepherd's crook and an oar depicted in it? I wonder if this could have been an input by the proprietor of the villa. Unfortunately this panel was damaged by a flash flood in 1994, causing a staining on the top of the oar held by the Triton in the centre of the panel. The introduction, by the flooding, of iron oxides and fertilizers chemically altered the composition of the grout between the tesserae and on the far western side of this room some of the mosaic floor has risen, bubbled up and blown.

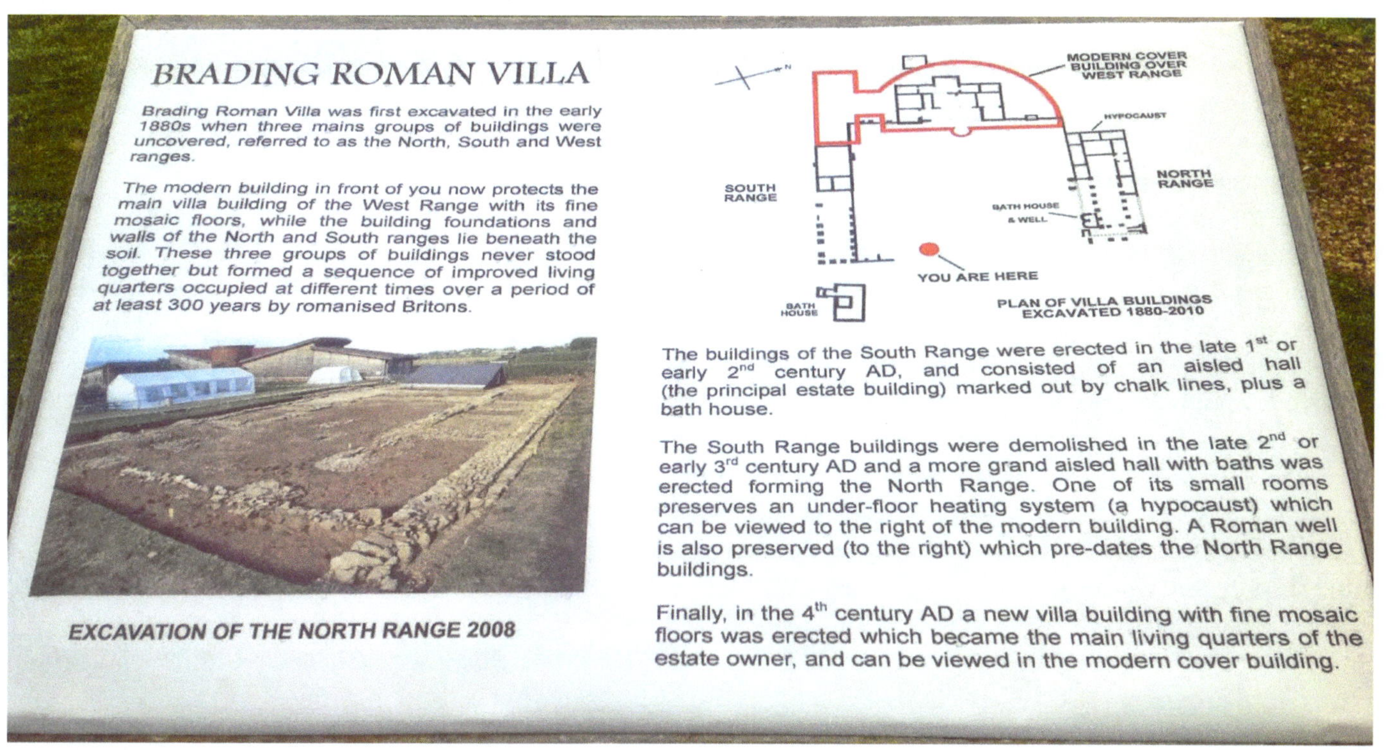

Excavation of the north range

CONCLUSION

At the period of time that these mosaics were crafted, late 3rd to early 4th century, the proprietor of the villa was, no doubt, extremely wealthy. But these extraordinary mosaics could well indicate that he was highly educated, well read and perhaps a man with a vision for the future. I can visualise that this establishment, at certain periods, would have been a place of education for the local inhabitants, especially for the young with their inquisitive and lively minds. They could have been tutored at the villa in Roman literature, Greek and Roman mythology and in science and astronomy. At night they could view the mysteries and the constellations of the sky, not forgetting that the sky then would have been free of the light pollution caused by increased urbanisation that obscures our views of the night sky today.

After the island was secured, Vespasian would have possibly left a small detachment of soldiers who would have worked with the Island's tribal leaders and elders to create a settled and prosperous, lasting administration. Recent archaeological excavations, coupled with a geophysical survey by English Heritage, suggest that this site has seen human activity over several thousand years. There is evidence for Neolithic and Bronze Age activity here. In all probability, at the time of the Roman invasion led by Vespasian, there was already a small farmstead here and over a period of time this would have begun to prosper. With increasing wealth the farmstead would have expanded to become a villa with a range of buildings to the north and to the south. There is evidence of crop farming for wheat, barley and oats. Animal bones, including that of cattle, sheep, pigs and goats, were also found during the course of archaeological excavations. Brading Haven at this period in time was a natural harbour and port. The villa could have gained extra wealth by controlling imports and exports from the port. Some of the exported local Bembridge limestone can be found in the construction of Fishbourne Roman Palace and other villas on the south coast of the mainland. Interestingly, Roman history tells us that between 286 and 296 AD, Britain was governed in turn by two usurper emperors, the first being Carausius who was assassinated by his own finance minister, Allectus. Allectus claimed himself as emperor and based his fleet of ships on the Isle of Wight. This came to an end in 296 AD when Allectus was defeated by the Caeser Constantius. The decisive battle was possibly at Calleva Attrbatum (Silchester), although it seems that Constantius did not reach Britain until the fighting was over. Therefore, by 296 AD, Britain was reunited once more with the Roman Empire. It is a possibility that all three of these men would have known and possibly stayed for a short period of time at Brading Roman Villa. A collection of coins found within the villa, and on the surrounding estate, starts in the reign of the Roman Emperor Domitianus, 81-96 AD. This collection runs through to the reign of Honorius, 393-423 AD which, perhaps, indicates some form of inhabitation over a period of 350 years. It seems possible that the villa's final destruction was caused by fire, but by what cause and when goes unrecorded. Eventually, the migration to Britain and the Isle of Wight by Germanic peoples from North Germany, Northern Netherlands and Southern Scandinavia would have introduced to the island a new culture with a different building technology, embracing wood and thatch. As the Island's elders died out, the Brading villa would have been lost from memory and consequently, with the ravages of time, disappeared into history.

As I break free from the embrace of this intriguing villa and make my way down the gentle slopes to catch the Island bus back to Ryde, a thought begins to bubble up in my mind, the thought being that two paths of human nature seem to march continually, side-by-side; one of the paths being the ability to create and the other path being the desire to destroy. This to my mind poses the question – is this then, as human beings, how we perceive evolution?

Chapter V

Newport Roman Villa

This chapter discusses the discovery, its evolution and final destruction of Newport Roman Villa on the Isle of Wight .My initial guide will be led by the archaeological and excavation reports and recordings of the villa in the mid and late 1920s.

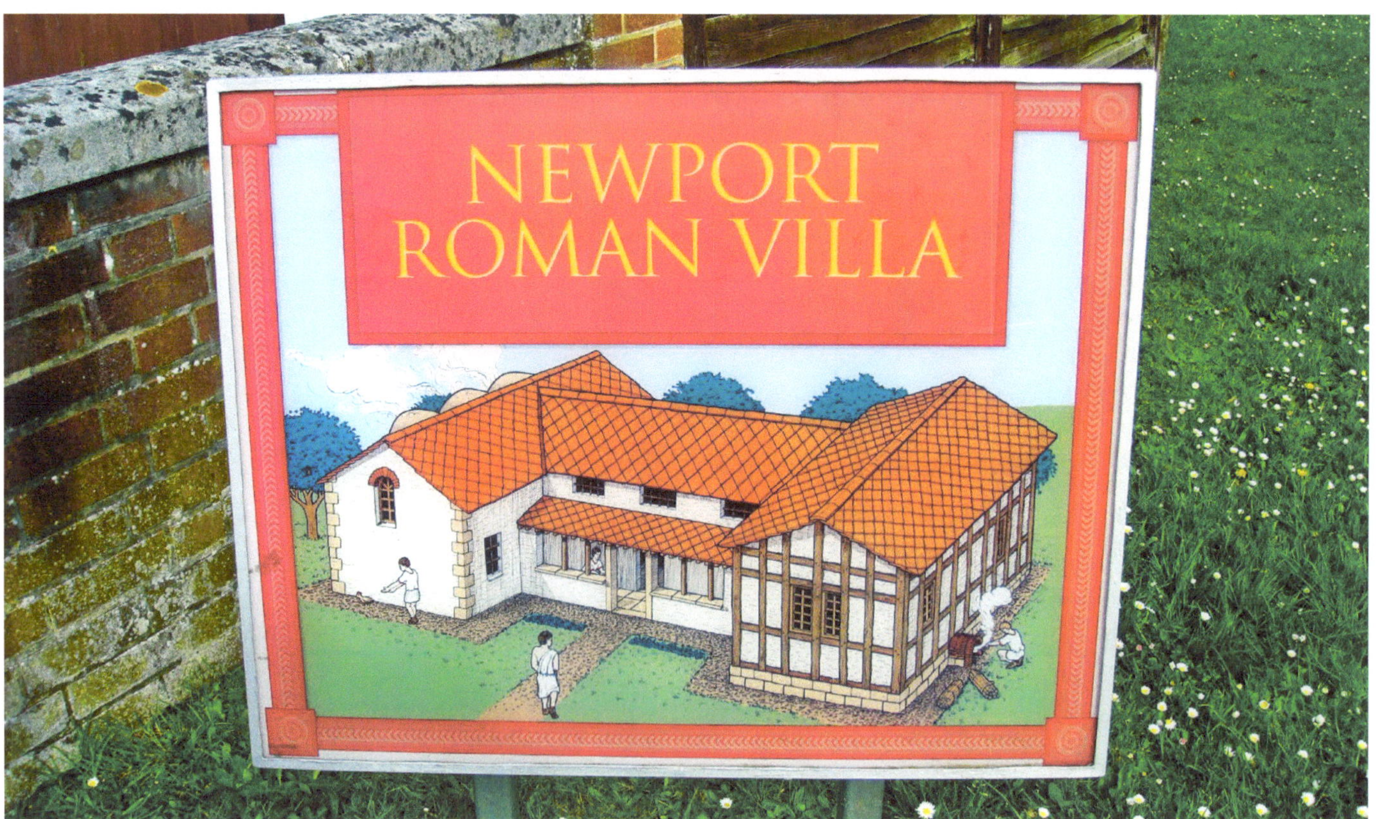

The entrance to Newport Roman Villa

ISLE OF WIGHT

The town of Newport is situated slightly to the north of the centre of the island at the head of the navigable section of the River Medina, which flows northwards towards the Solent. The town has a quay to which the tidal water reaches. It was built as a planned town in the 12th century AD and overlooks the Bowcombe Valley. This historic town now centres on two elegant squares with Georgian and Victorian architecture surrounding them. In 1180 AD the church of St Thomas of Canterbury (Thomas Becket) was built and lasted until 1854 when it was rebuilt with 14th century details.

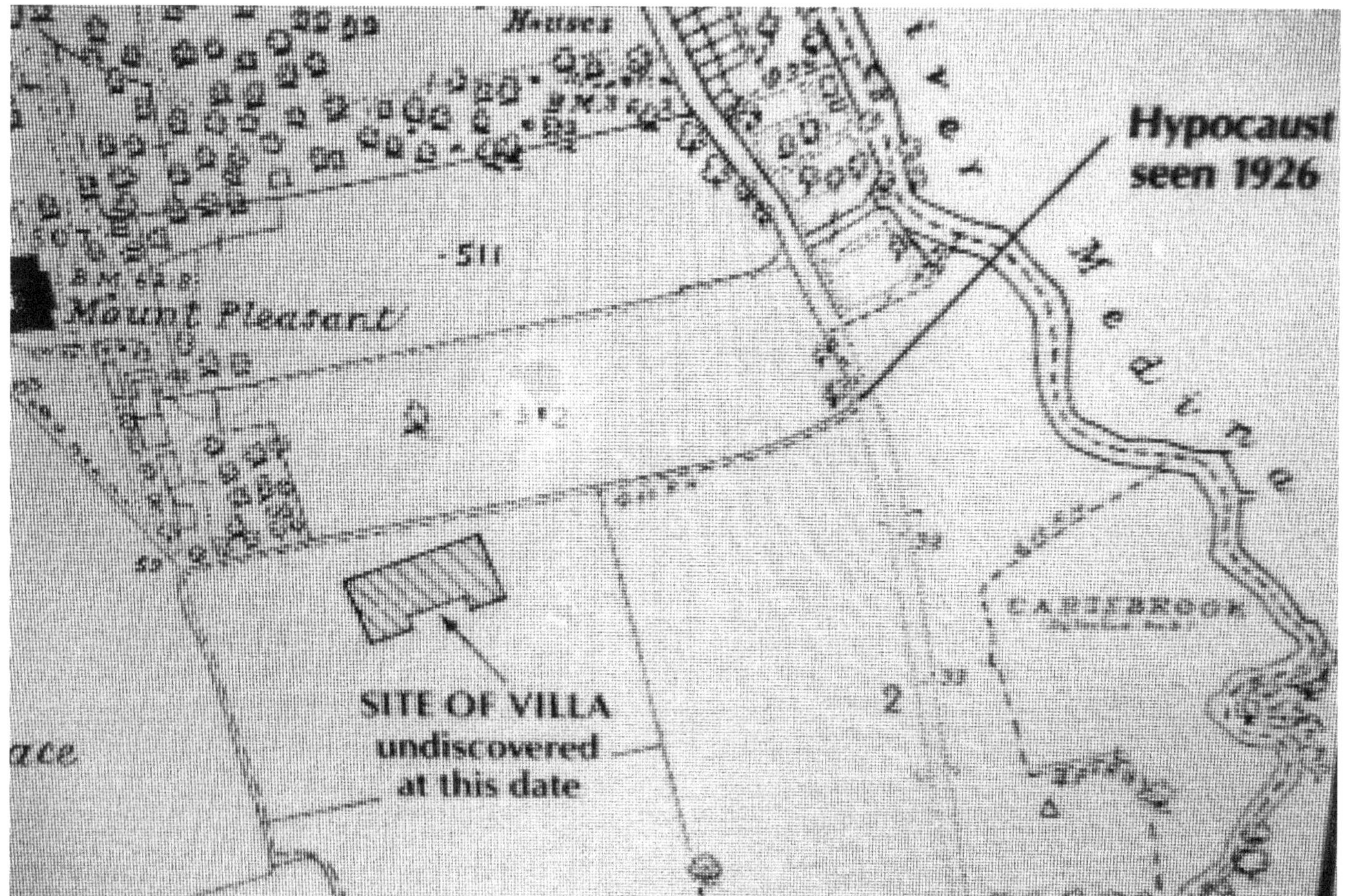

Location of the villa

It seems possible that the Isle of Wight had once been an independent region ruled by its own dynasty (Jutes?) until it was conquered and consequently Christianised by the West Saxons in the 7th century AD. In the Doomsday Book (1086) the island's name is recorded as 'Wit'. The Norman conquest of 1066 transferred the overall manorial rights of the island to William Fitzosbern, as Lord of the Isle of Wight. The island only came under the full control of the Crown when it was sold by the dying last Norman lord, Lady Isabella De Fortibus, to Edward the First in 1293 AD. Consequently the lordship became a royal appointment, with a short interruption when the first Duke of Warwick, Henry de Beauchamp, was crowned King of the Isle of Wight. King Henry VI assisted at the ceremony, placing the crown on the Duke's head. When the Duke died with no male heir, in 1445, his regal title expired with him.

The evolution of the island's current and accepted name is shrouded within the fog of the past, and for many years numerous explanations and theories have been offered up to the table of scrutiny through academic debate. The historian Suetonius records the island's name as Vectis, meaning lever/raised up, possibly from between the two arms of the Solent. The word 'Isle' was first used in the 13th Century and related to the Anglo-French 'ile', from the Latin 'insula'. Wight is a middle English word from the old English 'wiht' which could mean 'a living being/beings' (5th Century). Perhaps then this can be translated as the small Island of the living, levered up from beneath the sea.

THE INHABITANTS OF THE ISLAND

In all probability the Island's first inhabitants, because of the availability of a wealth of fresh seafood, would have settled near the coast. Eventually settlements/trading posts would have evolved along the Island's main rivers. Subsequently they have left us a shadowy realm of their lives, penetrated only by the dimmed beam of archaeology which has enlightened us about settlements at Brading and Knighton, close to the eastern Yar River, and another close to the River Medina at Newport. These early people may have been descendants of the Belgae tribe for artefacts consisting of bowls, butt beakers and bead-rimmed jars have been recognised as those used by these people. Century after century evaporated and the peoples of the Island began to leave more permanent footprints of their existence. Surviving landscapes of barrows from the early to mid Bronze Age were excavated. The early excavators discovered bronze metalwork assemblages and a number of ceramic forms. These have been interpreted to this period in time, based on known styles of object and vessel form. Sadly, coastal erosion has denied us knowledge of the content of numerous late Bronze Age and Iron Age sites.

Suetonius, the Roman historian from the early Imperial era of the Roman Empire, perhaps suggests in his writings that by the time of the disembarkation, in AD 44, of the Roman General Vespasian (the first Emperor of the Flavian dynasty, from AD 69-79) with his Second Legion (or part of), the Island was inhabited by two Iron Age tribes. If this is so, they were possibly factions of the Durotriges and Atrebates tribes. The Belgae may have formed part of the tribal domains of the Atrebates and at 43 AD were possibly still a subsidiary part of the Atrebates kingdom. Historians and archaeology suggest that the main tribe of the Durotriges were from what is now known as the County of Dorset and the Atrebates were settled in what is now recorded as the Counties of Sussex and Hampshire. Therefore, it is possible that the Island had a related tribal division. Although symbolism eludes the modern observer on this island, an endorsement of its ancestors can be interpreted by Iron Age coins that have been sucked up from its fields and consequently scrutinised with the passing of time. Later Iron Age coins suggest a stronger link with the Durotriges rather than the Atrebates, for at this point in time more coins relating to the Durotriges factions overshadow those of the Atrebates. Unfortunately, the coins relating to the Durotriges hold no inscriptions or definite images of regional Chieftains/nobility. It could well be that these coins were minted at Hengisbury Head (an Iron Age port), which is a headland jutting into the English Channel between the towns of Bournemouth in Dorset and Milford on Sea in Hampshire. An abundance of bronze coins have been excavated there and date from the pre-Roman period, suggesting a working mint under the control of the Durotriges tribe. Analysis of known Iron Age coin finds from the island would perhaps help to establish a chronological order of Iron Age activity and settlement.

The voice of history falls silent as to how the Island's inhabitants responded to Vespasian and his accompanying soldiers. Life upon this Island was full of enterprise and achievement as their fields were fertile for cattle, sheep and cereals. The rivers and seas were their arteries of communication and trade with Britannia and the Continent. Perhaps then, the peoples were subservient to the will of Vespasian and therefore the disruption of their lives would have been kept to a minimum. There seemed to be no Roman roads or Roman towns on this Island, or any indications of conflict, as no graves/pits containing evidence of violent deaths have been discovered. It is possible that Vespasian secured this Island for its strategic value, leaving behind a cohort to keep this Island secure, while he returned to the mainland to advance the arm of the Roman Empire through Dorset. Vespasian's first real violent resistance came from the warriors of the Durotriges tribe but the II Augusta 2nd Legion came down upon them with a heavy fist as skeletal remains, excavated near Maiden Castle, and possibly relating to this period in time, bear witness to a gallant but futile resistance. Vespasian would have been aware that any of the Durotriges warriors, who hoped to flee and perhaps regroup on the Isle of Wight, would have been confronted by the same fate as their compatriots. For Vespasian it would have been an objective to secure the south coast ports and its harbours.

NEWPORT ROMAN VILLA'S EVOLUTION AND DISCOVERY

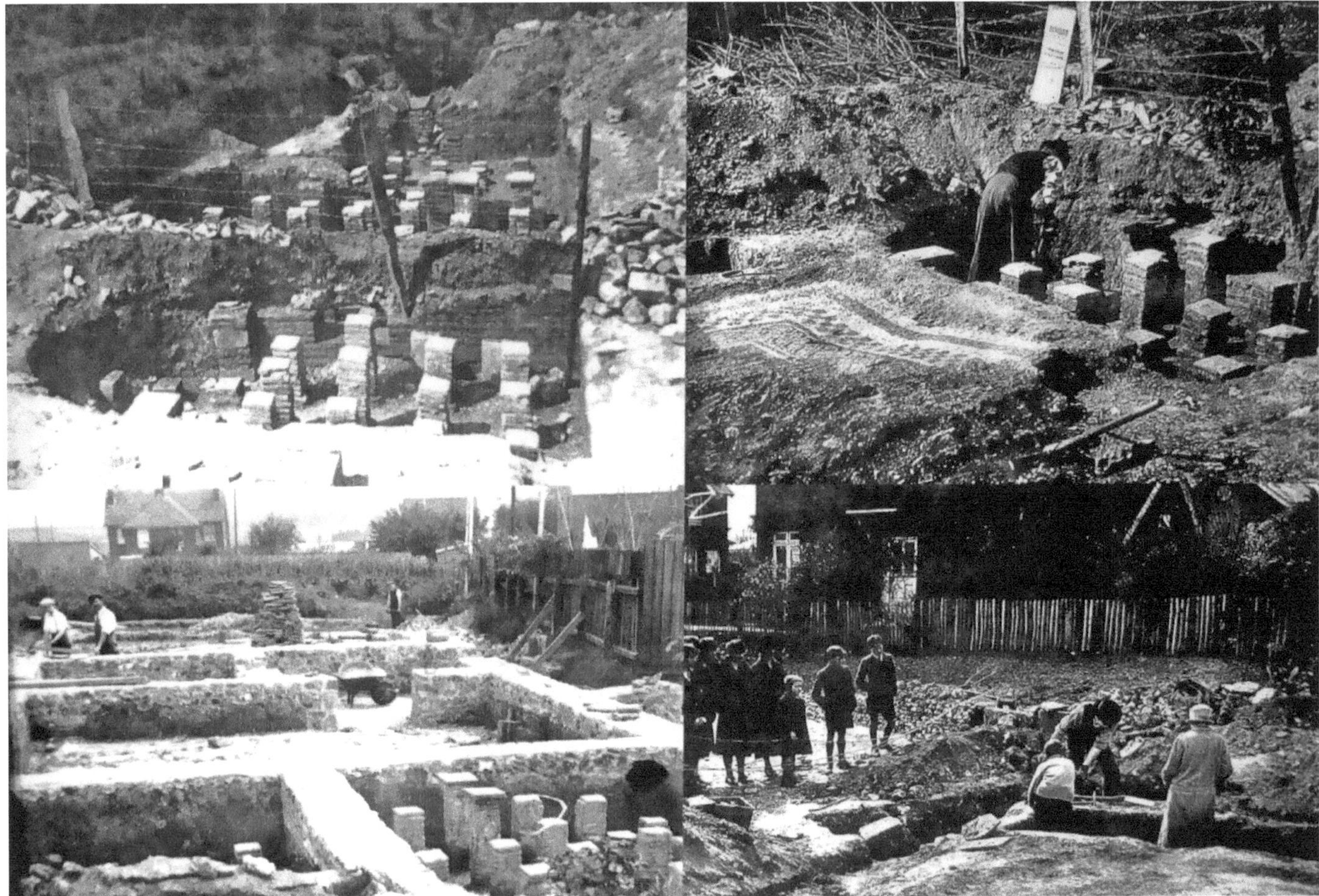

Views of the excavations during 1926-27

The villa, with its front facing to the south, was constructed on part of the lower slope of Mount Pleasant, which from here falls gently south east to the River Medina. This would have allowed the villa's patron, whose name still dwells within the shadows of time, extensive and commanding views over his estate.

The detective work of archaeology has placed its hands upon an ancient ditch concealed beneath the present villa. The ditch possibly relates to an earlier building constructed of timber and clay daub tempered with straw which consequently seems to have burnt down in the middle of the 2nd Century. In the deepening dusk of the 2nd Century, the decision was made to back-fill the ditch with clay; with this done construction of a new building began. But then, due to further excavations in the late 1980s, the construction date was revised to the mid 3rd Century.

The building materials used for the construction of the current villa's walls were flint nodules, chalk, upper greensand stone and limestone, with its enormous diversity of uses. It was used as aggregate for the walls and in block form for the quoins (external angles of the walls), door jambs (vertical portions of the door frames), and roofing slabs. The geology of this Island allowed all these materials to be sourced locally. Above the stonework, but now degraded, sill beams would have held a timber superstructure with waterproofed infill panels of wattle and daub. It has been suggested that the waterproofing could have existed of a lime wash and/or plaster. Archaeology also revealed a sparse amount of window glass mostly from the area of the corridor and from Room 5.They bore the colours of green, blue and a yellowish green. The building would have been a single storey construction with a corridor/verandah at the front giving access to the two projecting wings and to the rooms of the central range.

THE DISCOVERY

Unlike most of the villas I have written about, which were resurrected from within the delightful countryside of this green and pleasant land, the Newport villa dwelt within a local housing estate, its remains interred between Cypress and Avondale Roads. It was only in March 1926, when a Mr Cooper, a resident in Cypress Road, decided to erect a garage, that workmen found pieces of Roman tile in the foundation trench. They then proceeded to expose a portion of tessellated pavement. It was later conceived that this pavement related to the passage which gave access to the bath-house of the villa. Thankfully, Mr Cooper agreed to stop the building work until a decision was taken as to how to move the investigation forward. Excavation was decided upon and a promptly formed committee consented to the Island's architect and antiquarian, Mr Percy G Stone FSA, to be the director of operations. The concern about the funding of this excavation was alleviated when the Isle of Wight County Press stepped in to the breach and inspired locally interested residents to give generous donations. With the known and accepted excavation techniques available in that era, the mummified remains of the villa began to be exposed. In 1927, after an excursion further north into a neighbour's garden, the complete ground plan of the villa was revealed. Private enterprise, in the form of a Mr J C Millgate, saved the villa from being reburied, as he purchased the land and then generously financed the construction of a cover building for the villa's remains. After Mr Millgate's death and since 1961, the Isle of Wight County Council have taken on the responsibility of safeguarding the villa's heritage for many more generations of visitors to enjoy. Subsequently, in 2009, the County Council, with a £40,000 grant from English Heritage, made essential repairs and replacements to the villa's cover-building structure. The new roof was designed to improve the environmental conditions within the villa by reducing moisture levels which contribute to the build-up of algae on the mosaics.

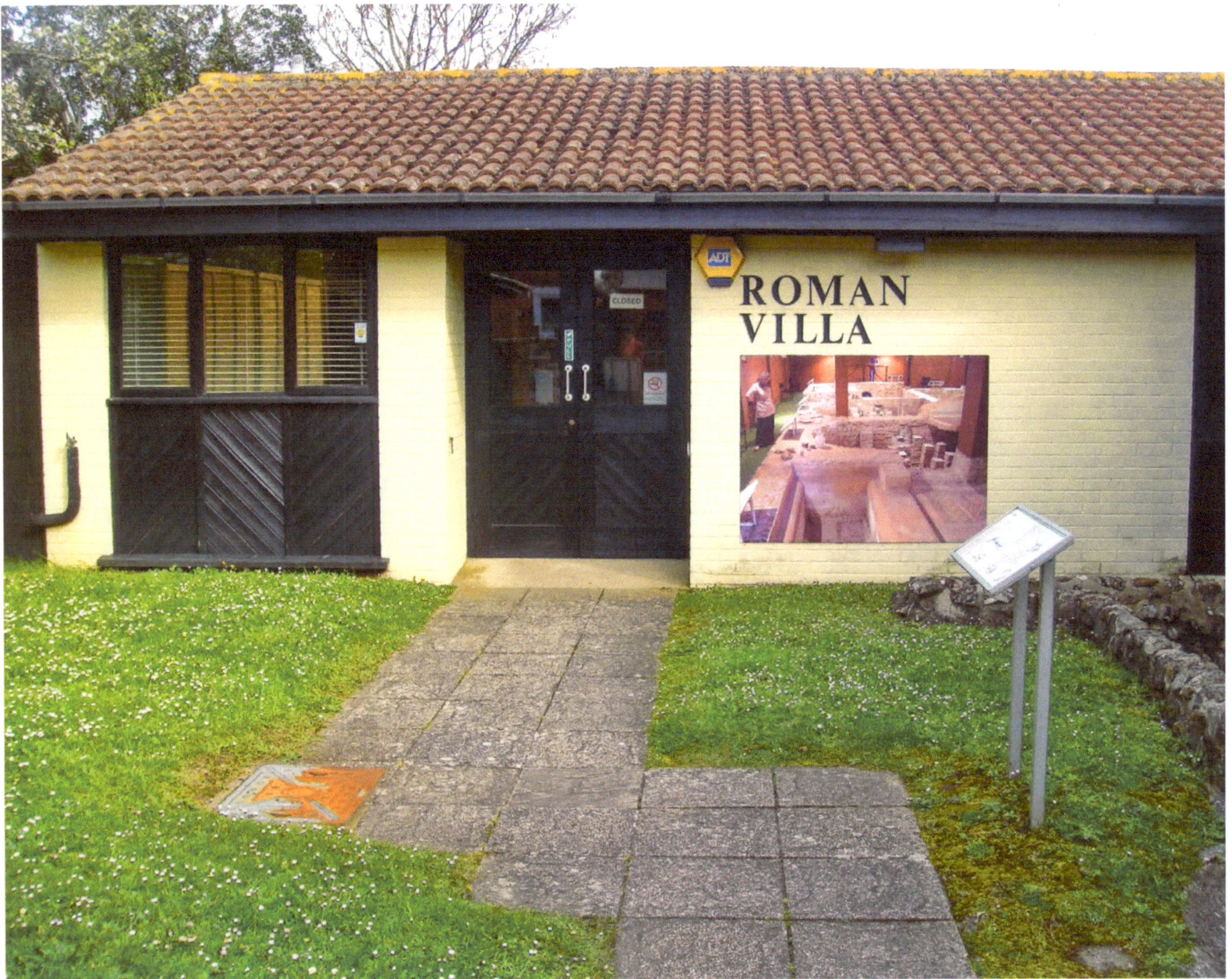

The villa coverbuilding

THE TOUR

As I drive deeper into the county of Hampshire I decide to park my car at the seaside resort of Southsea. From here I board the hovercraft which sweeps me across the Solent to the coastal town of Ryde, on the Isle of Wight. The bus to Newport awaits and I climb the stairs to the upper deck so as to enjoy the views of the journey. On arrival at the bus terminal in Newport, I amble the short 10 minute walk to Cypress Road.

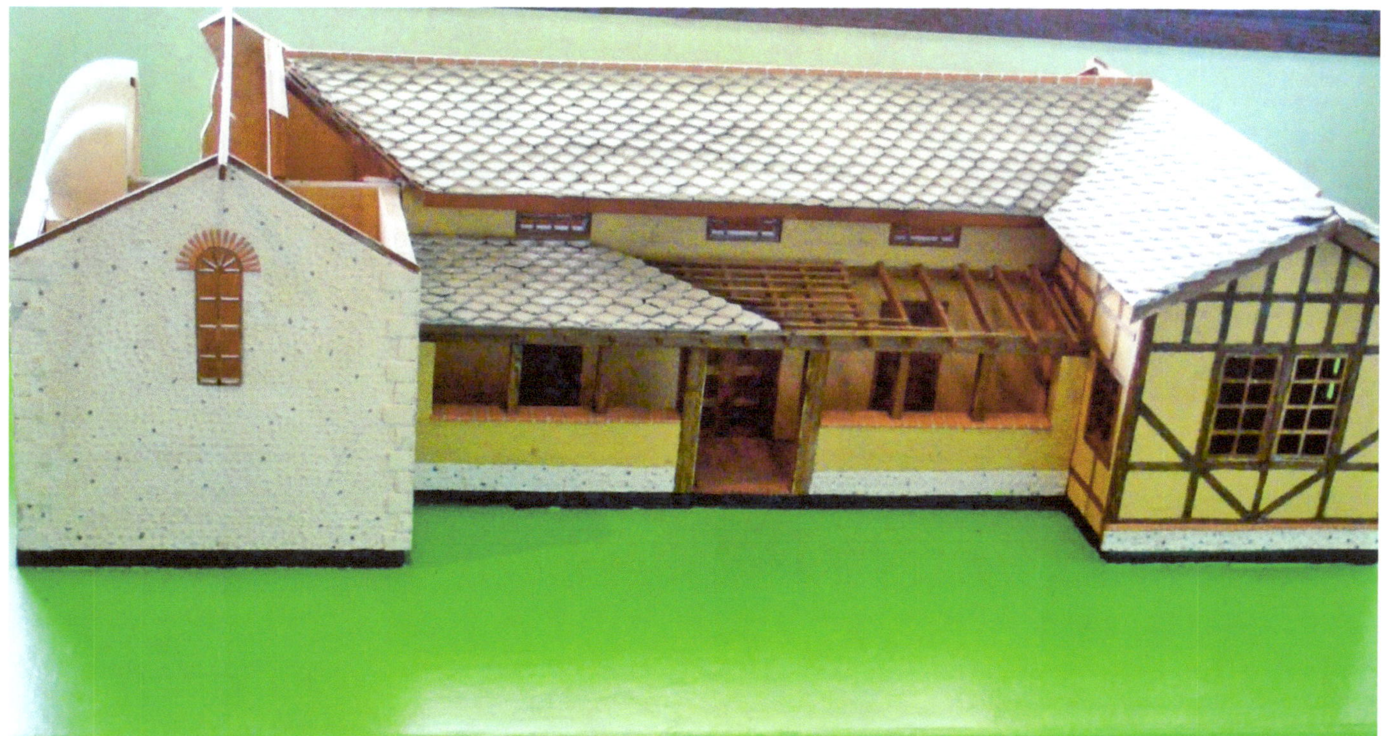

Model of the villa

On noticing the signpost to the villa I follow the short paved drive that terminates at the entrance. The buzzing energy of modern society is immediately exchanged for a calm and serene atmosphere as I stop and cast my eyes around the inside of the entrance lobby. The lobby is thoughtfully laid out with a good use of space and my eyes absorb a model of the villa, display cases containing artefacts and interesting books and souvenirs. Armed with my ground plan of the villa, I proceed to view the remains.

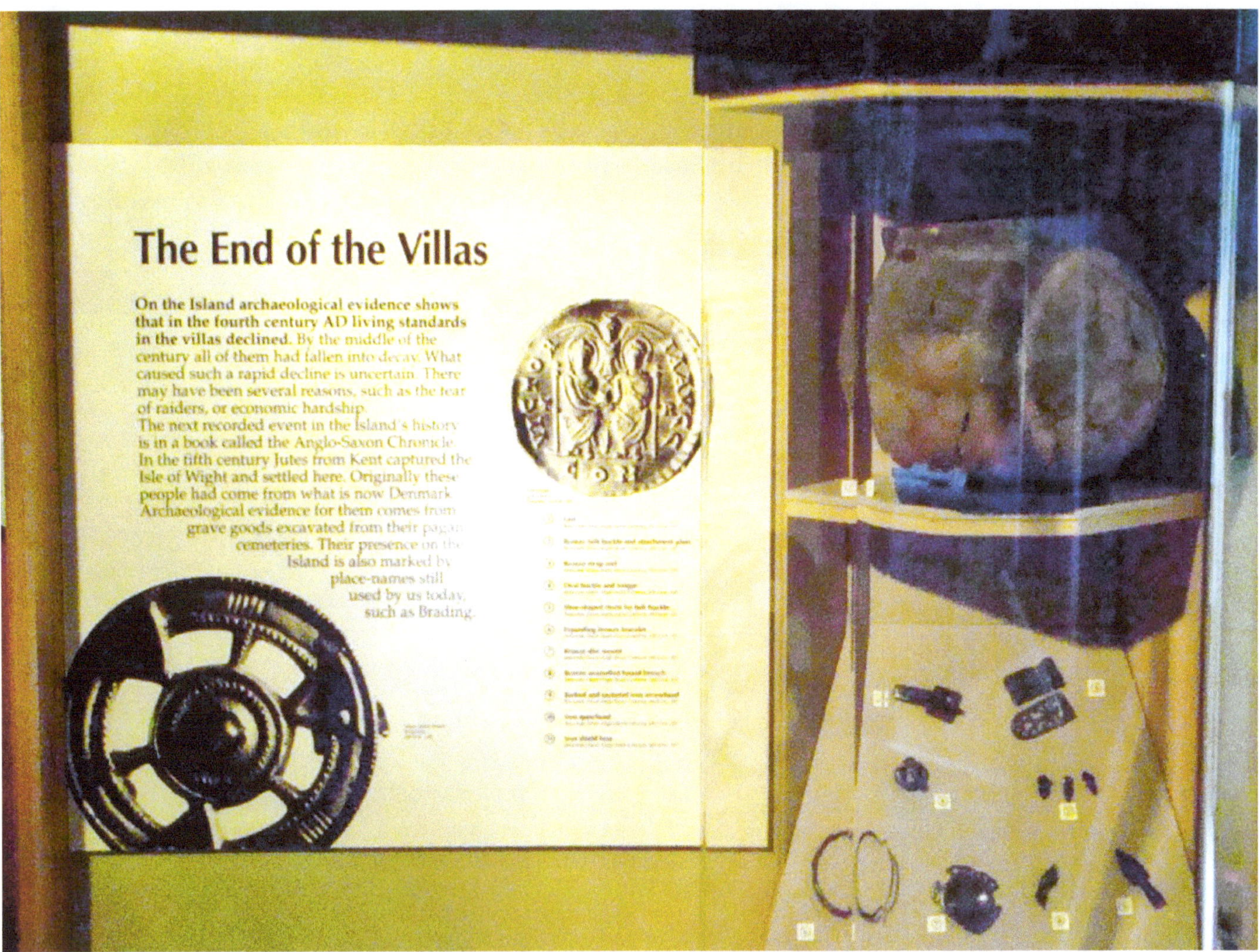

Artefacts

On entry to Room 1 (frigidarium), my attention is immediately engaged by a life-like figure on my right which is seated on a wooden bench. He appears to be resting after spending time weaving on a loom. Close to this reconstructed scene, and in the south west corner of this room, are the partial remains of a re-laid, but displayed in situ, mosaic. Most of the design has been lost in the passing of time so we are left with just a tantalising glimpse of its central panel. This central panel, working outwards, is protected by a four

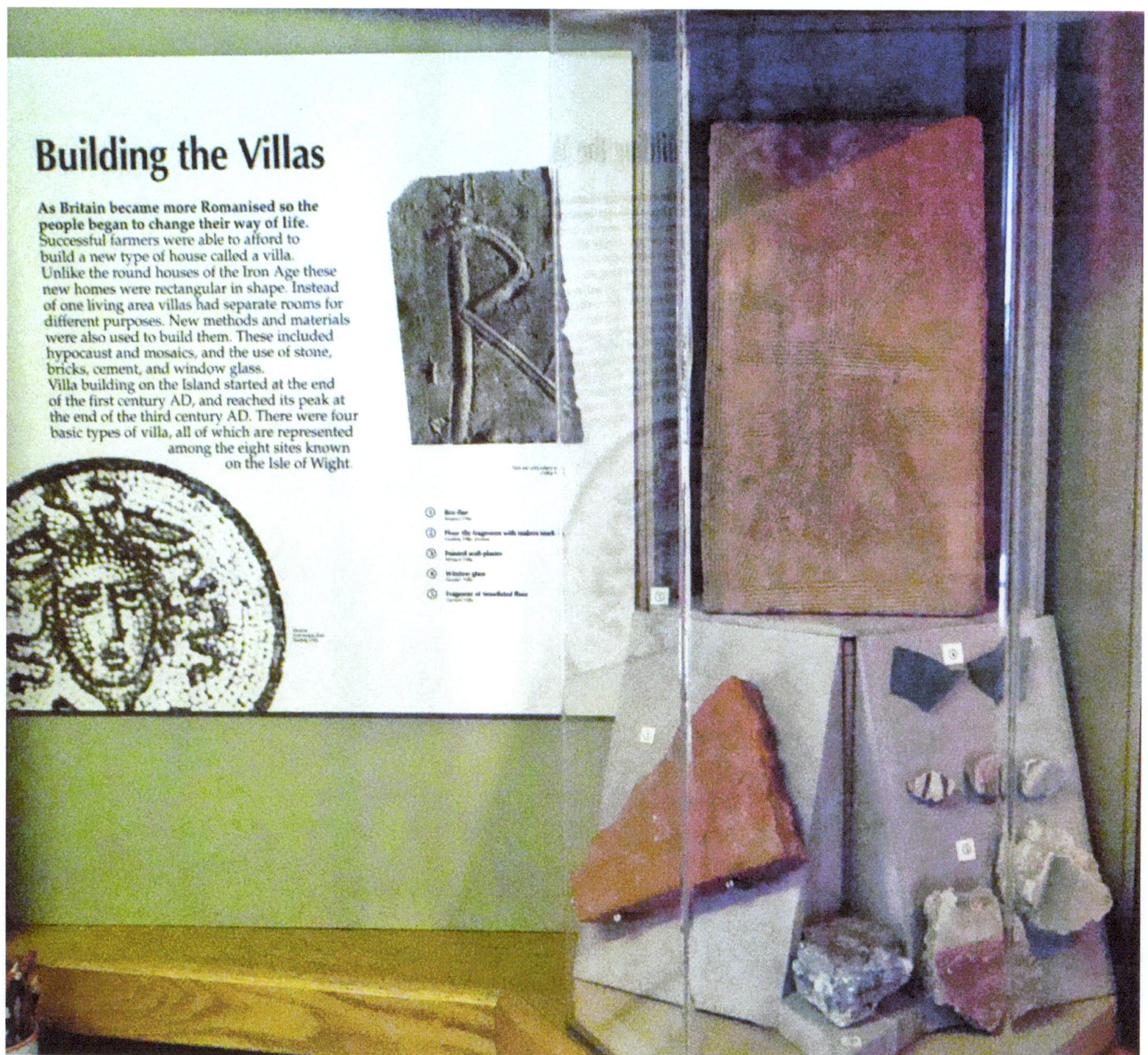
Building the Villas
As Britain became more Romanised so the people began to change their way of life.
Successful farmers were able to afford to build a new type of house called a villa.
Unlike the round houses of the Iron Age these new homes were rectangular in shape. Instead of one living area villas had separate rooms for different purposes. New methods and materials were also used to build them. These included hypocaust and mosaics, and the use of stone, bricks, cement, and window glass.
Villa building on the Island started at the end of the first century AD, and reached its peak at the end of the third century AD. There were four basic types of villa, all of which are represented among the eight sites known on the Isle of Wight.

Artefacts

strand guilloche. The guilloche is outlined with dark brown tesserae and the colours of the bands within are red, white and yellow. This, in turn, is surrounded by two triple fillets, one of white tesserae and the other of brown tesserae. My eye then gathers in a chequerboard pattern of red and white tesserae, which is itself encased in two concentric rectangles. Both are five-band (tesserae) deep, one of brown and the other of white. This mosaic then concludes with fragmented bands of brown and white tesserae. It is noted that all these bands have been constructed forming a series of right angles.

Beyond the male figure and behind the hanging curtain is Room 6, the Apodyterium. The remains of this room's mosaic floor, now much faded, contains bands of tesserae in red, white and dark brown. A simple guilloche design is noticed, which is outlined in dark brown; the colours of the strands in the guilloche are of red, white and yellow. Two white and two dark brown triple fillets surround this in alternate fashion. Continuing outwards and composed of larger tesserae are bands of red and then white, both bands being five strands deep. These lead to a band of eight strands deep in dark brown. At the northern end of this room are two additional bands of red and brown, both bands being of five strands deep. Also located in the west wing of the villa are the remarkably well preserved remains of the bath-house. This was the centre of recreational and social activities within the villa and the suite comprised of the following: a frigidarium (cold room) with a cold plunge bath, tepidarium (warm room), caldarium (hot room) with a semi-circular hot bath and a sudatorium (sweat room). All the warm rooms were heated by underfloor hypocausts and some of the pilae (floor supports) can be viewed today.

The early excavators, armed with their trowels and supported by their inquisitive eyes, recognised, from within the earth that crumbled away from the pilae as they worked, a number of small stones as tesserae. These tesserae were of red (tile), white (chalk) and grey (limestone) and led to the assumption that the now lost floors, which were laid above the hypocausts, were adorned with mosaics. Also retrieved within the pilae were fragments of painted wall-plaster. These were decorated with red, yellow, grey, green, brown and purple. All were painted onto a white background and enclosed within simple borders above a red dado. It percolates into my mind that perhaps the simplicity of the décor's designs served the purpose of trying to cement the atmosphere of tranquillity, so when the bathers took their leave from the bath-suite, their minds as well as their bodies were amply refreshed.

The information panels, displayed within the villa's remains, offer the visitor a descriptive and authentic aid on the interpretation of the lifestyle of the wealthy during the late 3rd Century and early 4th Century AD.

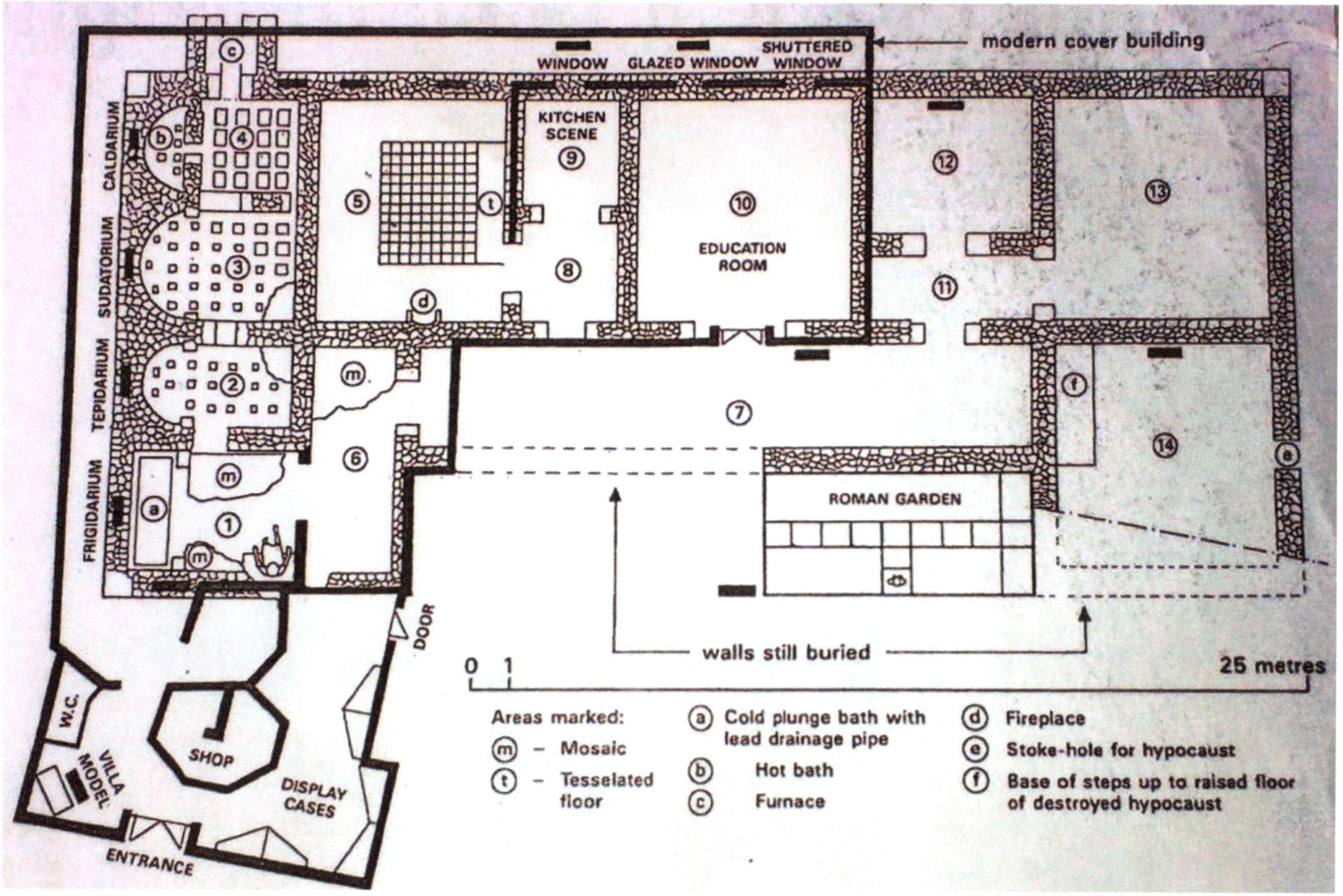

Ground plan of the villa

Of the 14 rooms within this villa, I feel that Room 5 is the one that stimulates thought and debate over how it was utilised during the villa's occupation. As my eyes glide over and around this room today they rest upon the artistic reconstructed three panels of design painted onto the back wall of this room. These are a warm and delightful reminder of the then fashion and personal choice of décor available to the villa's proprietor. More information on painted wall-plaster designs can be viewed on the information panel carrying the heading 'mural'. Intriguingly, below these painted panels a fireplace is noticed set against this southern wall. This is an unusual feature; it appears to have been a later addition, as its hearth rests upon the tessellated floor. The smoke from the fire, it seems, would have escaped through vents constructed under the eaves. Also noticed, at the bottom of the side walls, are the remains of plaster which is still adhered to the wall, although sadly the colours and design have been claimed by the passing of time. The floor of this room, part of which has been distorted by subsidence into an earlier pit, holds a tessellated rectangular panel of a chequer-board design constructed in red (tile) and white (chalk) which, on three sides, is surrounded by a white border. More red is noticed to the east of the floor and in a continuing band running along the room's southern edge. Next to Room 5, looking east, and connected with them by a doorway at the far end of this room's eastern wall, are two small rooms divided by piers.

Both these rooms (8 and 9) have simple tessellated floors of red and white tesserae. Room 9 has been thoughtfully reconstructed and furnished as the villa kitchen. As my inquisitive eye views this reconstruction, the tessellated floor of Room 8 is noticed in the background. Being armed with the ground-plan of the villa (purchased from the shop) is a huge asset in helping to understand the layout of the central and eastern rooms of the villa.

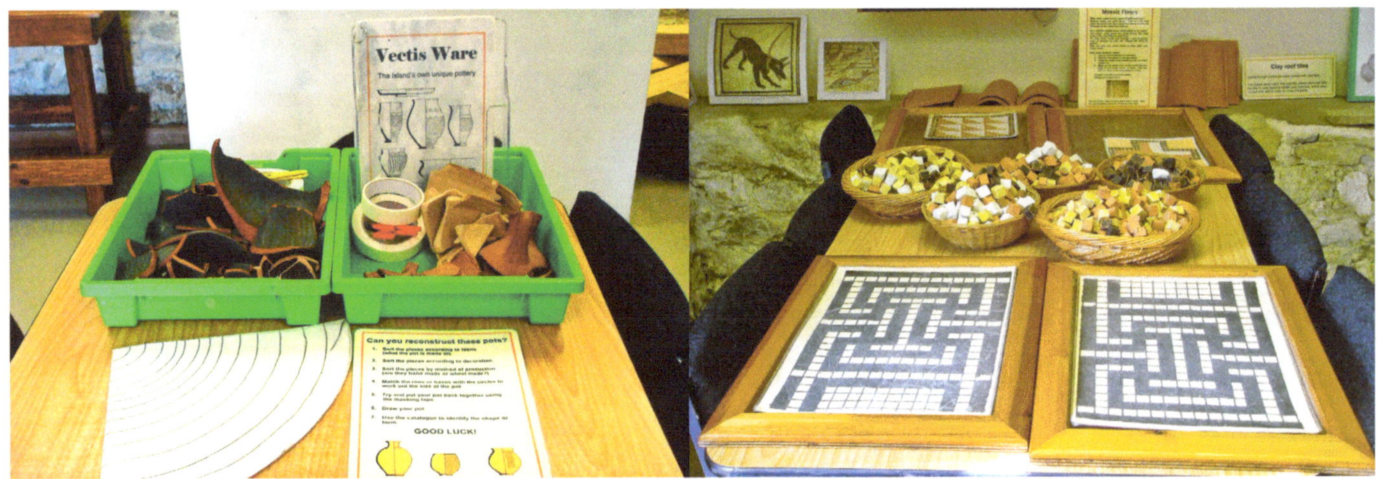

Education Room (Room 10)

The ground plan informs us that most of the western wing is absorbed by the rooms which relate to the bathhouse. Therefore, perhaps, the central and eastern rooms would have been utilised as the residential living quarters. These would have included dining and reception rooms, possibly bedrooms, and a kitchen, all accessible from the corridor (7). Room 10, entered from the corridor, is the central apartment of the villa (19 feet seven inches by 19 feet four inches) and unconnected with any other room. The last room to view within the modern cover building is now used as the education room (10). It is accessed from its southern side, which is the room's original entrance. As I enter this room my imagination becomes vividly alive, encouraged by the lingering atmosphere of fun, laughter and learning. There is an absorbing clarity and beauty about this room, full of all things Roman. There is a reconstructed kitchen and artificial food with menus. Mosaic making is available, as is a weaving loom, Roman board games and pieces of Vectus pottery to handle and reconstruct. These activities can be pursued while wearing traditional Roman clothes, all to be chosen from a rail containing tunics, stollas, pallas and birrus britannicus.

The next entrance from the corridor (looking east) opens into a short passage (11) which gives access to rooms 12 and 13. Room 14 seems to have had a hypocaust and is raised by at least two feet above the corridor level. A little of the original hypocaust remained and from within this, during the 1926/27 excavation, pieces of decorated wall-plaster were discovered. A small portion of the east wing remains buried under a neighbouring garden. My eyes are pleasantly rescued from flint walls and grass by a neatly laid out and presented Roman garden. The garden is overseen by a well-worn statue of the Roman goddess Flora. Flora is the fertility goddess associated with spring and her festival, Floralia, was celebrated from 28 April to 3 May each year and symbolised the renewal of the cycle of life.

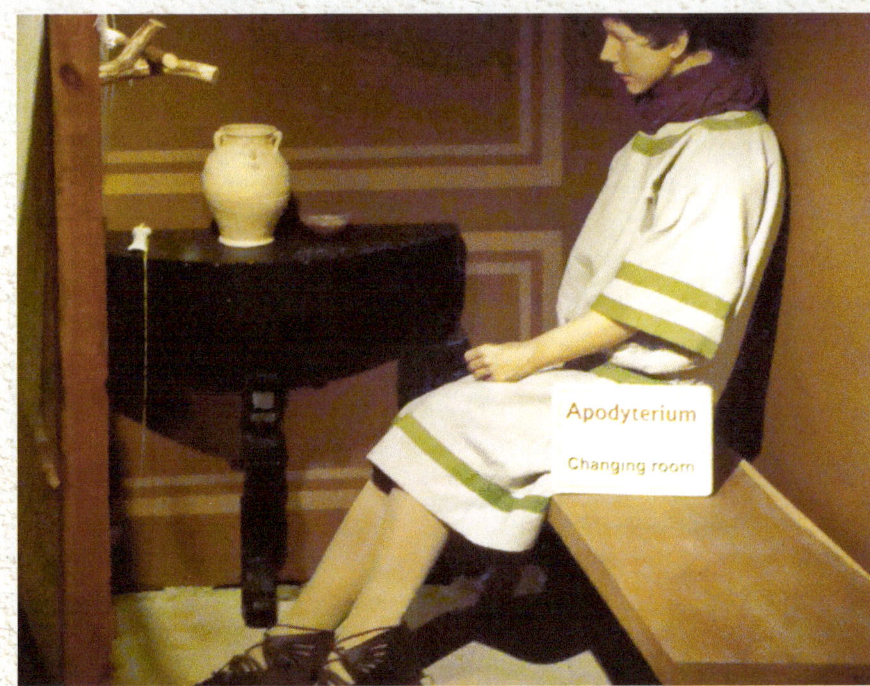

Room 1 - Frigidarium

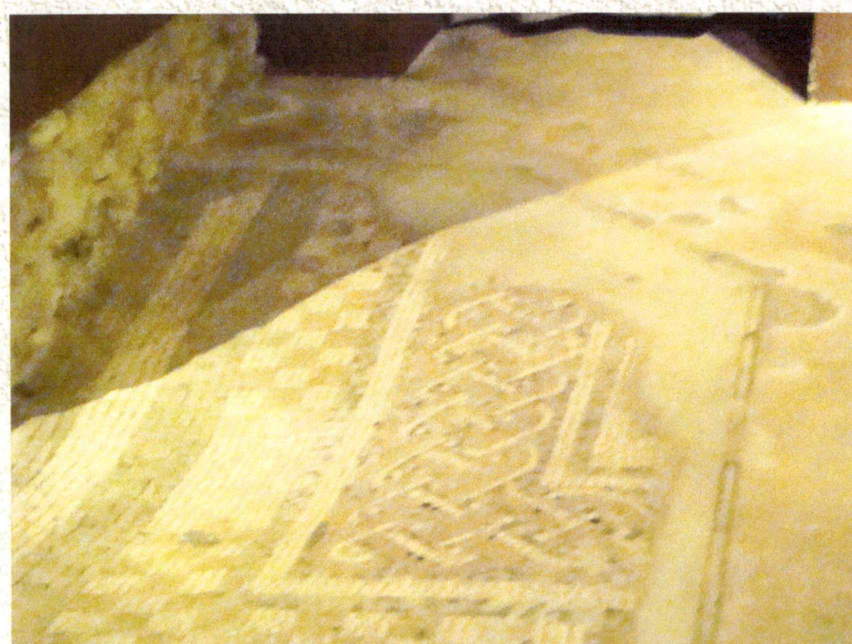
Mosaic Room 1 Frigidarium

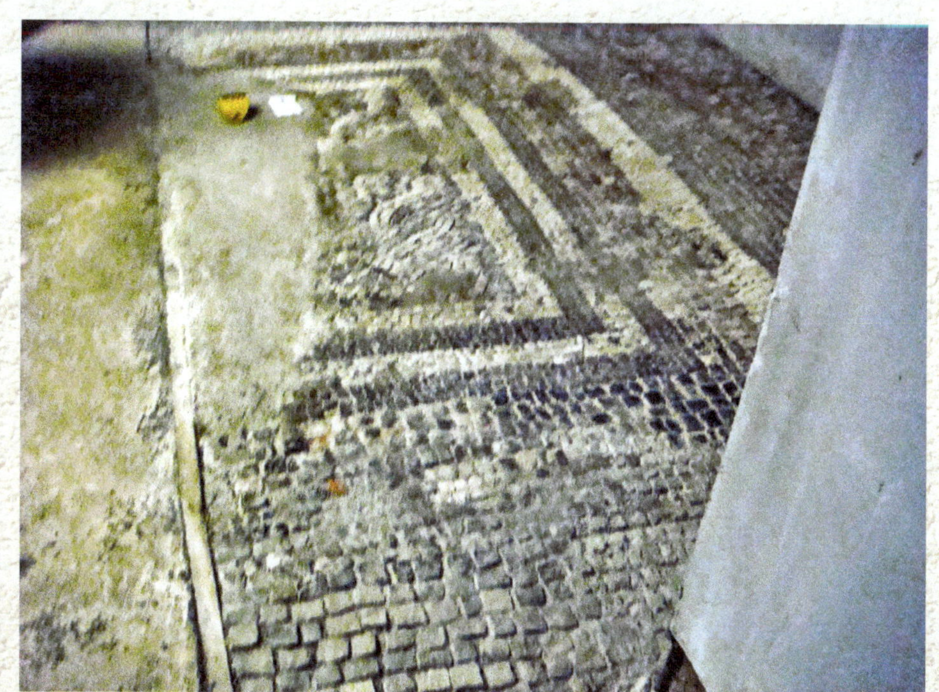

Room 6 Apodyterium

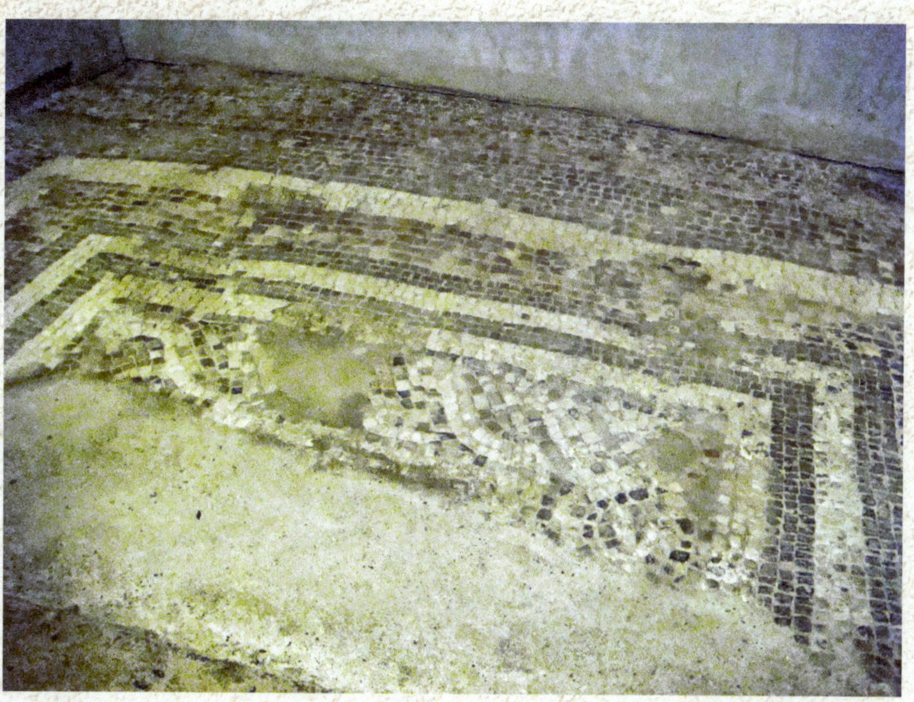

Room 6 Apodyterium

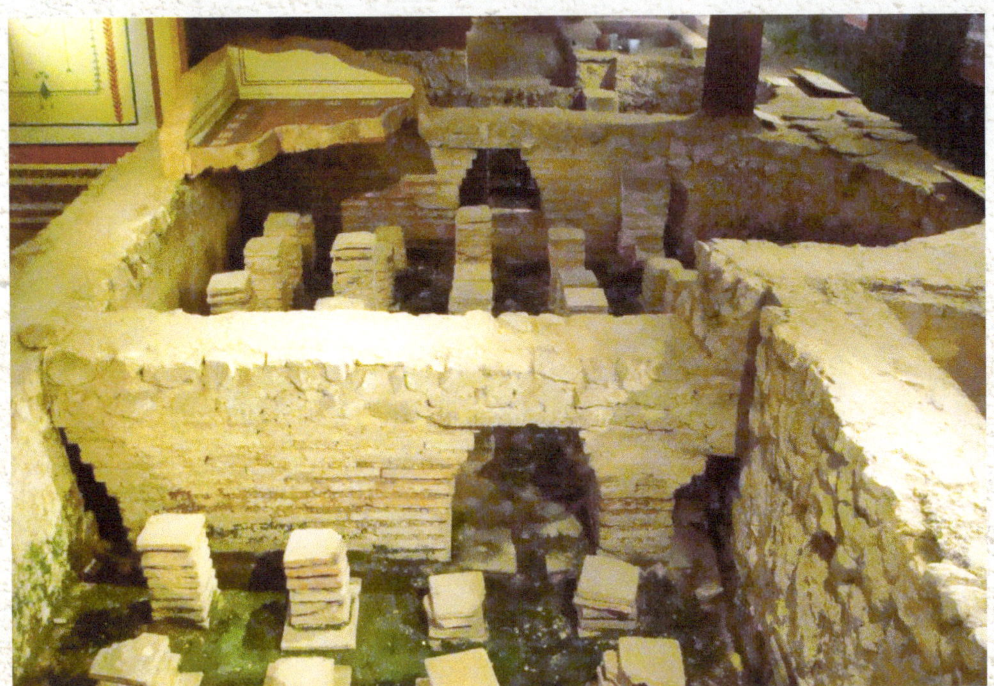

The Hypocaust

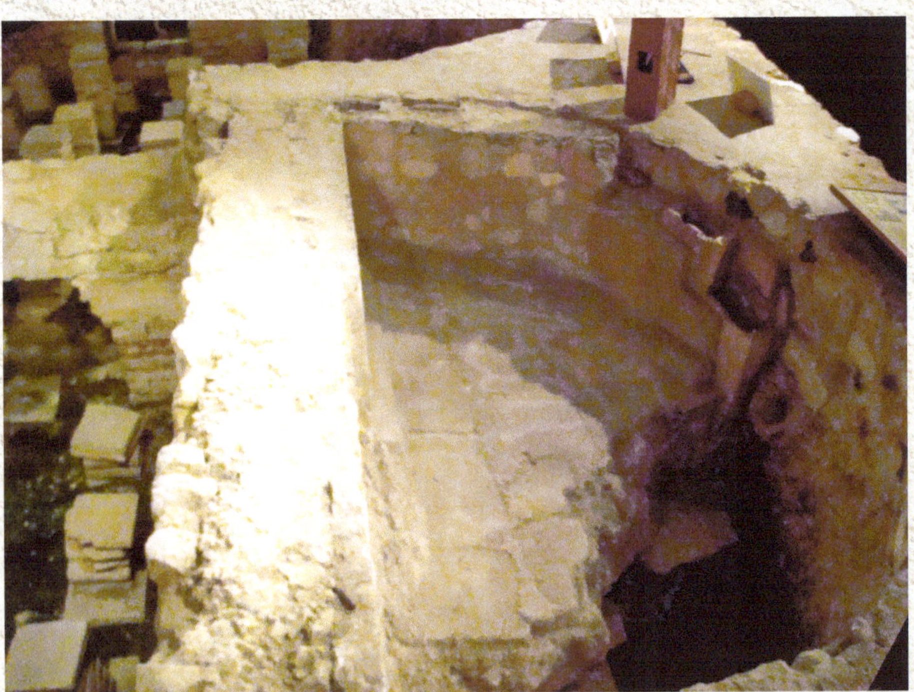

Bath

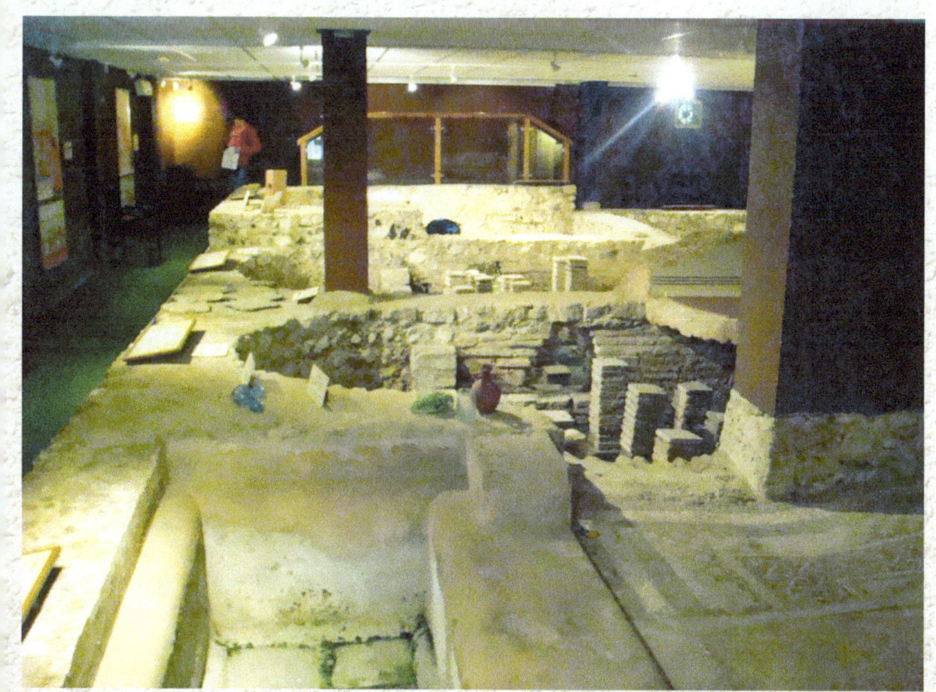

View of bath suite

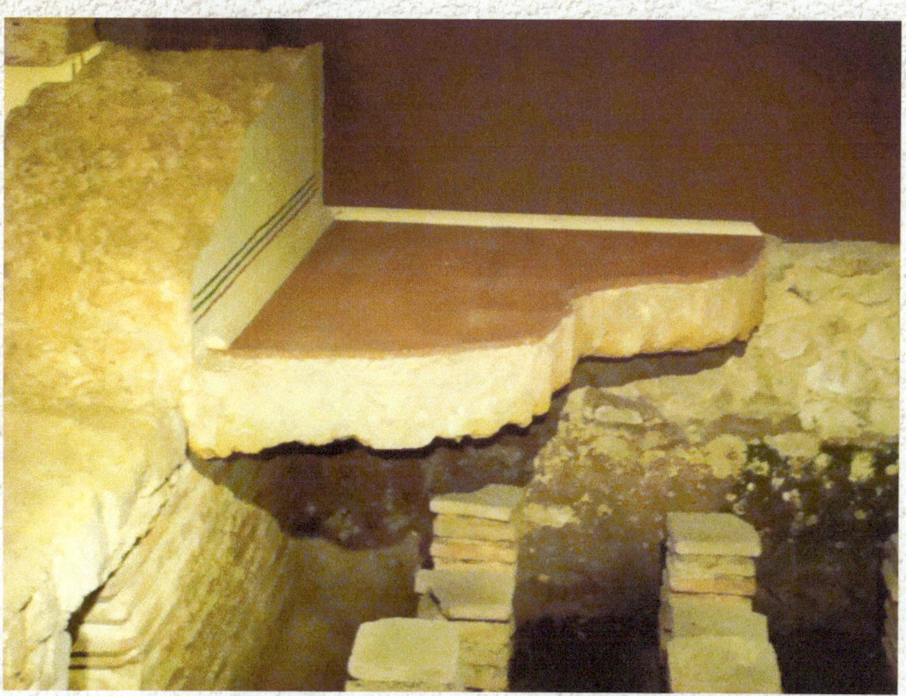

Reconstructed floor in bath house.

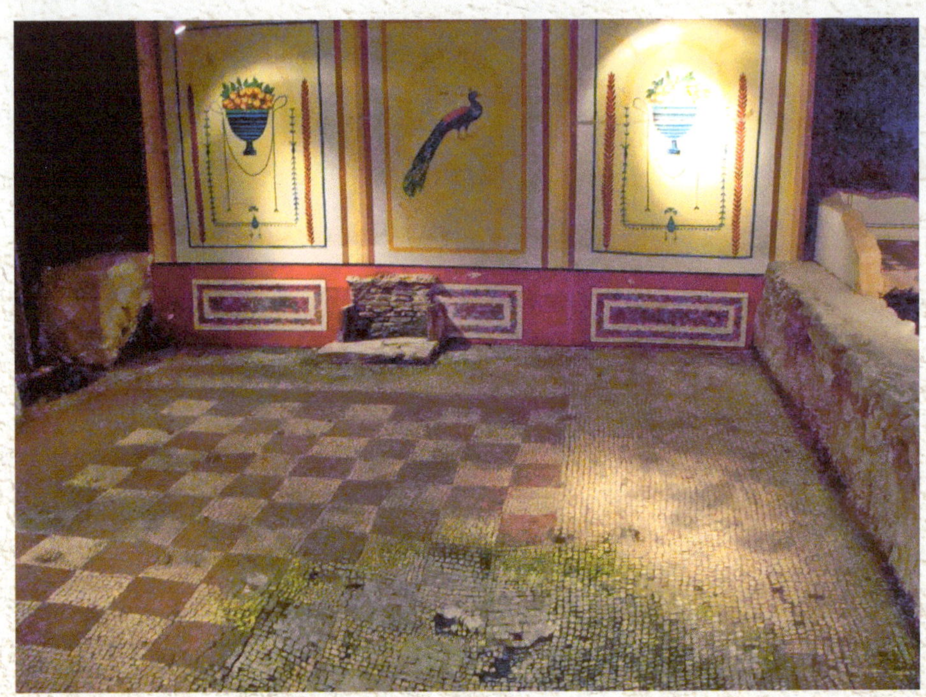
Room 5 Newport Roman Villa.

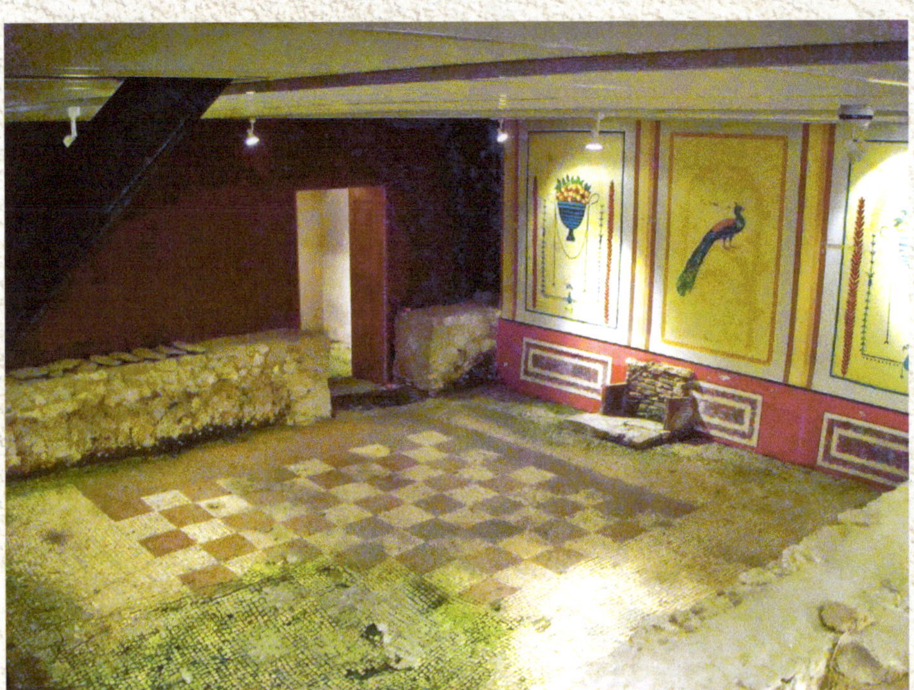
Room 5 Newport Roman Villa.

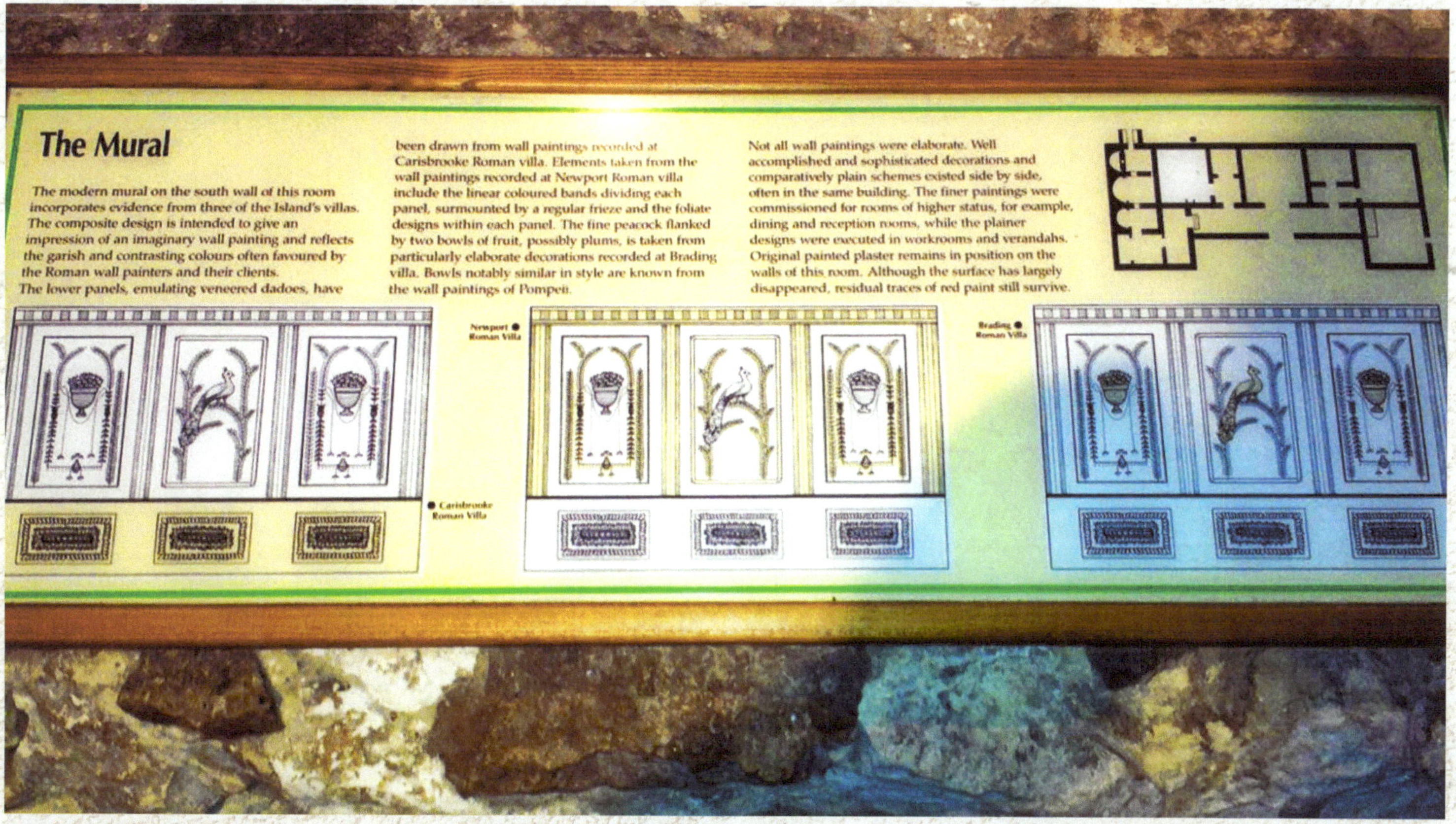

The Mural

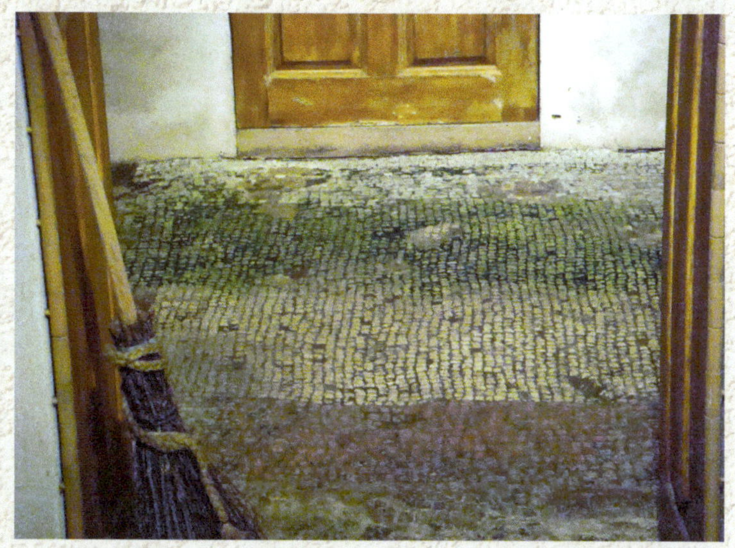

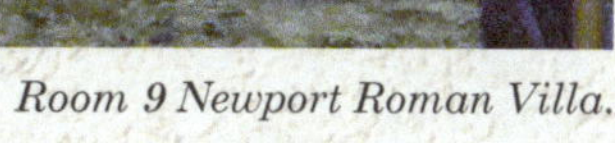

Room 9 Newport Roman Villa.

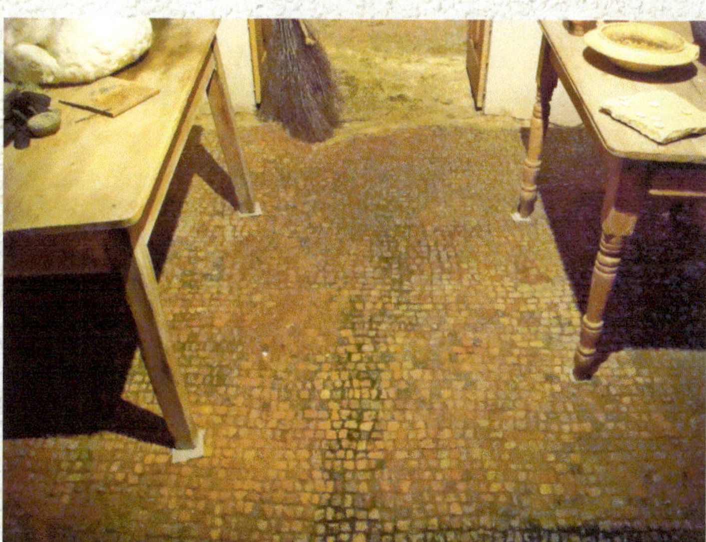

Room 8 Newport Roman Villa

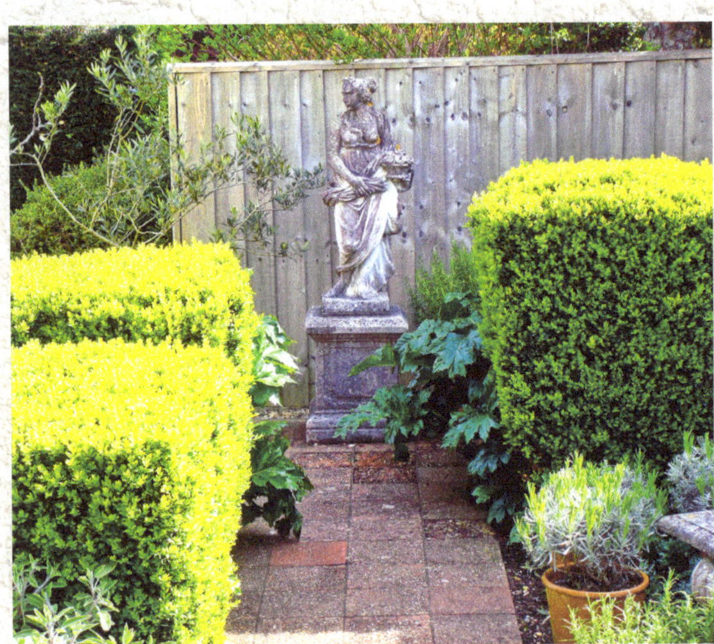

View of the Roman Garden

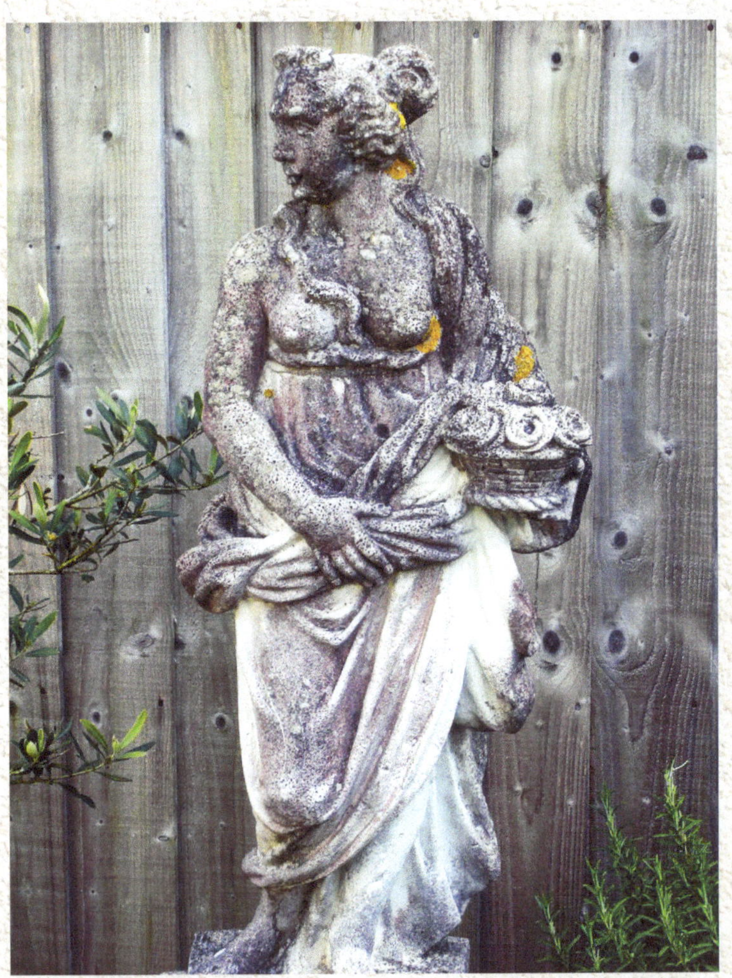

The Roman Goddess Flora

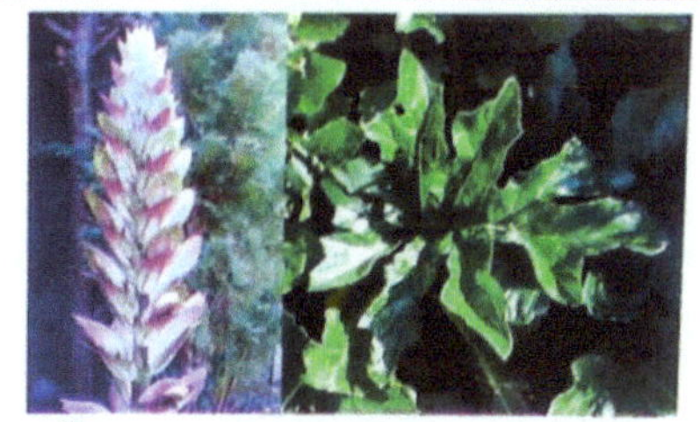

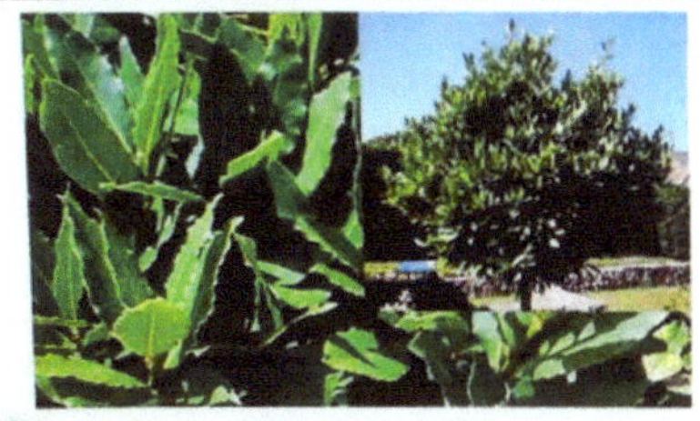

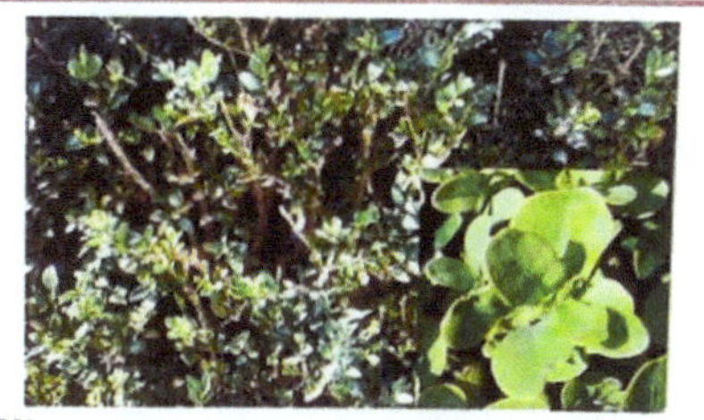

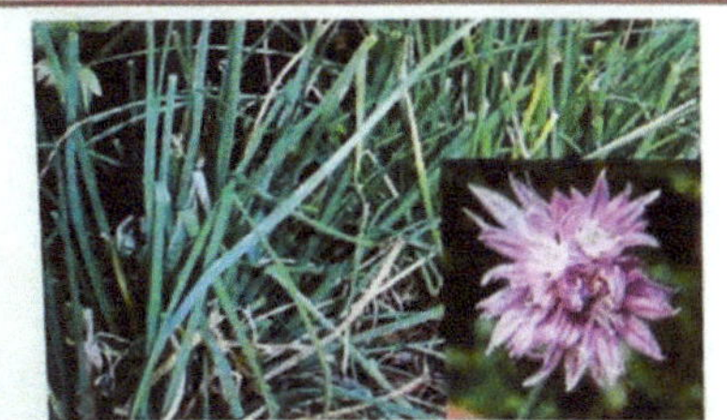

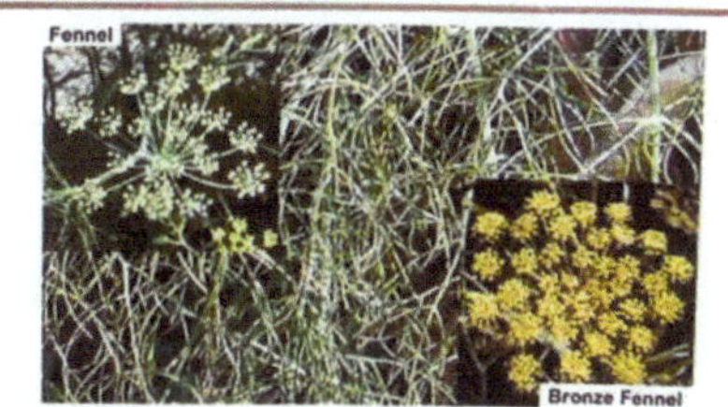

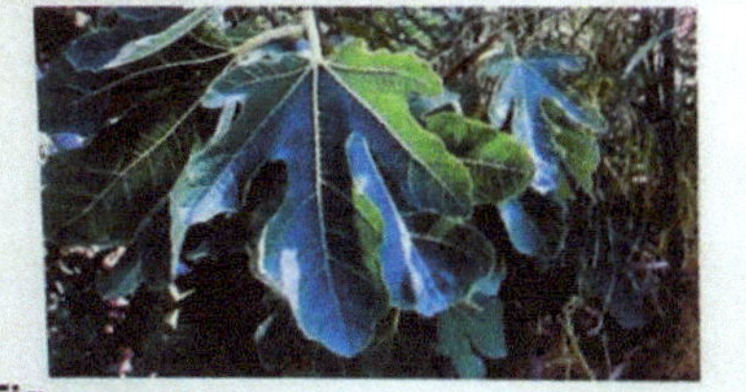

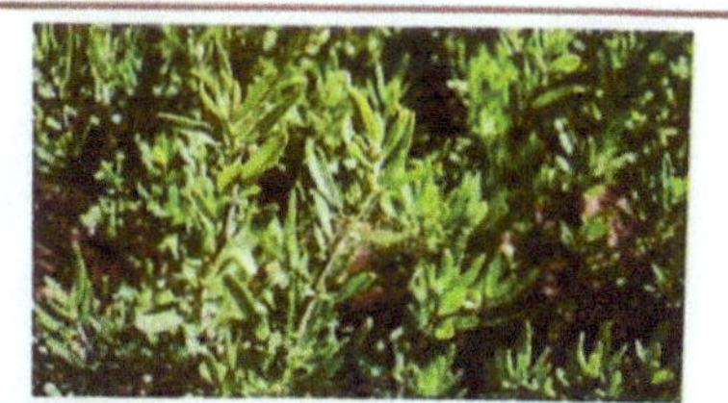

Plants of the Roman Garden

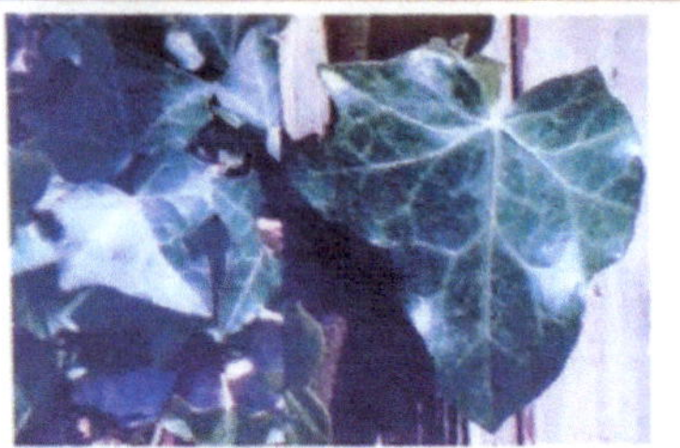

Ivy
Ivy was used extensively as a decorative plant. It was also used to produce a black hair dye and a lice poison.

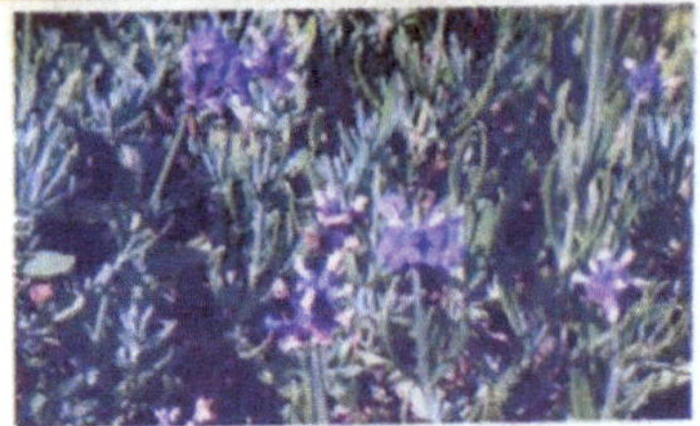

Lavender
Lavender gets its name from the Latin word lavare meaning to wash. Lavender oil was added to bath water to cure headache and faintness.

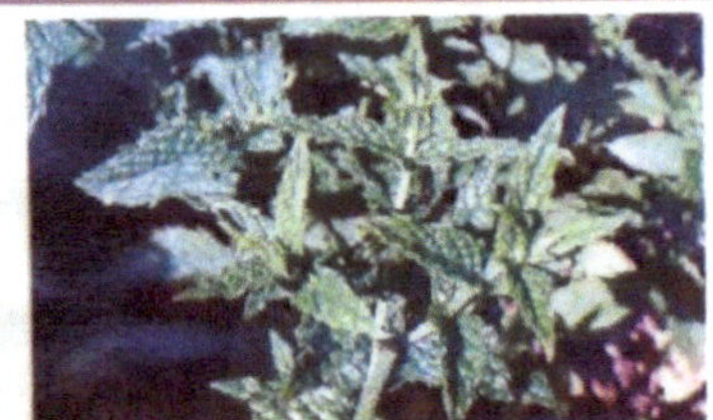

Mint
Mint was used to flavour wine and sauces and was thought to be good for the stomach. A paste of mint and honey was often taken to sweeten the breath.

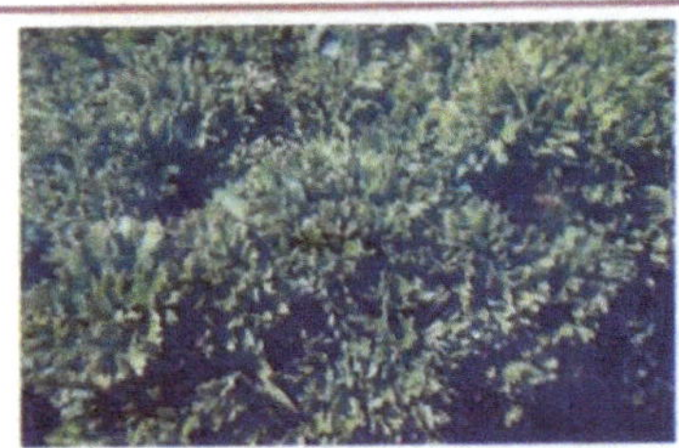

Parsley
Parsley was put in ponds to revive ailing fish. It was also used to flavour sauces.

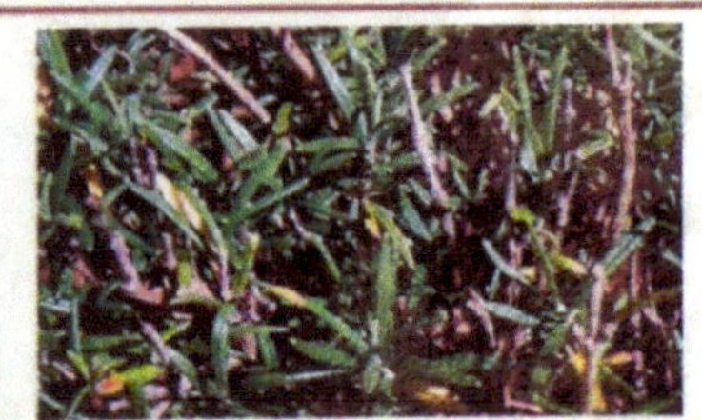

Rosemary
Rosemary was used to decorate crowns and garlands. It was also boiled in water and taken before exercise to warm you up.

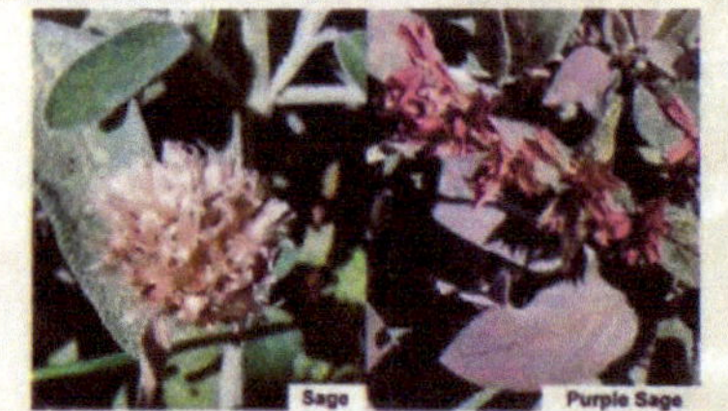

Sage
Sage was a sacred plant and was gathered with ceremony. Sage gets its name from the word salvere to save. It was used on wounds and ulcers.

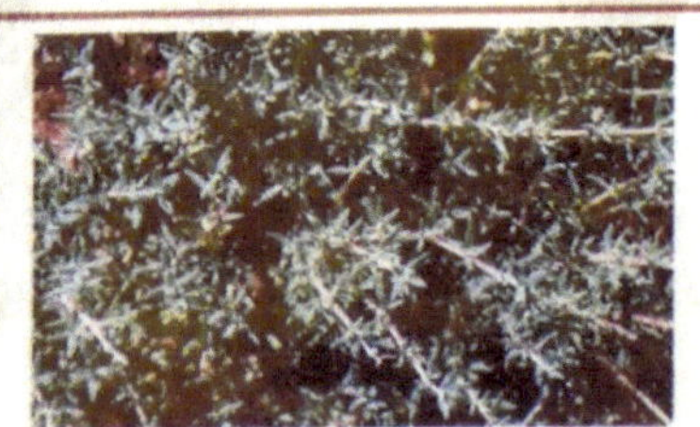

Thyme
Roman Soldiers added thyme to their baths to give them vigour. Thyme was also used to ease belches, and as an antidote for snake bites.

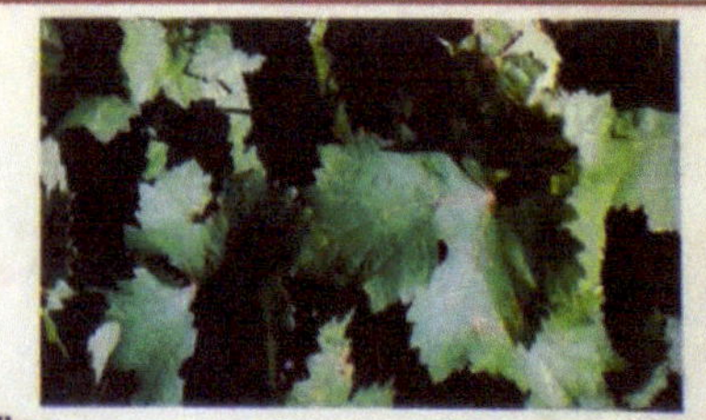

Vine
Vines provided grapes for the table and shade for pergolas. Fresh white grapes were often given to those recovering from illness.

Plants of the Roman Garden

CONCLUSION

With a lack of coins and pottery which can be firmly dated after 320 AD, it suggests that the villa's life as a high status residence was relatively short, perhaps no more than 50-80 years. As for the coins, the latest one which was found was discovered outside the west wall and was of Helena (after 328 AD). The pottery consisted of local ware, New Forest ware and some samian ware. The New Forest ware would not have been in use before 275 AD. The latest piece that has been dated (4th Century) was part of a mortarium.

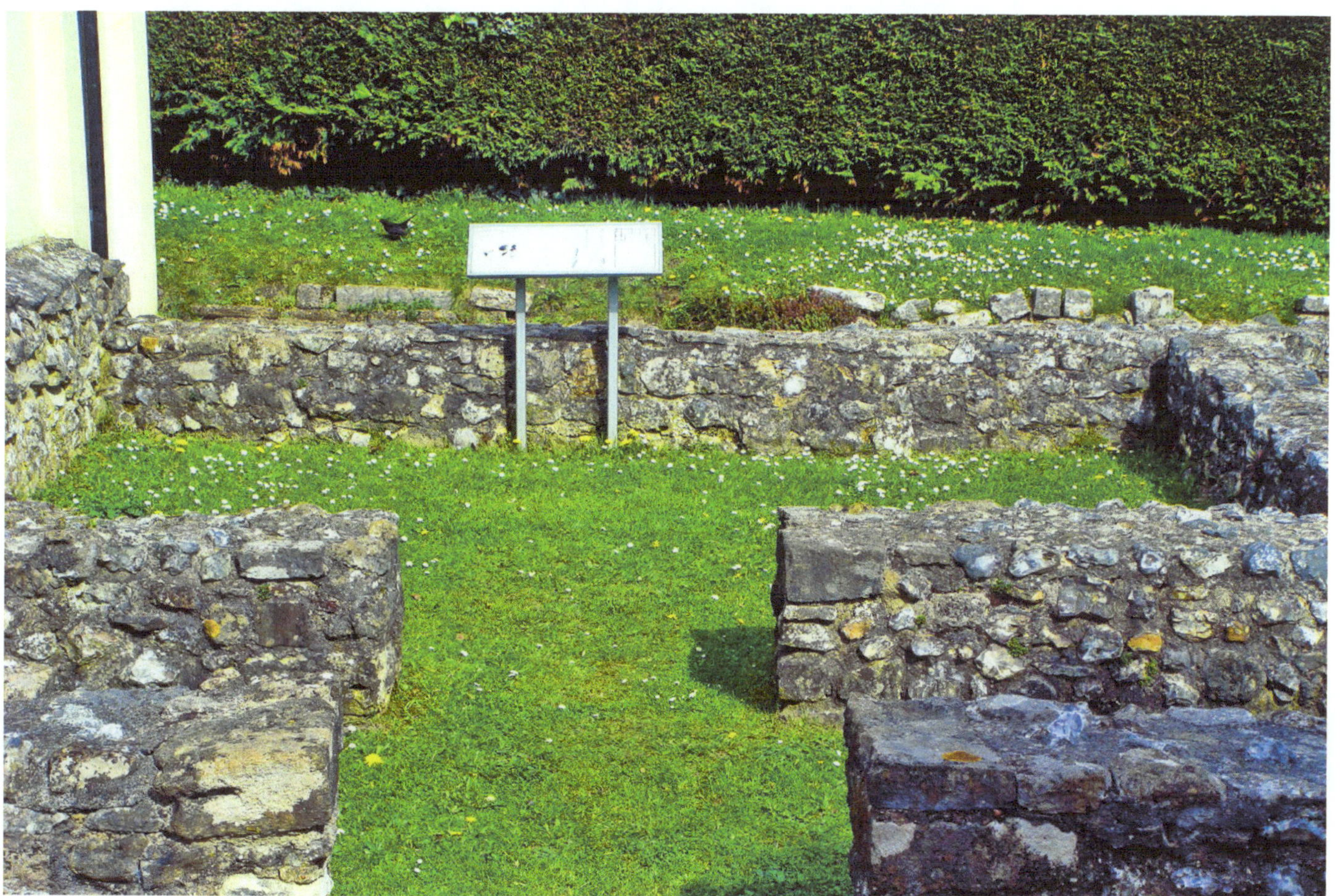

View of the Roman Garden

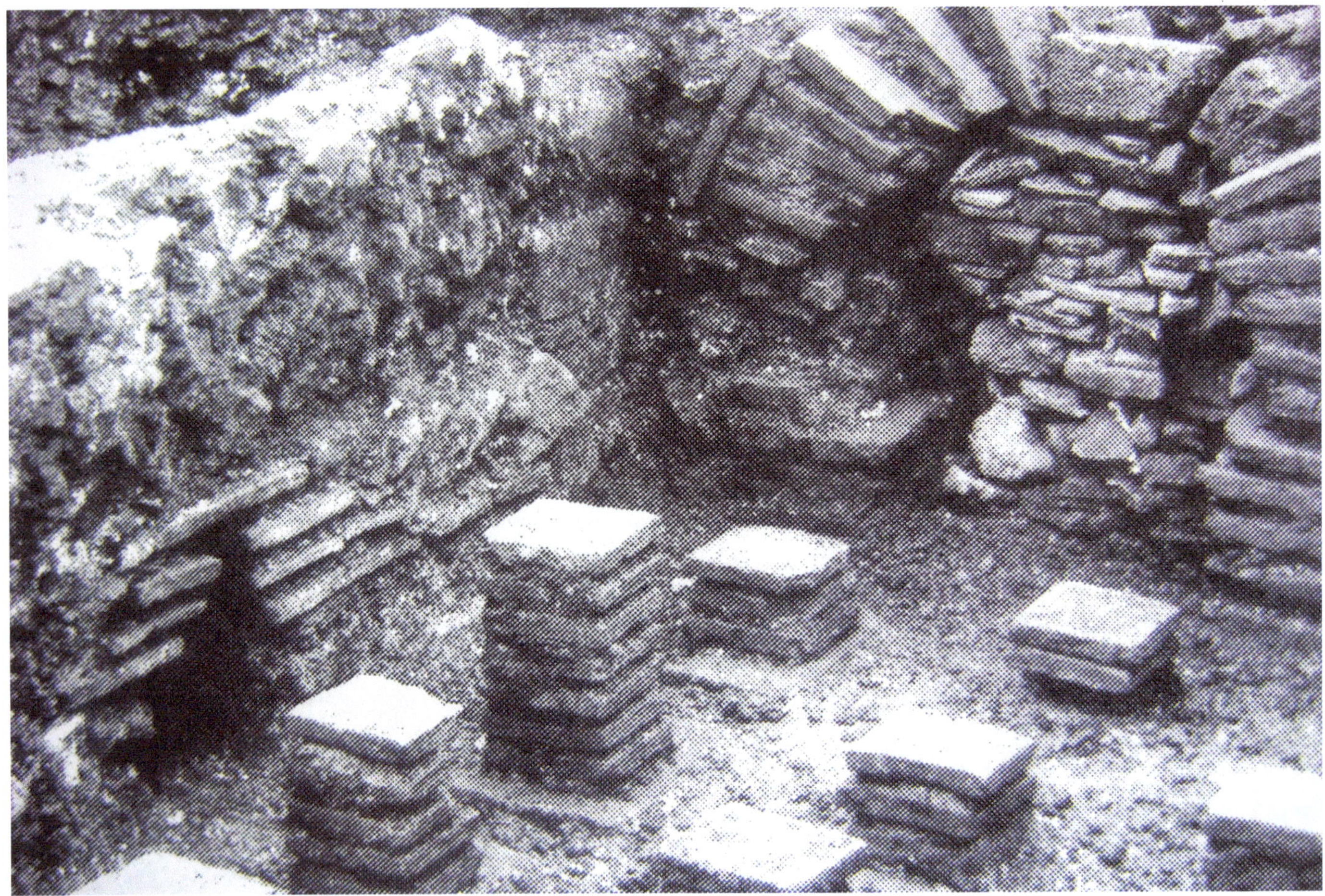

The hypocaust blocking, Percy Stone 1926

Perhaps the demise of the Newport villa was a gradual process fuelled by a continuing and declining prosperity. It seems that the trade routes of the Island were being disrupted by the then three most powerful Germanic peoples, the Jutes, Saxons and the Angles. The villa and its estate, being close to the head of a navigable river, would therefore have been vulnerable to spasmodic pirate raiding parties. The coming of the eerie evening mists, and the engulfing dark of the nights, would have helped to sow the seeds of fear that the villa would become a rewarding target for the raiding pirates. Consequently, perhaps then the wealthy family sought a more secure home further inland and their villa became the responsibility of an estate manager. The signs that the villa's conventional life of some luxury were beginning to falter is indicated when the excavation reports of 1926/27 are scrutinized. The bath range seemed to go out of use as the hypocaust arch was blocked/sealed with slabs of stone. The rooms of the bath-house could then have been utilised as store-rooms for grain and produce, for the blocking up of the heating system would have kept out destructive vermin. It is possible that the fireplace in Room 5 was constructed to replace the heat that would have been denied from the adjacent, redundant bath-house. Life at the villa was certainly becoming less sophisticated. Room 10 seems to have been utilised by a blacksmith, as ashes and a quantity of iron slag were excavated from within it. Interestingly, two coins were discovered from within this room. A coin of Tetricus (271-273 AD) was rescued from the ashes of the blacksmith's fire. The other, a bronze coin of Postumus (258-267 AD) was recovered from the stolen floor. Intriguingly, the excavation reports inform us that the floors in Rooms 10, 11, 12, 13 and 14 have been totally obliterated and that no recognisable signs of any underlay were visible. Bearing in mind the discovery of painted wall plaster in the remnants of the hypocaust, in Room 14, it is not beyond the realms of possibility that these floors were decorated with mosaics and that they were sensitively removed to be re-laid elsewhere.

Eventually, following the pirates, the immigrant settlers would have come bringing with them their own building technology using wood and thatch. They had their own pagan gods and their own mythology brought to life by their gifted orators and story-tellers, using poems and riddles that would have kept the memories of their ancestors fresh in the minds of the younger generations. All through this culture change farming would have remained the most important focus for the future and, I feel, there would have evolved an interlacing and interlocking relationship with the earlier islanders; gradually the trade routes would once again have flourished.

By the early 5th Century Bede's ecclesiastical history suggests that the Island was completely settled by the Jutes. A place now, perhaps, of peaceful living, the population continued to farm the land and pay homage to their chosen pagan gods. Many generations would have lived and died appeased by this accepted existence. Then in 661 AD a storm laden cloud of Christianity briefly descended upon this Island led by the violent hand and mind of Wulfhere, the first Christian king of all of Mercia. It is chronicled that on an enforced return to the Midlands by Wulfhere, paganism was once again embraced by the Islanders.

Then in 685 AD, the violent priests of Christianity returned; this time they were led by the West Saxon king, Caedwalla of Wessex, who viewed the Islanders as apostates. The historian Bede suggests that paganism on the Island was obliterated by these West Saxon invaders who were spurred on by their belief that on their deaths a heaven of eternal joy awaited them. Bede also tells us that Caedwalla vowed to give a quarter of the Island to the church if he successfully conquered the Island. Interestingly, Caedwalla abdicated from his kingship in 688 AD, travelled to Rome and was baptised by Pope Sergius I. Days later

Caedwalla died and his remains were laid to rest in St Peter's Church, Rome.

Perhaps then, with the construction of the now lost churches of worship to this new religion, the peoples of this scenic and picturesque Island were granted a settled peace in which to continue living their lives. Architectural historians remind us that two churches on the Island, St Georges at Arreton and All Saints at Freshwater, contain some recognisable Saxon construction.

As season after season, year after year, and generation after generation tumbled into obscurity, the inhabitants settled down within the firm embrace of Christianity, but then in 789 AD another devil's brood gathered upon their horizon … the Vikings.

Conclusion

More Romano-British mosaics, many of which have been rescued from the farmer's plough and from the mouths of mechanical diggers when towns are being redeveloped, survive within the sanctuary of numerous museums. Some of these museums are located in buildings which themselves have an interesting and intriguing past. One example being the Taunton Museum, in the county of Somerset, where the museum has been constructed within the 12th century Great Hall of Taunton Castle. Within this museum, a rescued mosaic from Low Ham Villa's bath complex demands one's attention. Dido, Queen of Carthage, and the Trojan hero Aeneas, are the main characters of this mosaic. The story is based on Book IV of Virgil's Aeneid. This mosaic, within five narrative panels, tells the story of a tragic love affair.

St Albans (Verulamium), in southern Hertfordshire, also has a museum displaying Romano-British mosaics, including a rare semi-circular shell mosaic dated to 150 AD. But the real jewel of St Albans lies within Verulamium Park, near the museum and housed in a cover building – an 1800 year old hypocaust and its covering mosaic floor. This mosaic formed part of the reception/meeting rooms of a large town house.

I recommend a visit to the Dorset County Museum in the town of Dorchester (Durnovaria). The museum is located in High West Street and can be found in a purpose-built, Gothic-inspired building constructed in 1883. This museum contains a large geometric pavement which was discovered in 1905 in Durngate Street, Dorchester, and was relaid on the floor of the Gallery. Consequently this is one of the few places in Europe where one can walk upon a Roman mosaic.

Also worth an hour or two of one's time is a visit to the Corinium Museum in Park Street, Cirencester, perhaps to correspond with a viewing of the Roman Villa at Chedworth. This museum is home to one of the largest collections of Romano-British antiquities and includes mosaics excavated from Corinium, which was Roman Britain's second largest city.

In conclusion, in the spring of 2016 I will start gathering material towards the composition of a third book that will include many mosaics which are to be found in museums across England. My progress will be posted on my blog, 'read-roman mosaics'.

www.ingramcontent.com/pod-product-compliance
Lightning Source LLC
LaVergne TN
LVHW070214110826
845147LV00003B/571
* 9 7 8 1 9 1 0 2 2 3 4 6 8 *